Also by Judith Milner and Patrick O'Byrne

Brief Counselling: Narratives and Solutions
Assessment in Counselling

Also by Judith Milner

Women and Social Work
Working with Violence (with Steve Myers)

Also by Patrick O'Byrne

Constructive Social Work (with Nigel Parton)

3RD EDITION

Assessment in Social Work

Judith Milner

and

Patrick O'Byrne

palgrave
macmillan

First edition 1998
Reprinted seven times
Second edition 2002
Reprinted five times
Third edition 2009

Published by
PALGRAVE MACMILLAN

Palgrave Macmillan in the UK is an imprint of Macmillan Publishers Limited, registered in England, company number 785998, of Houndmills, Basingstoke, Hampshire RG21 6XS.

Palgrave Macmillan in the US is a division of St Martin's Press LLC, 175 Fifth Avenue, New York, NY 10010.

Palgrave Macmillan is the global academic imprint of the above companies and has companies and representatives throughout the world.

Palgrave® and Macmillan® are registered trademarks in the United States, the United Kingdom, Europe and other countries.

ISBN: 978–0–230–21862–8

This book is printed on paper suitable for recycling and made from fully managed and sustained forest sources. Logging, pulping and manufacturing processes are expected to conform to the environmental regulations of the country of origin.

A catalogue record for this book is available from the British Library.

A catalog record for this book is available from the Library of Congress.

10   9   8   7   6   5   4   3   2
18 17 16 15 14 13 12 11 10

Printed and bound in Great Britain by
CPI Antony Rowe, Chippenham and Eastbourne

Contents

List of Tables and Figures

Tables

Figures

Acknowledgements

The authors wish to thank the following (in alphabetical order) for their generous assistance in the preparation of this edition:

Marian Barber, Eoin Byrne, Tom Cahil, Stephen Foy, Sue Hadley, Jon Neville, Mary O'Byrne and Pam Walker.

Members of the Woodhouse team, Leeds: Fiona Henry, with Emma Chadwick, Michael Danahar, Paul Frier, Farrah Khan, Jo Robinson and Lindsey Taylor.

We want to thank Steve Myers for his enthusiasm, encouragement and generous help with library searches.

Thanks also to Catherine Gray and Kate Llewellyn at Palgrave Macmillan.

Also, the authors and publishers wish to thank SAGE publications, London, Los Angeles, New Delhi and Singapore, for permission to use Table 8.2 from O'Connell, *Solution Focussed Therapy* Copyright © SAGE 1998, 2005.

Every effort has been made to contact all the copyright-holders for material in this book, but if any have been inadvertently omitted the publishers will be pleased to make the necessary arrangement at the earliest opportunity.

Introduction

As with the second edition, the major revisions in this book reflect the revisions in government guidance on how to undertake high-quality assessments. Following a series of audits which raised concerns about the effectiveness of social work assessments in determining appropriate interventions (for an overview see Ward and Rose, 2002), there has been a huge number of papers and substantial amendments to the legislation. *Valuing People: A New Strategy for Learning Disability for the Twenty-First Century* (Department of Health, 2001c) heralded government's vision of care, one in which learning-disabled people would be given a voice about how they were cared for. The buzzwords in this paper – rights, independence and choice – echo in subsequent government publications and legislation. The latter includes four major new acts: the Children Act 2004, the Mental Capacity Act 2005 (in Scotland, the Adults and Incapacity Act 2000), the Children and Adoption Act 2006, and the Mental Health Act 2007. Alongside this legislation sits a number of papers setting out the outcomes expected from assessments, chiefly: *Fair Access to Care Services* (FACS) (2003), the *Every Child Matters* series (2005), *Our Health, Our Care, Our Say* (2006), *Every Parent Matters* (2007), the Health and Social Care Bill (2007) and *Valuing People Now* (2008). As fulfilling desired outcomes depend on good quality assessments, government also provides assessment frameworks, most notably the Common Assessment Framework (for children and families) and the Single Assessment Process (for adults in need). Additionally, the guidance on risk assessments has been amended and enlarged with an emphasis on safeguarding. Thus assessment work has to assess *need* within a context of choice and supported decision-making, which allows people to take *risks* at the same time as it has to minimize any risks through partnership and improved intra- and inter-agency working.

We acknowledge at this point that since devolution Scotland and Wales have their own laws and government guidance. These are made clear in Chapters 10 and 11, but for brevity the main processes described in this book are those used in England.

The new climate of thinking is congruent with social work values and aims but the delivery of outcomes is dependent not only on high-quality assessments but also on the provision of high-quality resources. Government guidance on how assessments must be undertaken, along with a plethora of assessment tools, does not necessarily clarify or simplify the task. Not only are the resources identified in collaborative assessments – for example, the provision of respite care in the home – not readily available but the increased emphasis on assessment activity has had the effect of reducing social workers to case managers at the expense of them gaining confidence and experience in direct work with service users (see, for example, Cleaver and Walker, 2004). Other complexities of assessment work include the problem that it is difficult to identify strengths when service users are described as 'vulnerable people', although service users rarely divide neatly into cared-for and carer categories, and it is difficult to assess community and environmental needs and strengths when government guidance encourages the use of psychological assessments alongside social work assessments.

This book embraces these complexities, integrating these issues throughout each chapter through the use of numerous case examples of contemporary dilemmas from the authors' own assessment practice; and learning exercises aimed at promoting reflexive practice. Additionally, the complexities of anti-oppressive practice, not least the problems in assessing outcomes, are discussed, and the psychology relevant to decision-making is detailed in relevant chapters. There are also two new concluding chapters addressing the impact of new legislation and government guidance on *assessment in children's services* and *assessment in adult services*. The research into performance indicators and method outcomes is also described and each chapter includes pointers to the relevant sections from National Occupational Standards for Social Work.

Despite the increasing complexity of assessment work, we hope that this book provides social work students and practising social workers with clear and accessible information on how to undertake collaborative assessments which lead to effective and appropriate interventions.

A new feature of this edition is the inclusion of thinking points and learning exercises. While it is hoped they will inspire the strong student to develop a critical appreciation of the material, developing reflective practice takes time and experience. Therefore, it is hoped that social work lecturers and practice teachers will use the thinking points and learning exercises with students in the first place.

CHAPTER I

Assessment in the Twenty-First Century

What this chapter is about

In this chapter we will look at the difficulty of defining assessment. How theory and research influence social workers' hypotheses about the focus of assessment will then be addressed, as will the impact of a massive amount of legislation and government guidance in recent years and the complexities arising out of the emphasis on managing risk.

MAIN POINTS

➤ Definitions of assessment.

➤ Psychology versus sociology.

➤ What is normal?

➤ How hypotheses are formed and checked.

➤ The changing legal context and its impact.

➤ Evidence-based effective practice.

➤ Handling uncertainty in complex assessments.

Defining assessment

Although Crisp *et al.* (2005) found that there was no universally agreed definition in social work, most textbooks on assessment offer some definition related to one or more of the five stages of assessment proposed by us in the previous edition of this book (Milner and O'Byrne 2002). Coulshed and Orme (2006) said it was an ongoing process in which the service user participates, the purpose of which is to understand people in relation to their environment; it is the basis for planning what needs to be done to maintain, improve and bring about change. Kemshall (1998) said it is a process of professional judgement or appraisal of the situation, circumstances and behaviour of the service user and it might involve risk assessment, while Griggs (2000) said it is about ascertaining need.

More comprehensively, Smale *et al.* (1993) held that realistic assessment has: to address the whole of the task, to engage in ongoing negotiations with the full range of people involved in the situation and their possible solutions and to address both the change, care and social control tasks so as to go beyond the individualization of social problems as the focus for assessment and intervention. Compton and Galaway (1999) described assessment as the collection and processing of data to provide information for use in making decisions about the nature of a problem and what is to be done about it. It is a cognitive process: it involves thinking about the data, and the outcome is a service plan which provides a definition of the problem for work objectives or solutions to be achieved, and an action plan to accomplish the objectives. For Hepworth *et al.* (2002) assessment is a fluid, dynamic process of receiving, analysing and synthesizing new information as it emerges through the entire course of a given case.

The *Framework for the Assessment of Children in Need and Their Families* (DoH, 2000) says it involves analysis, judgement and decision-making, but in its explanation of these aspects it speaks of judgement in the analysis section and decision-making in the judgement section. We hope our definition will help to clear up some of the difficulties.

Our definition

Assessment in social work is a five-stage process of exploring a situation by:

1. *Preparing* for the task.

2. *Collecting data*, including perceptions of the service user, the family and other agencies of the problem and any attempted solutions.

3. *Applying professional knowledge* (practice wisdom as well as theory) to seek analysis, understanding or interpretation of the data.

4. *Making judgements* about the relationships, needs, risks, standard of care or safety, seriousness of the situation, and people's capacities and potential for coping or for change (is the progress good enough?).

5. *Deciding* and/or recommending what is to be done, plus how, by whom and when, and how progress will be reviewed.

In this definition, *analysis* is about making sense of events and statements, arriving at an overall picture and an understanding of what is happening and perhaps giving some thought as to how the situation has come about, using one or more of the theoretic 'maps'. *Judgement* is about what is good enough and what is not, what is dangerous and what is reasonably safe, what is of a reasonable standard and what is not. *Decision-making* is about future action or inaction and aspects of that action, with a plan for carrying it out and reviewing it. Described thus it seems almost simple, but of course it is anything but in most cases. Even the question of what data to collect, what is relevant, what is enough, and so on, makes the very start of the process difficult and many of the frameworks that have been written are little more than checklists to ensure nothing relevant is forgotten in stages 1 and 2 of work with particular service user groups. Where it is needed most – in stages 3, 4 and 5 – there is less guidance. We will return to examining frameworks in Chapter 3; first we consider some of the debates over what knowledge informs the process.

How working hypotheses are developed

Traditionally, social work texts have expressed agreement that assessment is a key element in social work practice, in that without it workers would be left to react to events and intervene in an unplanned way (see for example Coulshed *et al.*, 2006). Having agreed on the centrality of assessment in the social work process, some texts, over the last twenty years, then dismissed the subject in a few pages. Apart from some brief homilies on counterchecking facts and hypotheses and the necessity of reassessing wherever appropriate, most writers made a list of information-yielding sources and then departed from the subject to other aspects of the social work process. The exceptions include Middleton (1997), Clifford (1998) and Parsloe *et al.* (1999), who have written books specifically on assessment.

However, gathering information, sifting it carefully and coming to an 'objective' and 'accurate' conclusion is by no means as unproblematic as this infers; assessment has never been the scientific, easy to learn activity that many writers pretended. For example, Coulshed and Orme (1998) compared assessment with a social study that 'avoids labels and is reached as a result of logical analysis of data which has been carefully and systematically collected' (p. 3). They implied that editing needed to be done but made no suggestion as to how this skill could be acquired, although editing shapes the way information is collected and selected for the initial assessment (Sheldon, 1995), and later information is processed selectively and discretely if it fails to confirm the initial hypothesis (Reder *et al.*, 1993; Milner, 2008b).

CASE STUDY: THEORY INTO PRACTICE

Mohammed and Tracy's children were removed from their care following discovery that Mohammed was violent towards Tracy, that their home lacked some basic amenities, and that they regularly entertained large numbers of young people who were known to misuse substances. Mohammed and Tracy obtained the tenancy of a more suitable house in a nearby town, the address of which they kept from their previous acquaintances. They were angry and upset throughout the subsequent child protection assessment process, being particularly aggrieved at what they perceived as a lack of acknowledgement of their efforts to meet the concerns which had led to the removal of their children. After Mohammed beat Tracy again, she ejected him from the house and was hopeful that she would regain the care of her children. She found the questions asked as part of the continuing assessment offensively intrusive and tended to respond in either an angry or a tearful manner. The social worker accepted that Tracy had done everything demanded of her but continued with care proceedings on the grounds that Tracy's 'hostility' would make it impossible for her to work with social care if the children were returned on a supervision order.

■ How could the information collected by the social worker have been interpreted differently?

Viewing assessment as unproblematic and unbiased in itself created a gap between theories of problem causation and intervention, a gap in which the service user was often squeezed to fit the social worker's ideas about the nature of people and how best their problems could be addressed. Denney (1992), for example, found in his study of probation reports that many of the assessments seemed to contradict the form of work being advocated. The most commonly used interventions were largely individual rather than social, although there have been some protests:

> If we are to maintain the integrity of 'community' care, 'social' service and 'social' work, we have to confront the constant tendency that we all have to regress to the individualization of people's problems. (Smale and Tuson, 1993, p. 30)

Similarly, Barber (1991) also expressed dismay at the tendency towards 'reductionism' in which social work became equated with casework and individual solutions were found within the psychopathology of individuals and their interpersonal 'relations. Present institutions train several kinds of persons – such as judges and social workers – to think in terms of situations. Their activities and mental outlook are set within the existing norms of society; in their professional work they tend to have an occupationally trained incapacity to rise above 'cases'. Harrison (1995) refers to this as the 'forensic gaze', suggesting that it gives rise to 'placebo solutions'. He illustrates his point with the example of a refugee mother of five children.

Mrs Rusha lost half her family, struggled through a civil war, fought her way to England, studied in the evenings for a decent job and then popped out to the shop, leaving a 10-year-old in charge of the family. She was then 'threatened' with parenting skills training.

This was a solution firmly embedded in a belief that family pathology is the key to much abuse and neglect rather than one, minority, analysis of the context of abuse. Why the preoccupation with individual casework? Scourfield (2003) makes an important point about the impact of theory and research on the development of working hypotheses: '[S]ocial workers take up *selected and condensed messages* from this literature, which are passed on to colleagues through occupational cultures' (p. 111, our emphasis). For example, he found that persistence of psychodynamic ideas about the emotional wellbeing of children in social work practice meant that social workers dig for sexual abuse as an explanation of current family dysfunction: '[I]t seems that social workers want to get beyond the surface of observable family situations to find unpleasant secrets rather than locate causes of problems that can lead to helping strategies' (Scourfield, 2003, p. 127). 'Digging' for secrets is not only subjective data collection but is also deeply resented by service users:

> They failed me with my sexual abuse. My social worker never even turned up for the court case, even though she promised. I took an overdose after the court case and then she turned up … before, she was just digging, thinking it was something else, like a problem at home. (Milner, 2004a)

It also skews the assessment, leading to inappropriate interventions being prescribed.

CASE EXAMPLE

Nadia, a girl subjected to a single sexual assault by a peer acquaintance, was assumed to require counselling due to the traumatic nature of the event. She was referred to a group for girls who had been sexually abused, yet left after one session because the rest of the group had been systematically abused by members of their families over a long period of time, an experience she could not relate to. Nor did the therapy address her specific needs. Questions were asked about her 'denial' (a psychological concept of dubious validity) as she had been subsumed into a category 'abused' without any sense of the complexity and individuality of her own experience. She had been constructed as a victim, which became her identity with all the expectations of this (Myers and Milner, 2007, p. 2). As psychological explanations locate problems and solutions within people, they categorize rather than individualize people.

There are several important assumptions being made here:

Checking assumptions 1

The counselling offered to Nadia is predicated on assumptions that sexual abuse is always traumatic, that it is likely to be repressed (so the person will deny or forget much of it), and that it needs to be sensitively drawn out through the counselling process before the person can 'move on'. Check out the basis of this assumption by reading:

Storr, A. (1966) 'The concept of cure', in C. Rycroft et al. (eds) *Psychoanalysis Observed.* Harmondsworth: Penguin.
Bass, E. and Davis, L. (1988) *The Courage to Heal: A Guide for Women Survivors of Child Sexual Abuse.* New York: HarperCollins.

Dolan, Y. (1991) *Resolving Sexual Abuse*. New York: Norton.
Jones, D. P. H. and Ramchandani, P. (1999) *Child Sexual Abuse: Informing Practice from Research*. Oxford: Radcliffe Medical Press.
Selekman, M. D. (2002) *Living on the Razor's Edge*. London: Norton.

Barber (1991) complains that the problem with much casework theory is that the sole unit of concern and the focus of all analysis is the individual. The research by Sinclair *et al.* (1995) into assessments of young people accommodated by a local authority also expressed concern about the tendency of 'traditional' assessments to concentrate on searching for the origins of past problems. They comment: 'However it is defined, assessment was commonly associated with identifying a problem, the purpose of which was to find an appropriate resource or solution' (Sinclair *et al.*, 1995, p. 130). Given that resources available to social workers have always been restricted, it is not surprising that they have been lured into locating the solution within the individual. There are several reasons why social workers find a broad, social assessment particularly difficult to undertake and present successfully to their managers.

Assessment of individual need is affected by expediency because there is pressure on workers to construct their assessments so that they fit into existing resource provision, although this is not quite what is envisaged in the original Department of Health guidance (1991). The pressures of expediency may mean that it is easier as a consequence to subsume some individual needs under more general family needs when one is faced with uncooperative family members. For example, Bebbington and Miles (1989) found that a combination of poverty and lack of available social support led to children being accommodated, and 'most people enter residential care because of the relationships they have, or do not have, in their social circumstances and not just because of their individual characteristics' (Smale and Tuson, 1993, p. 26). Similarly, mental health problems are more likely to result from a range of adverse factors associated with social exclusion than from individual characteristics (DoH, 1998, p. 6).

When faced with the miseries of poverty, inadequate housing and poor employment conditions, it is easier to seek psychological explanations for events rather than explore complex interactions between the social and psychological dimensions of problems. The 'psychologizing' of social problems in this way has been referred to as 'therapy to help you come to terms with your rats' by practitioners who are only too aware of the fate of an accurate assessment. Agency function rarely permits social workers to address major problems rooted in social deprivation, while, at the same time, holds them responsible for attempting to operationalize a care plan that is not founded on a realistic social assessment.

Equally damaging is sociological reductionism (attributing all social phenomena to social structures alone), as a number of child deaths in families of different cultures demonstrate (see the Climbié report as an example of these). Indeed, research shows that a different approach to child protection assessments is taken depending upon whether the subject of inquiry is a case of physical or sexual abuse – the former tending to focus on parents and the latter on children (Corby, 2000), although this creates difficulties where children are victims of adult sexual abuse but have also been encouraged to sexually abuse their younger siblings. Should the assessment focus on the child's needs or other children's safety (Myers and Milner, 2007)? Scourfield (2003) looks at how working hypotheses are developed from feminist sociological research into sexual violence, with men seen as a threat to children. He found that social workers interpreted the research in a way that formed a rigid template for assessing safety: sexual offenders were viewed as inherently recidivist and thus exempt from the fundamental tenet of social work – universal respect; thus women who refuse to leave such partners are constructed as failing to protect rather than as women in need. This distorts the reality of sexual abuse for mothers, who typically vacillate between believing their partner's assertions of innocence and their children's disclosures (Milner, 2004a). This does not necessarily mean that a mother is either in denial or failing to safeguard her children (for a fuller discussion see Turnell and Essex, 2006).

Checking assumptions 2

What evidence do you have that sex offenders are inherently dangerous and recidivist? Check this out by reading the following:

Craig, L. and Hutchinson, R. B. (2005) 'Sexual offenders with learning disabilities: risk, recidivism and treatment', *Journal of Sexual Aggression*, 11: 289–304.
Grubin, D. (1998) *Sex Offending Against Children: Understanding the Risk. Police Research Paper 99*, London: Home Office.
Soothill, K. *et al.* (2000) 'Sex offenders: specialists, generalists, or both?', *British Journal of Criminology*, 40; 56–67.
Hanson, R. K. (2004) 'Sex offender risk assessment', in Hollin, C. R. (ed.) *The Essential Handbook of Offender Assessment and Treatment.* Chichester: Wiley.

Checking assumptions 3

How likely are child sexual abusers to become adult offenders? Check the evidence for this by reading:

O'Callaghan, D. and Print, B. (1994) 'Adolescent sexual abusers; research, assessment and treatment', in Morrison, T., Erooga, M. and Beckett, R. (eds) *Sexual Offending Against Children: Assessment and Treatment of Male Abusers.* London: Routledge.
Hackett, S. (2004) *What Works for Children and Young People with Sexually Harmful Behaviours?* Barkingside: Barnardo's.

There remains a rightful place for psychological explanations in assessments; the real issue is to remain cautious (Sutton, 2000) and avoid blaming or pathologizing individuals by ascribing to them the cause of their difficulties that stem from injustice, disadvantage and deprivation. Barber (1991) clearly argues that external difficulties cause and interact with internal difficulties.

How does this happen?

The 'social' frequently becomes 'psychological' and vice versa; the disempowered develop 'learned helplessness', for example, and resource improvement may not be a helpful solution on its own. Many service users either 'lack the purchasing power to seek solutions to their problems or are constrained by the courts to submit to social work' (Barber, 1991, p. 29). Common to both instances is a lack of control over some of the important events in their lives, and therefore a 'psychology of empowerment' is useful. Powerlessness generates despair, listlessness and lethargy, people internalising the views of oppressors, blaming themselves and developing dysfunctional, self-defeating thought processes and behaviours so that, in Freire's (1972) terms, 'the oppressor lives inside'.

Social work hypotheses underpinning assessment are encouraged by what has been called an 'individual dependency-led model' (Dalrymple and Burke, 1995), leading to what Lindow (2000) refers to as 'clientism'; that is, simply by *being* a client of social services, people's judgements about themselves and their differences are seen as inferior to those of social workers, who become the experts in problem-solving. None of us are objective in our assessments as we tend to weight some piece of evidence more heavily than others, particularly negative information. There are also two other effects of this *selective attention*: vivid, distinctive or unexpected data are perceptually more salient. The subjects of social work assessments are most likely to encourage these effects, the reason for their referral being usually one which is distinctive. As they will initially be seen when they are at their 'worst' (an overload of negative information), they will then present the assessor with an initial impression that is difficult to dislodge.

Thus service users' potential and possible solutions are often ignored. This leads to social workers clinging to their hypotheses and interventions in the face of considerable failure. For example, child protection social workers who hold strong beliefs about the importance of attachments in healthy personality development undertook lengthy assessments consisting of ten sessions with parents discussing their attachment experiences, without ever once observing the parents parenting their children. The results were that mothers not uncommonly were prescribed counselling to come to terms with previous experiences of sexual abuse before their children could be returned home, despite the mothers exhibiting many mothering skills and capacities (for a fuller discussion see Milner, 2001). Similarly, Dobash *et al.* (2000) base their understanding of domestic violence on a concept of male abuse of power, with interventions predicated on the principle of challenging abusive men in groups. Their research into the men's analyses of their behaviour revealed that the men located their violence in domestic discord and desperately wished to stop arguing and fighting with their partners; and that their narratives were so impoverished that they did not understand the concepts of male power underpinning the prescribed group 'challenging'. Dobash *et al.* (2000) reframe these findings as more 'denial' in need of further challenging. The group work interventions researched had a high dropout rate; however rather than reassess in the light of service user views, the authors recommend more of the same, but backed up by a court mandate (now known as Integrated Domestic Abuse Programmes (IDAP) and run by probation services) The working hypothesis that domestic violence is the mis-use of male power over known women has become so entrenched in social work assessments that female violence or couples fighting is constructed as 'fight-ing back' and totally ignored (for an overview see Milner, 2004a, 2008b). For example, faced with permitting a father to care for his children after his partner left the home following the couple's extensive fighting when they were both coming down from drugs, a female social worker said: 'We did everything we could to keep the children with the mother and get her to separate from the father. It goes against everything I stand for to have had to place them with the offender [the father].'

Checking assumptions 4

To what extent is female violence always a defensive response to men abusing their power? Check this out by reading the following:

McKeowan, K. et al. (2001) *Distressed Relationships: Does Counselling Help?* Dublin: Marital and Relationship Counselling Services.

Grady, A. (2002) 'Female-on-male domestic abuse: uncommon or ignored?' in Young, R. and Hoyle, C. (eds) *New Visions of Crime Victims*. Oxford: Hart.

Muptic, L. R. et al. (2007) 'An exploratory study of women arrested for intimate partner violence: violent women or violent resistance?', *Journal of Interpersonal Violence*, 22: 753–74

Milner, J. (2008b) 'Working with people who are violent towards their partners: a safety building approach', *Journal of Family Therapy*, 30: 29–53.

Lindow (2000) suggests that pessimism and persistence with an original planned intervention is caused partly by the compartmentalized thinking that character-izes much service delivery, the latter imposed largely by legislation which is based on preventing something rather than enabling independence – a shift towards risk assessment. Also, treating people in separate groups according to age or impairment or defined status can powerfully enhance *stereotyping*. There can be some truth in stereotypes – indeed, people give strong signals by the way they present themselves, indicating the categories to which they consider themselves to belong. The danger is that information on which categorization is made may be faulty because of the selective attention errors mentioned above, or because differences from a stereotype that indicate a person's uniqueness may be ignored. For example, a social worker with a stereotype of Asian fami-lies to do with the importance of family networks assessed an Asian woman as depressed owing to social isolation because she had no links with her extended family. This completely ignored the fact that she had made a conscious decision to move away from her family, whom she saw as the cause of her problems in the first place.

Primacy effects work on stereotyping in a peculiar manner. If the first impression is a good impression – which will be weighted heavily for both distinctiveness and primacy effects – a halo effect can sometimes operate in which a person's very positive characteristics colour one's perception of their various other characteristics. This is quite different from picking out positives as well as negatives in assessment work and can have grave consequences when too much is expected of people. Another inherent danger in stereotyping is that it tends to produce negative as well as positive self-fulfilling prophecies about people. Putting people into erroneous categories tends to perpetuate myths about them, as has been amply demonstrated by research into social class, race and gender effects on educational achievement. The results of research into social work attitudes shows that social workers are, like everyone else, susceptible to stereotyping effects, with concomitant self-fulfilling prophecies. Davis and Ellis (1995) found that when social workers were responsible for allocating scarce resources, they labelled people who appeared knowledgeable about their entitlements as 'demanding' and those who tried to exercise choice or challenge workers' judgements as 'fussy' or 'manipulative'.

We suggest that in new situations, social workers routinely ask themselves 'How is this person similar to others – how might they be categorized?' and then ask 'How are they *different*?'. The most common way in which service users are categorized is by age, but this is not always helpful:

CASE STUDY: THEORY INTO PRACTICE

Jeff is a young man who physically abused his partner but had also been sexually abused by his foster father and was about to lose his job; so should he be the subject of a risk assessment or a needs assessment?

Cassy, aged 15, is her disabled mother's primary carer but was being physically abused by her alcoholic father; so should she be assessed as a young carer or as a child at risk of significant harm?

A risk assessment would probably mean that neither of their own descriptions of themselves would be considered: Jeff viewed himself as a child in need while Cassy viewed herself as an adult with responsibilities. If they were to be appropriately compartmentalized for service assessment and delivery, Jeff would be best served by a children and families team and Cassy by an adult care team; although their particular risks and needs do not actually compartmentalize neatly.

While social workers remain within a problem-solving narrative which pays little attention to the complexities of assessment, it is very difficult for them to make social rather than individual assessments, as the former would highlight what is currently well hidden; that is, the moral issues involved in making judgements about what is and what is not desirable social behaviour. It is not surprising, therefore, that social workers tend to drift towards psychological reductionism, to analysing and working on the individual service user. And this service user was for a long time most likely to be a woman. Despite service user compartmentalization, the bulk of carers are women (for an overview see Williams, 1993), as are service users (for an overview see Braye and Preston-Shoot, 1995), although most people's lives are more complex.

CASE EXAMPLE

Lynne's mental and physical frailty cast her as needy (deserving), vulnerable, dependent and incompetent. The influence of scarce resources meant that when her son lost his flat through unpaid rent and moved in with her, he was recruited as her main carer. She then had several hospital admissions following overdoses and facial bruising which she told neighbours were caused by her son but which she vigorously denied in hospital. A reassessment of her as victim of adult abuse floundered on the possibility of further risk to Lynne of re-abuse and the loss of her main carer. In actual fact this family's relationships were more complex than carer and cared-for. They were interconnected in that they both were grieving the recent deaths of Lynne's husband and older son; they were interdependent in that the son needed a home with his mother and she depended on him to pick her up after falls and arrange medical treatment; and neither of them had any other close emotional contact. Thus they were simultaneously vulnerable and competent and their desires for independence and choice were stifled by assessments which were framed in the 'either/or' of needs/risk.

The changing legal context and its impact on practice

The sweeping reforms embodied in the welfare and education legislation enacted in England in the early 1990s, with the emphasis on the family and its informal networks as an essentially private arena for the provision of care – a new view of the family, as an independent economic unit – clarified the distinction between assessment and intervention but added a new set of values for social workers. (The legislation varies in Wales, Scotland and Northern Ireland. For examples of how assessment practice is affected see Cree and Myers, 2008.) These included partnership, empowerment, multi-agency cooperation, and value for money. Assessment was separated from interventions, which became 'care planning', the former being focused on the identification of the objectives of care and the problems to be tackled, and the latter being focused on the actual selection of appropriate means to meet these needs.

However broadly welcome the new legislation was to social workers, it had two major influences on assessment practices. First, by separating assessment from intervention and social workers from much 'hands-on' intervention, it removed them from the source of their practice theory. Second, it made their values explicit. It did not increase resources, suggest new interventions or state how the people social workers traditionally 'individualized' were to be increasingly valued by society. While providing much-needed definitions of assessment, the new legislation had the effect of leaving social workers in a vacuum between the old and new styles of working and/or encouraging a checklist mentality. Some of the blame for the vacuum lay however with agency management, whose role was to equip staff for change; the law itself cannot directly govern practice.

Although all the major pieces of legislation (the Children Act 1989, the National Health Service and Community Care Act 1990, and the Criminal Justice Act 1991, the Education Reform Act 1993,) emphasized assessment as a separate and important activity, with both the Children Act and the National Health Service and Community Care Act having the same ideological underpinnings, it was the latter which most clearly spelled out precisely what is meant by assessment: '[T]here has clearly been detailed thinking on the purpose and nature of assessment activity and this is reflected in the impressive range of documents which have been produced by the SSI on this topic' (Sinclair *et al.*, 1995, p. 42).

Although s. 17 of the Children Act (1989) gave local authorities a general duty to safeguard and promote the welfare of children in need, there was little reference to the assessment of children 'in need' in the guidance accompanying the Act (Tunstill, 1993). As a consequence, women, who were most likely to be on the receiving end of assessments, were subject to a bewildering variety of formats depending on the location of the social worker within a specific specialization with its own particular assessment definition. Take, for example, the following hypothetical scenario of Mrs Edwards:

> Mrs Edwards is a depressed black woman living in poor material circumstances with three children, two of whom have problems at school, and a partner who is due to be paroled from prison where he is serving a sentence for aggravated burglary. She has no near relatives, although she is a regular churchgoer.

By 1996, Mrs Edwards could have found herself subjected to several varied and contradictory assessment formats depending upon which part of the welfare services first came into contact with her. For example, her mental health needs might have been assessed under the provisions of the NHS and Community Care Act 1990, but she may equally have received a risk assessment under the provisions of the Mental Health Act 1983. Similarly, the needs of her children could have been assessed in terms of either s. 17 or the risks to them estimated under s. 8 of the Children Act 1989. Additionally, there was the possibility that her children would be assessed under the provisions of either the Education Act 1981 or the Education Act 1993, depending largely on whether their special educational needs were determined to be worthy of specialist educational support or whether they fell into an exclusion from school category.

Mrs Edwards might well have been assessed under the provisions of the Criminal Justice Act 1991 to determine whether she was able to reduce the risk of her partner reoffending. She was also entitled to an assessment of her own needs under the Carers (Recognition and Service) Act 1995.

Following guidance relating to the NHS and Community Care Act 1990, the hypothetical Mrs Edwards's first assessment would probably be undertaken by a care manager. This assessor is charged with aiding her empowerment through the rights of citizenship, the right to self-determination, dignity and individualization. Her limited choices were to be maximized and her individual aspirations and abilities realized, and the 'assessment process should be as simple, speedy and informal as possible' (Department of Health, 1991, 3.3). Additionally, Mrs Edwards should have extended choices as a potential service user and be involved in a participatory assessment process (Social Services Inspectorate, 1991). Baldwin (1993) argued that choice was to be defined as knowledge and experience of three or more options.

After assessing Mrs Edwards's needs according to these principles, the care manager would come up against the reality that community care in the form of, say, respite or domiciliary care was in short supply and probably available only for 'deserving' or 'high-risk' cases. So this woman would have a high probability of facing child protection case conference scrutiny of her mothering as a means of converting her into a high enough risk case to obtain access to scarce resources (Denman and Thorpe, 1993; Milner, 1993), an experience which could hardly be anything but humiliating. In this assessment arena, despite the parental partnership prescription of the Children Act 1989, the development of participation would be restricted and ambiguous, and its focus limited and not always welcomed by families (Thoburn *et al.*, 1995).

The reality of providing resources for Mrs. Edwards meant that although '[p]ackages of care should be designed in line with individual needs and preferences' (Meredith, 1993, p. 41) and despite the fact that '[a]uthorities are aware that assessment systems must centre on the needs of users and carers rather than the requirements of services' (Audit Commission, 1992, p. 36), neither of these considerations would be likely to be implemented. The latter one would be particularly difficult to achieve in our scenario because of the prescription not to discriminate on the grounds of cultural needs (see for example Home Office *et al.*, 1995, p. 5). Despite the official guidance, interventions and assessments for black people were particularly underdeveloped and inappropriate for these potential service users (see for example Ahmad, 1990; Denney, 1992).

Between 1990 and 2000 numerous Department of Health guidance papers appeared dealing with mental health, looked-after children, modernization of social services, frameworks for action with various service users, national service frameworks, and quality strategies. 2000 brought the *Framework for the Assessment of Children in Need and Their Families*, a document that still sets the principles for assessment in child protection work, and on which the modern *Common Assessment Framework* is based. The Common Assessment Framework followed the Children Act 2004 and the *Every Child Matters* agenda and its guidance papers. The Children's Act (2004) requires local authorities to have regard for the importance of parents and other carers in improving children's wellbeing and requires them to liaise with other services for this purpose. The Act has initiated Local Safeguarding Children Boards (LSCBs) which are now producing impressive clear guidance, definitions and flowcharts. (These documents will be considered in detail in Chapter 10.) In theory, once one agency records information concerning any referral, it is expected, with consent, to share the information/assessment with other agencies that may become involved in the case so that the service user does not have to repeat the history and basic data.

Meanwhile, in adult services for care in the community, the *National Framework for Older People* (2001c) proposed that by 2004 there should be a *Single Assessment Process* (SAP) for all adults. This scheme is still being developed with talk of moving adult assessment on to a Common Assessment Framework (not to be confused with the Common Assessment Framework for children). The adult Common Assessment Framework may incorporate the Health Service assessment process and be managed jointly by Health and Local authorities. In 2005 the *Fair Access to Care* document proposed a framework for the allocation of care in the community services, based on the risk of loss of independence, immediate or long-term. Four categories of risk of such loss – critical, substantial, moderate and low – would decide the amount of help needed. However, limited funding may mean that only the higher categories will receive help.

The Mental Capacity Act 2005 (DoH, 2005b) stresses that capacity is to be presumed, and not to be ruled out because the person makes an unwise decision. The 2006 document *Our Health, Our Care, Our Say* spelt out differing levels of care for those leaving hospital. In that same year the paper *Guidance on Person-Centred Integrated Care Planning* reinforced the policy of healthcare and care provided by local authorities being coordinated with joint management networks by 2008. Also the paper *Independence, Choice and Risk* placed a new emphasis on supporting service users' decisions and choices about their care. The Mental Health Act (2007) further strengthened people's rights while safeguarding the public. The direct payments to service users, first proposed in 1996, is now making an impact in some areas, although there are concerns about how they will be rationed if local authority budgets are cut. Some managers may be concerned over loss of control – fewer than fifty areas have paid out any real money as yet, and a further Green Paper is expected during 2008.

It is good that much of the recent government guidance stresses not only interagency collaboration (although that is not without its problems) and it has put more emphasis on assuming people's competence and ability to respond to useful help, on better collaboration with service users and their families and on paying more attention to people's own expertise. There will be much more detail on this in Chapter 11.

(A full outline of current laws and procedures in England and Wales is presented in Chapters 10 and 11.)

THINKING POINT

- To what extent will the single assessment process simplify Mrs Edwards's assessment?
- In what ways will it enable the assessing social worker to provide her with choices and independence?

Evidence-based practice

A further complication in assessment work is the growing trend to promote evidence-based practice. While the definition of this is being widened to include not only research but also government guidance, the work of theorists and other writers, and practice wisdom and experience, there are two main strands to evidence-based practice; the *first* being research evidence into problem causality, evaluation for knowledge as opposed to accountability (for a fuller discussion of the purposes of evaluation research see Lewis and Utting, 2001). This 'evidence' influences the 'facts' selected during the assessment process, determining whether the focus is on needs, risks, potential or resources. For example, the evidence from *attachment* studies provides an explanation for dysfunctional behaviour at any stage of the life span (for an overview see Howe, 1995) and is widely used in assessments, particularly in adoption, guiding and informing a range of interventions aimed at fulfilling attachment *needs*. Other evidence provides possible indications of increased *risk*, for example, the link between early cruelty to animals and subsequent abusive behaviour in adulthood (for an overview see Lockwood and Ascione, 1998). In the case of the former, biases necessarily creep in – mainly to do with neglecting the wider social context of families as intrapersonal relationships are explored (Jack and Gill, 2003); while in the latter, a checklist mentality is encouraged – despite prediction checklists being shown to be crude and unreliable measures of risk (for an overview see Corby, 2000, pp. 186–9). Thus, simpler diagnosis is achieved at the expense of false certainty – a certainty that is hidden as social workers rarely make clear their preferred theories about the nature of people to the service users they are assessing. This denies the service user the possibility of participating fully in an assessment. When given this opportunity, they often define themselves differently. For example, when we advertised a domestic violence service for adults who wished to change their abusive behaviour, we found that three of the first ten adults to avail themselves of the service were women in same-sex relationships. As other programme designs were underpinned by 'evidence' that domestic violence is the result of the abuse of male power, interventions consisted of groups for heterosexual men and refuges/support services for heterosexual women, thus effectively denying resources to lesbian, gay and bisexual people.

The *second* strand of evidence-based practice takes a more pragmatic view, being concerned primarily with effective practice. Chapman and Hough (2001) see this concern as arising partly from an increase in the probation service's caseload which coincided with pressures of cash limits and partly as a reverse of the 'Nothing Works' pendulum. Outcome research indicates that some probation interventions are more effective than others (see for example McGuire, 1995) and this shifts the focus of assessment work away from needs in favour of extensive assessments of risk of harm, offender motivation, and the targeting of effectiveness-based work using specific models such as that devised by Kemshall (1998). Similarly, outcome research indicates particular intervention effectiveness in other areas of social work; see for example, Macdonald (1998) on child protection, Macdonald (1997) on mental health, Buchanan (1999) on young people with behavioural disorders. Details on outcome research into the effectiveness of particular social work methods is included at the end of the 'map' chapters, Chapters 5 to 9.

Evaluation research undertaken to establish accountability ('Did It Work?') is often regarded as particularly sound research because of the impartiality of the 'stand aloof' researcher (Lewis and Utting, 2001; Newburn, 2001) but biases still exist. Macdonald (2000) suggests that synthesizing the effectiveness literature is fraught with difficulties in that literature reviews often contain biased summaries, that much of the research is out of date at publication, and that it is rarely updated in the light of new evidence. And as Webb (2001) points out, evidence-based practice is limited by the complex phenomena involved; for example, much decision-making is not rationally determined or subject to control. There is also 'a degree of ambiguity over the extent to which "what works" for children is the same as "what works" for families and "what works" for society as a whole' (Glass, 2001, p. 17).

Smith (2004) makes the important point that whatever the evidence, some practitioners are not only more skilled than others but also better at deciding what evidence is relevant to a particular case, thus success may not be evidence that a particular theory works but simply that the worker is skilled:

> What matters or should matter in making choices among theories is whether a given theory is helpful in a particular context in relation to a particular problem, not whether it has consistently demonstrated its predictive power. (Smith, 2004, p. 16)

In making a choice of a particular theory or specific research findings, the practitioner also needs to be aware that others involved in the case may have different preferences. This is especially true where the assessment is a joint or team one (Trevithick, 2007). At least this may limit the contributions of some practitioners where they lack the status of others; at worst it will confuse the service users.

Uncertainty

Despite the growing volume of frameworks and checklists, for the busy social worker trying desperately to keep up to date with all the new information contained in the research literature and the procedures and responsibilities laid down in government guidance, selecting what information is relevant to them remains the biggest problem in assessing for a specific purpose (either risk or needs) and being fair. The social work literature, research evidence and government guidance has been, and sometimes remains, vague about how this task is to be undertaken, yet it is central in that the process controls the nature, direction and scope of social work intervention; an intervention that may well affect a service user's entire life.

It is rarely possible to have a single purpose when dealing with families in trouble. Their real-life situations involve the assessing social worker in attempts to achieve a satisfactory balance between diverse needs, recognized risks and restricted resource provision, or between considering whether some intervention should be attempted as against the restraints of time. And there always exists the tendency to drift not only towards psychological reductionism as a placebo solution to inadequate resources, but also towards risk assessments as a response to continuous public castigation of social work efforts. Despite the principle that individuals should be allowed to assess the risks to themselves, should an elderly person be found to have died alone at home it is likely that social work will be found culpable. A study of care provided for elderly people (Sinclair *et al.*, 1990, p. 176) found that:

> Social workers were predominantly concerned with the degree to which clients were 'at risk'. So in order to assist decisions about staying at home or moving to residential care, workers examined depression, mental confusion, the client's failure to behave prudently, the effects of living alone while being physically ill or disabled, and environmental factors such as trip hazards or poor heating.

Risk predominates in the assessments of elderly people being discharged home from hospital. Clark *et al.* (1996) found that older people were less concerned about their safety than professional assessments indicated, being more concerned with coming to terms with their disabilities and retaining some control over their lives. This in no way follows the recommendations for comprehensive assessment outlined by Challis *et al.* (1990), which included physical and mental health, attitude and outlook, environmental and social circumstances, views of their most pressing problems and desired solutions, and identification of retained abilities and strengths.

There are, however, some welcome trends in all these added complexities. The revised assessment framework for children in need and their families (DoH *et al.*, 2000c) shifted the focus of assessment away from deficit identification by recommending that the assessing social worker build on family strengths as well as identify difficulties (1.33). It also explicitly encouraged assessment of family *and* environmental factors; for example, exploration of the wider context of the local neighbourhood and community and its impact on children and their parents; and identification of community resources (2.16). This helps to counter the tendency of psychologizing families; at the very least, the potential value of church attendance for our hypothetical Mrs Edwards would be seriously considered in the assessment process; while, optimally, her poor material circumstances will be addressed. Similarly, guidance on care leavers now stresses that assessment is a process requiring continual planning (DoH, 1999). The Mental Capacity Act 2005 has begun to improve how mental capacity is considered, and in child care work the guidance from some LSCBs is becoming clearer and more balanced – see for example the West Yorkshire Consortium's Procedures Manual (2007) on www.procedures.leedslscb.gov.uk.

Whatever the difficulties with the effectiveness research, it has at least identified the core skills of successful assessment work. These include being punctual, reliable, courteous, friendly, honest and open: 'Staff who lack integration between their values and behaviour lose credibility with the people with whom they are working' (Chapman and Hough, 2001, 1.53). Similarly, the DoH (1999b) identifies listening, being non-judgemental, having a sense of humour,

straight talking, and being trustworthy as essential elements of good professional practice (3.40). This brings assessment work back to basic social work
principles and considerably clarifies the task.

Being straightforward with people and embracing the complexities of their
lives actually helps make sense of the sometimes competing requirements in
assessment activity. Despite their similarities, people are actually very different
in how they deal with their difficulties and so do not fit neatly into existing categories of service provision. Nor do they define themselves as carer or
cared-for, or abused or abuser, or competent or vulnerable. These categories
are more blurred in the everyday realities of their lives. Service users are capable of making assessments about their own needs, risks, and the resources they
would find useful; thus being potentially able to do much of the work for
the assessor – even where risk factors are high, such as in cases where child
abuse is strongly suspected but denied (Essex *et al.*, 1996). This is recognized
in the guidance on adult abuse (DoH, 2000a) where it is recommended that
social workers assess their assessments by learning from experience – including
user/carer views on how interventions have worked for *them* (3.19), reflecting
what Lymbery (2001) refers to as the breaking down of barriers between service users and social workers to create a 'new professionalism' that encompasses
values of empowerment, advocacy and anti-oppressive practice as part of everyday social worker thinking. We examine anti-oppressive practice more fully in
the following chapter.

As for uncertainty, we see it as a positive element. We invite social workers to
resist the pressure for certainty because *uncertain is how things are*. It is striving
for certain ground under our feet that causes stress, not the uncertainty itself.

SUMMARY

- A preoccupation with individual casework has inhibited the development of
  social assessments.

- Assessments have tended to locate the problems of family dysfunction not only
  in individuals, but also in individual mothers.

- Assessment practice is beginning to move towards a balance of interests and
  external factors and more respect for service users' attitudes and views.

- 'Borrowed' knowledge from psychiatry and psychology has been the major
  influence on social work assessments. Even where there is an obvious
  psychological dimension, the balance between internal and external factors
  needs careful consideration.

- Legislation defines assessment as an activity separate from intervention.
  Assessment activity is defined differently in each new piece of legislation.

- Differing emphases on risk, needs, resources and options make it difficult for
  social workers to develop an overarching framework for all their assessments.
  A dual focus on risk and safety is easier to accommodate in assessment
  frameworks than needs and risk.

- Assessments are best evaluated for their effectiveness in terms of the resulting decisions on service users' lives.

- Social workers need to learn to live with uncertainty and to communicate it to others while stating firmly what their own professional experience tells them should be done.

FURTHER LEARNING ACTIVITIES

1. Take the most cherished idea that underpins your understanding of the nature of people and search for evidence that undermines this idea.

2. Take any situation that you are aware of and consider your understanding of what went on. What was the balance of psychological and sociological factors in your analysis?

3. List some of the merits of uncertainty and of certainty.

4. Debate: In their everyday lives, are people more similar or more different?

FURTHER READING

Clifford, D. (1998) *Social Assessment Theory and Practice: A Multidisciplinary Framework.* Aldershot: Ashgate.

Parsloe, P. (1999) *Risk Assessment in Social Work and Social Care (Research Highlights).* London: Jessica Kingsley.

NATIONAL OCCUPATIONAL STANDARDS

For students working with the British National Occupation Standards for Social Work (see Appendix):

- This chapter relates to *practice* elements 1.1; 5.1; 11.1–4; 18.1–3.

- With which of the *knowledge* requirements in the Appendix does this chapter help you?

CHAPTER 2

Anti-Oppressive Practice

What this chapter is about

In this chapter we examine the origins of anti-discriminatory and anti-oppressive practice in the radical social work of the 1970, and how it has been developed by Dalrymple and Burke (1995), Thompson (2003a, 2006a) and Burke and Harrison (2002). The complicated nature of power is then discussed and the interplay between the various 'isms' is examined. The implications for assessment are detailed, particularly the importance of negotiating perceptions and recognizing diversity. There follows a critical comment on the lack of an adequately agreed definition of what constitutes equality; the nature of knowledge; and the fluidity of social divisions which complicates anti-oppressive practice. The chapter concludes with suggestions on the basic elements of effective anti-oppressive practice, those which promote genuine partnerships in the assessment process.

MAIN POINTS

> ➤ Wider theoretical issues: origins of AOP and ADP, the complexities of power.
>
> ➤ The 'isms': class, race and gender (the 'big three') and other social divisions such as religion, sexuality, disability, age, and language.
>
> ➤ The implications for assessments: negotiating perceptions, similarities and differences, systems theory, and acknowledging diversities.
>
> ➤ Critical comments on 'correct' anti-oppressive practice, equality and rights.
>
> ➤ Outcomes in research measures and the effectiveness of anti-oppressive practice.

Wider theoretical perspectives

Anti-discriminatory and anti-oppressive practice has its roots in the radical social work movement of the 1970s which was informed by humanistic and social justice values, raising awareness of how poverty and deprivation affected the lives of service users. The 1980s saw an increased awareness of inequalities arising from gender and ethnicity as well as class, culminating in the seminal work of Hugman (1991), who drew attention to the inadequate concept of rights which had underpinned citizenship in Western liberal democracies (p. 215) and the inequalities arising from this. Anti-oppressive practice is based on a belief that social work should make a difference so that those oppressed may regain control of their lives and re-establish their right to be full and active members of society. To this end, say Dalrymple and Burke (1995), practitioners have to be political, reflective, reflexive and committed to promoting change. Reflection and reflexivity mean that they need to be critical of their everyday practice to ensure that they do not abuse their power, but having a commitment to challenging inequalities is viewed as central to effective anti-oppressive practice (Burke and Harrison, 2002, p. 230). Anti-discriminatory practice (Thompson, 2003a, 2006) focused more on managing diversity on the grounds that the result of negative discrimination is generally one of oppression, thus avoiding too narrow a perspective of equal opportunities. Central to both anti-oppressive and anti-discriminatory practice is the notion of empowerment and emancipation.

Thus, social work practice has moved away from traditional approaches emphasizing a need to diagnose the problems of individual people and their families (largely through psychological knowledge) towards a more emancipatory form of practice which locates those individuals within their social contexts, particularly the structural patterns of society that perpetuate inequalities (for a fuller discussion see Thompson, 1993, 1997, 2003a, 2006). The traditional values of social work have been accommodated to some extent; for example, unconditional acceptance becomes respect for clients' dignity and strengths, self-determination becomes promotion of choice, and non-judgementalism becomes non-discrimination and anti-oppression. However, combining individualism, social collectivity and an understanding of oppression in all its forms involves also accommodating overlapping psychological and social theories, creating a practice tension that is not easily resolved. At the most basic level, psychological theories underpinning different methods of interventions, those which social workers commonly use to 'shape' their assessments, were developed primarily as means by which individuals could be better understood by 'experts'. Attempts to graft on notions of empowerment to existing theories ignores their inbuilt Eurocentric and professional bias.

Despite their benevolent intentions, these theories 'essentially reflect the power relationships that exist between us all' (Dalrymple and Burke, 1995, p. 11). These existing power relationships are basically white, male, healthy, employed and Western-dominated. McNay (1992) suggests that, while all oppressions are important, gender, race and class are more central to the profit base of our economy and therefore have a greater effect on how lives are lived and dominated (for example, by the exploitive division of labour). Although advocating that other social divisions should be extended, Payne, G. (2006) still considers race, class and gender as the 'big three'. Clifford (1994) writes that the material basis of social divisions is a governing factor in understanding real lives, going on to suggest that good practice requires the participation of workers whose personal experience of oppression gives them a counter-hegemonic understanding of material as well as cultural and personal differences. By this, some sense of 'fit' is implied between the different levels of anti-oppressive theory – materialist social theory, strategic practice theory and working concepts – which Dalrymple and Burke (1995) maintain should respond to the reality of both service users' and social workers' lives. Similarly, attempting to reduce the complexities of this practice tension to personal prejudice or structural disadvantage, what Thompson (1998) refers to as psychological and sociological reductionism, can actually increase discrimination; a rigid interpretation of social structural oppression having the capacity to dehumanize social work and result in formulaic interventions (see for example Featherstone and Trinder, 1997) as much as a rigid interpretation of psychological knowledge has the capacity to story an individual *as* a problem (see for example White, M., 1995). We will address these complexities but this chapter will first examine what the various forms of oppression have in common, in particular the abuse of power.

Power

Power is a significant element in every relationship and a main motivating influence. Indeed, all relationships, whether between one individual and another, between one group and another, or between rulers and subjects, can be said to be the result of power. In social work, power may be legitimately used to empower others in anti-oppressive practice or illegitimately used to oppress others in malpractice. Power is also an element in the competitiveness of life, of the struggle for resources, employment and education. Social workers, too, can experience a lack of power, and this can help them to understand service users better, but, crucially, the concern for social workers is when power is used to exclude and marginalise: '[W]e must recognise the power of social workers in terms of knowledge and expertise; access to resources; statutory powers; and influence over individuals, agencies, and so on' (Thompson, 1996a). In work with marginalised people, we seek to counteract negative images of self, negative life experiences, blocked opportunities and unrelenting physical and emotional distress, Thompson (2003a, 2006) argues that it is essential to take a three-track approach that links the personal (P) with the cultural (C) and structural (S). P refers to personal/psychological factors and also to practice and prejudice; C refers to culture, commonalties, consensus and conformity; and, S refers to structural aspects, social forces or the socio-political dimension. Thompson describes P as being embedded in C and C in S, yet as all interacting with each other:

> It would be naïve to assume that professional practice can make major changes at the structural level. However, empowerment, by assisting people to take greater control over their lives, can have a significant impact at the personal level, thereby making a contribution at the cultural level and, in turn, playing at least a small part in undermining inequality at the structural level. (Thompson, 2003a, p. 221)

It is optimistic to think that empowerment can be actualized just by minor tinkering with social workers' preferred theories. Traditional family therapists and psychodynamic counsellors have not readily addressed the complaints of feminists and black people that their theories lack an appreciation of the impact of patriarchal power on women and the impact of racism on black people. Their adaptations have been largely cosmetic and have done little to make social workers more confident about what empowerment, partnership and choice actually consist of (see for example Macleod and Saroga, 1988; Cavanagh and Cree, 1996). It is naïve to underestimate the difficulties in operationalising empowerment strategies – powerful people (and powerful theories and methods of intervention) are resistive to yielding power: 'Power concedes nothing without demand...the limits of tyrants are precise by the endurance of those they oppress' (Douglas, quoted in Dalrymple and Burke, 1995, p. 14). Social workers are not in a position to *give* people power, and their aim to *help reduce* the powerlessness that individuals and groups experience is likely to be limited by other individuals' and groups' investment in power positions *and* in the complex nature of power.

There is an important psychological legacy left by powerlessness that includes lethargy, despair and listlessness – 'learned helplessness' – and, as Freire (1972) called it, a 'culture of silence' in which there is an apparent acceptance of servitude and dependence. The marginalized subscribe to the myth that they get what they deserve, and internalize, and are possessed by, feelings of alienation and worthlessness. For example: 'It is practically impossible for a lesbian, gay or bisexual person who has grown up in British society *not* to have internalised negative messages about their sexuality' (Davies, 1999, p. 55). Social workers can unconsciously reinforce this message through well meaning attempts to recognize diversity; for example, the commonly used term to describe young people 'as confused about their sexuality' is not used to mean 'that a person has doubts that they are gay and considers that they may be heterosexual; it is a code for thinking about being gay' (Milner and Myers, 2007, p. 2). As Hicks (2007) points out, seeing lesbians, gays and bisexuals as fixed types with needs that need to be understood and met by social workers neglects the important question of the power of social work to *produce* these categories.

Powerlessness is not necessarily expressed in terms of easily defined oppressed groups; it is much more diverse and complex. Indeed, Foucault questions the relevance of ideas about power as primarily repressive by counterposing the idea of power as productive (see for example Sawicki, 1991). Modern developments of power operate in subtle terms through self-regulation. For example, it is difficult to see quite 'who' is oppressing mothers as the psychology underpinning 'good enough' mothering has become internalized. Mothers operate within a 'discourse' that does not need the so-called experts of child-rearing necessarily to be on hand for advice (for a fuller discussion see Ingleby, 1985).

Similarly, children, a perhaps easily identifiable oppressed group, are not entirely powerless. Foucault considers resistance and power to be interrelated. Marshall (1996) discusses the relevance of the 'discourse' in which children place themselves as necessary for understanding the complexities of their power relationships. Thus, a child at school might be seen to be oppressed in terms of teacher discipline but may be acting in a children's discourse in which the teacher's power discourse is irrelevant. Marshall cites an example of a classroom incident involving young children and a female teacher in which two young boys temporarily positioned the teacher as a subordinate through the use of sexually explicit language. The teacher was unable to reassert control as the dichotomy between adult and child had been redefined as one between male and female, wherein the males are more powerful. The author concludes:

> Thus, through some discourses, children are able to enact strategies that gain power for themselves in relation to adults and can be experienced by adults as powerful. However, in the context of institutional adult authority these [strategies] may produce situations where children are excluded [from school] and can be seen as *powerfully powerless*. (Marshall, 1996, p. 104, our emphasis)

Appreciating that service users can be oppressed but, simultaneously, 'powerfully powerless' helps social workers to understand their own sense of frustration and powerlessness with looked after children who truant, abscond or continue with the 'undesirable' behaviour that led them to enter the care system in the first place. These are not merely damaged and powerless children in a simple relationship with a powerful welfare network; they are active participants in the various facets of their lives, exerting power often outside the linear relationship with the professionals in the Welfare network (see for example Barrett, 1997; Taylor, 2004). Similarly, social workers will be familiar with service users who are the most easily identifiable as oppressed – poor, old, downtrodden, disadvantaged families – who exhibit resistance through the only power mechanism available to them, the people Dale *et al.* (1986) refer to as 'passive-resistant'. This form of resistance can be very powerful indeed. Cockburn (1991) suggests that we need to recognize power as multidimensional in that it is spread around and that almost all of us share in it a little. Similarly, she argues that power is not always negative in that it can mean capacity as well as domination.

The 'isms'

It is clear that some 'isms' are more powerful than others at various times. Measured on a simple scale of 'isms' training, we would suspect social workers in the 1980s to have been more likely to have undergone race awareness training than any other. One reason for this situation could, perhaps, be that black men have much in common with the most easily identifiable powerful group in our society – white men. There are suggestions that masculine solidarity will make blackness the most important issue, deflecting attention from the issue of male power. As two white, male probation officers say, 'There is more that joins men across class and disability, and even race and sexual orientation, than divides them' (Cordery and Whitehead, 1992, p. 29). We return to the commonality of male experience later in this chapter but question here whether it sufficiently addresses the complexities of race and gender.

THINKING POINT

1. What do you consider to be your ethnic identity?

2. What leads you to this choice?

3. To what extent do you think your answer provides a satisfactory representation of the 'real you'?

4. What are your reasons for this?

(For more information see Payne, G., 2006.)

In the 1990s feminist critiques placed gender more centrally in the anti-oppression debate (see, for example, Butler, 1990; Mullender, 1996; Fawcett *et al.*, 1996), with practice wisdom incorporating notions that are pro-feminist. Not only is it potentially oppressive to promote any particular 'ism' in that it creates a hierarchy of oppression that elevates one form of discrimination above others – it also ignores the interrelatedness and complexities of the various 'isms", most notably race, gender, class, age, disability, and sexual orientation. More recently mentalism, clientism, and linguistic oppression have also received attention (see for example Thompson, 2006); elites and religion are also increasingly being recognized as social divisions (Payne, G., 2006). Aldridge (2006) notes the decline in the social significance of Catholicism in the UK and examines the roots of Islamophobia, suggesting that religion is a cultural resource on which individuals and groups draw for identity, motivation, mobilization and legitimacy; and that as such is a volatile and unpredictable resource which has the capacity for both increasing social cohesion and conflict. The effects of immigration on UK populations will increase religious diversity as much as ethnic diversity and further complicate anti-oppressive practice.

THINKING POINT

1. How does your religion or non-religion relate to your ethnic identity?

2. To what extent would you say that you had chosen your own religious or non-religious identity?

3. Is there a cultural bias against religious minorities?

4. If so, is this based on hostility towards their beliefs and/or practices?

5. How would you distinguish between religious hostility and racism?

(For more information see Payne, G., 2006.)

The interrelatedness of the 'isms' is evident in our earlier scenario of Mrs Edwards and her family (p. 14). For example, if we take seriously that to 'separate racism and sexism is to deny the basic truth of black women's existence' (Dalrymple and Burke, 1995, p. 17), how do we seek to understand our hypothetical black woman discussed earlier? And is this complicated by the possibility that the assessing social worker may be black or white, male or female, heterosexual or homosexual, young or old, and thus have different personal experiences of oppression and power *vis-à-vis* not only the potential service user but also their own institutional authority? Black people, whether male or female, have to negotiate at least three different social contexts: *mainstream* (white) processes, in which they constitute a *minority* (racism), and within that minority context, they also have to negotiate *black cultural* agenda, which can be as diverse as Rastafarianism or Seventh Day Adventism. Their strategies for negotiating these different contexts (like the schoolchildren discussed earlier) will not always be displayed in power and oppression terms which social workers would recognize as appropriate to their positions as service users. For example, for black children, Boykim and Toms (1985) argue that 'the mainstream socialisation has to be negotiated *in lieu* of the minority and black cultural agenda'. These agendas clearly conflict with the mainstream one and, for that matter, also *with each other*. Blyth and Milner (1996) show that black boys' positioning of themselves in a racial and masculinist context in school may seem threatening to white male teachers who are concerned with the mainstream disciplinary context. Channer (1995), on the other hand, highlights the importance of religion, the cultural context, as the main issue in Black African Caribbean school achievement, while Hussain (1996) emphasizes the importance of religion in transcultural fostering. These are power contexts that are largely ignored in most social work assessments yet are a source of strength for black people to alleviate their oppression in the other two contexts. With adults, race, class, gender and sexuality interrelate powerfully with obvious categories masking hidden ones. Myers (2007a) gives the example of a black, severely disabled woman at a conference who chose not to attend a workshop on her 'obvious' categories. Instead, she opted to attend a workshop for lesbians as this was the only category that other people would not automatically assume for her (p. 78).

Ageism, particularly, tends to be regarded as an additional category which increases the treatment of old people as non-persons. There is a dehumanisation inherent in old age as 'negative images of and attitudes towards older people, based solely on the characteristics of old age itself, result in discrimination' (Hughes and Mtezuka, 1992, p. 220). Ageism is compounded by the fact that assessing social workers may have some similarity to potential service users in that they are black or white, male or female, heterosexual or homosexual, but they are never old. Although they can remember what it was like to feel the oppression of youth, they can rarely anticipate what it will be like to be old. Perhaps worrying about their own futures, they tend to homogenize older people as automatically ill and deteriorating, inflexible, miserable, unproductive and dependant although older people actually find old age a better experience than anticipated (O'Leary, 1996). Sexuality tends not to be considered in the assessment of needs of older and disabled people (Myers and Milner, 2007):

> Being disabled following a stroke means, apart from anything else, I'm more dependent on my children. My relationships with my lesbian friends have changed

dramatically. My daughter is in a way relieved that she can think of me as granny instead of a lesbian, I'm respectable, I've even got a sort of status, but it means keeping quiet about the most important part of my life. I'm well looked after, but if I want to go to a gay pub or a woman's day concert, I have to arrange things with my friends, sneaking around like I did when I was a teenager. (Cited in Young, 1999, p. 154)

The 'isms' also compete in complex ways. This is not so much in creating 'deserving' categories of service users but in constructing people as either/or; as victims or perpetrators, cared-for or carers. For example, mothers' needs are often neglected where they are receiving services for a disabled child (Read, 2000), the organizational structuring of social work departments serving to separate 'isms' and create competition. Disability teams rarely have the word 'family' tacked on in the way that children's teams do. The team in which the assessing social worker is located probably influences whether disability and age are prioritized or gender and class. In the latter, the evaluation of gender, through feminist empowerment models, has shifted from highlighting mothers' perceived deficiencies, allowing men to disappear (see for example Milner, 1993) to a tendency to construct men as either threatening or useless (Scourfield, 2003). This is particularly evident in risk assessments where violence is an issue and there is need to construct one person as a perpetrator. Similarly, Wise (1995) cites an example of a young working-class woman, deserted by her violent husband, impoverished, isolated and unhappy, who deals with her despair by getting drunk and forgetting to come home to her young children. She argues that a feminist empowerment model would ignore the fact that the children are the most vulnerable people in this situation. And that a men-as-threatening model underpinning assessments of domestic violence ignores the reality that same-sex violence exists at similar levels to heterosexual violence in intimate relationships (Renzetti, 1992; Leventhal and Lundy, 1999), and the levels of female-on-male violence (Milner, 2004a, 2008; Dutton and Corvo, 2007).

However complex, unequal power relations are still at the root of social injustice and have replaced 'libido' as the core force in understanding human relationships. Those who benefit most from any relationship are those with the most power (McNay, 1992), so an assessment of, for example, mothering needs to look at a woman's lack of power and resources, rather than at her personality, or at least at the interaction between these two aspects. And if she is black, then black culturalism mediates this through how racism compounds her powerlessness and through membership of community groups that can provide a source of strength and group solidarity. Additionally, Thompson (1998, 2003a, 2006) draws our attention to the importance of oppression through the use of language. The most powerful people, those who can enter people into stories about themselves, also create the language used in this process; language is, indeed, man-made (Spender, 1986), reflecting racial and gender divisions. There is also interplay between language and social structure, with language helping to reproduce social values. For example, feminine is a 'marked' category in language where there are pairs of words, such as actor and actress. The word 'actor' functions as neutral term but 'actress' is formally marked as feminine. Close examination of descriptions in case records will usually indicate 'marking' for subjects who are neither male nor white. For example, Denney (1992) shows how the word 'space' has different meanings for black and white subjects of probation reports. For black subjects, space is used to describe physical space, whereas for white subjects it indicates ontological space in which the subject can explore feelings and have space to think. There is also linguistic derogation of women with other pairs of words that do not match, for example, fathering and mothering.

There are also linguistic gaps, such as a dearth of expressions that refer to women's sexual activity in a positive way. For example, women cannot be 'virile', although there are many pejorative words such as 'promiscuous'. The lack of words for many of the activities of women and black people creates silences in which whole areas of experience of people's experiences are ignored (Maynard and Purvis, 1995).

What the various 'isms' have in common is the core value of equal opportunity. Any effective assessment needs to consider the impact of its absence and the absence of equal access to resources. Any fundamental solution to the problems of oppressed groups must include policies that address all elements of oppression. These policies are difficult to formulate because of the complexities mentioned earlier and because of vested power interests, so social workers need to be aware that their efforts to develop anti-oppressive practice will not necessarily be well supported. Agency policies and procedures are as much a barrier to partnership initiatives in child protection work as are family characteristics (Thoburn et al., 1995; Cleaver and Walker, 2004). Social workers' responsibility to practice anti-oppressively is not reflected at other organizational levels (for an overview see Coulshed et al., 2006).

Additionally, assessments need to examine how oppression might be affecting the service user's functioning in the mainstream context. How can we overestimate the sheer grinding stress of experiencing daily injustice for any reason and of feeling devalued because of gender or race? How can we overestimate the psychological effects of being hated, despised, regarded as only fit to service others and discriminated against in housing, education and jobs? The task is enormous but recognizing this helps social workers to begin the first steps towards operationalising anti-oppressive practice.

Implications of anti-oppressive practice for assessments

Dalrymple and Burke (1995, p. 120) propose that an ethical framework for assessment needs to include the following:

- Assessment should involve those being assessed.
- Openness and honesty should permeate the process.
- Assessment should involve the sharing of values and concerns.
- There should be acknowledgement of the structural context of the process.

- The process should be about questioning the basis of the reasons for proposed action, and all those involved should consider alternative courses of action.
- Assessment should incorporate the different perspectives of the people involved.

Negotiating perceptions

If assessment findings are to be considered valid, to have 'truth', the authors' assumptions and biases must be addressed. Likewise, if an assessment is to show a valid understanding of the subject, it must address the 'differences' gap between writer and subject, their mutual subjectivity, their different backgrounds and experiences of life. Social workers have needs too, and if these are not met they function less well. As Nice (1988) has suggested, social workers are taught and expect, like mothers with their families, to put the needs of others above their own. Recognizing their own feelings lays upon them the charge that they are bad social workers. How we function can have an impact on how we see the functioning of others, so any meeting for assessment purposes involves the meeting of two complex subjective worlds.

Social workers also come from the world of the agency, and service users usually have ideas about those agencies that colour how they see social workers and affect the emotional impact they each have on the other. A social worker who overidentifies with agency procedures risks losing sight of the subjectivity and special needs of the user, while a social worker who overidentifies with agency policy risks unfairly rejecting individual need and failing to challenge and improve those policies. On the other hand, a social worker who overidentifies with service users risks failing in responsibility to the agency and in the fair assessment of priorities. To strike a balance between what the service user wants and what intervention the agency considers sufficient for satisfactory functioning requires recognition of our own values, feelings and biases, and the ability to engage in dialogue with the subjective world of service users in an open, reciprocal way (Sainsbury, 1970). For example, Richards (2000) comments that a user-centred approach requires information-getting and provision that is meaningful to an older person and sensitive to their efforts to analyse and manage their situations; and that these efforts are often revealed in narrative form which can be overlooked in an agency-led assessment.

A conversation, what Freire (1972) refers to as a 'critical dialogue', can be developed in which experiences are shared and differences acknowledged. A shared narrative encourages the development of mutual understanding, deficits in mutual understanding can be acknowledged and a 'moral dialogue' ensue. Where this dialogue is not achieved and service users are perceived as uncooperative, the conclusions reached by assessors are greatly affected. For example, a key factor in whether abused children are accommodated or allowed to remain with parents is often whether the parents are cooperative, that is acknowledge the evidence of harm done, accept responsibility for their part in causing it and agree to measures to avoid its reoccurrence, including a programme for monitoring and/or changing their behaviour (for an overview of the research findings see Platt, 2007). This dialogue has been found to go more smoothly where parents conform verbally and agree a plausible explanation in comprehensive risk assessments. It seems more likely that a parent who conforms in this way will form a positive relationship with the assessing social worker, and it is this relationship that appears central to the outcome (Holland, 2000). Thus the outcome of the meeting between social worker and service user is crucially affected by whether their relationship is oppressively adversarial or anti-oppressively cooperative; the social worker has responsibility for promoting cooperative working. In making assessments for services, too, there needs to be *negotiation* over issues of fairness, need and availability of resources as understood by both sides. For example, it is important to explore how an old person's need for day care relates not only to the carer's need for a respite break, but also to the availability or otherwise of culturally appropriate services.

Where there is a difference of gender, race or class between social worker and service user, there seems to be a tendency to focus unduly on deficit and/or risk rather than on *strengths* and seeking to establish how people's control over aspects of their lives can be increased. We all, social workers and service users alike, have unmet wants, and if these are ever to be met we must make our story visible and look at the stories of others, to see our situations not as 'no exit' places but as places capable of reform. In this way, we can gain an awareness of where our oppressions are located and of how structural as well as psychological obstacles operate, and have a sense of our ability to be agents of change and locators of resources. This requires the capacity to deal with self-blame, to attribute problems to unfair structures rather than people when that is the case, and to develop necessary supportive networks.

By and large, we attribute our successes to our own efforts and our failures to events outside ourselves. However, we judge other people oppositely. This is called an 'attributional bias'. The first part of this, attributing positive outcomes to stable, personal factors and negative outcomes to unstable, external factors, is called 'a self-serving bias' (see, for example, Miller and Ross, 1975). This is actually a healthy thing because it not only helps us to make sense of unexpected events, but also protects our self-esteem and public image. The social worker who is named in a child death inquiry will probably see this as resulting from a lack of resources or bad luck, while all other workers will probably be quite sure that their assessments would have been better. The tendency to attribute causes oppositely when observing other people is called 'fundamental attribution error'. This arises from *overattribution* and *defensive attribution*, both of which can serve to insulate observers from anxiety. If other people are considered *personally* responsible for their misfortunes, the same fate cannot befall the observer. This means that we are all predisposed to victim blaming – even where the 'victim' is clearly constrained and controlled by situational factors. Thus, it can be seen that we have an inbuilt tendency to prefer social work interventions that locate the problem within the subject. It is not only that it is easier to 'work' on the subject rather than social circumstances; it also makes us each feel more individually secure.

Thus, social workers need to avoid blaming and, instead, identify service users' competencies and to affirm their experiences, so that self-confidence can grow. This requires asking for their stories; listening to and taking them seriously helps to build confidence and a sense of being valued. This can be achieved quite simply through offering written assessments for editing by the service user, taking care to avoid *recording distortions*. Prince's study of agency records (1996) found that 'Records actually occupy a "hot seat" in the power relations between social workers, their managers and consultants, and functioned not only as an index of power but also as a bearer of meanings, codes, resources and emotions' (p. 180). Once something is written down, it gains authority and causes individuals to be captured and *fixed* in writing. This is particularly important since recording has become diagnostic rather than simply factual. Records can create the impression of the possession of an objective and detached view that does not actually exist. With the introduction of service user access to files, there is also a reluctance to record assumptions, although they remain in the social worker's head. This manifests itself in the form of Chinese whispers in the inter-agency group or the use of euphemisms in reports, particularly court reports. Euphemisms may seem kinder to the service user but have the disadvantage that they are difficult to challenge, although one 90-year-old woman agreed broadly with the assessment recommendations but asked her assessing social worker to remove the word 'frail' from her description as she had a more robust view of herself.

People also need the assertiveness to communicate their wants. Many women, particularly, suppress their own wants, so workers need to take extra care to seek them out. This is even more so with older women and especially where the social worker is male. Men and women often view satisfaction differently (McNay, 1992), and it is therefore often necessary to facilitate mutual listening by such means as circular questioning.

As it is neither possible nor necessarily desirable to provide, for example, every poor black female service user with a poor black female social worker, there will inevitably be large gaps between service users and social workers. This will be even more obvious when differences in sexuality, religion and culture are considered. However, anti-oppressive practice dictates that workers *acknowledge* and seek to *bridge* these gaps. An openness about one's own culture and values and about one's lack of knowledge of the other person's beliefs is essential at the beginning of any involvement. This is then followed by an invitation to service users to help the social worker see life as they see it.

CASE STUDY: THEORY INTO PRACTICE

Katie, is a young, black, out lesbian. She is assessing Jennifer, a elderly disabled black widow. In line with the recommendation to 'take account of the strengths the older person can bring to bear on their needs' (Single Assessment Process, DoH, 2002, Annex A, p. 2) she has identified Jennifer's membership of her local church choir and involvement with bible groups as a source of support and opportunity to make a contribution. It becomes obvious as the conversation develops that Jennifer's understanding of the bible means that she considers homosexuality to be sinful.

- What are the essential considerations for anti-oppressive practice in this scenario?
- To what extent should Katie be open about her beliefs and values?
- Which dimension of anti-oppressive practice is most useful here?

Social workers ought not to be too proud to ask the service user to help them understand how class, race or gender factors are affecting their situation. Without such a humble, 'one down' stance, male white social workers, for example, will rightly be seen by women and black service users as coming from another world (see for example Jordan, 1989; hooks, 1991, 1993). Equally, it is important that class is examined; social workers are sensitive to the effects of personal poverty on service users but less attention is paid to the impact of living in impoverished communities. For example, there is evidence that social workers routinely neglect the environmental dimension in their assessments of children and families in need (Jack and Gill, 2003).

Social workers have been criticized for failing to acknowledge the strengths and coping strategies of minority groups. We suggest that one way this can be corrected is by respectfully asking the service users to share their story of struggle and survival in the face of social structural inequity, by asking not only about their wounds, but also about their capacity for self-nurturing, not only about their lack of a sense of entitlement and justice but also about the strengths derived from their membership of their community group, and also any stresses that that membership might sometimes cause (for example see Denborough *et al.,* 2006, who describe the work of service users as 'experience consultants'). Sometimes, says Strom-Gottfried (1999), the *absence* of difficulties in a particular area of functioning can constitute a strength. This work involves social workers sharing some similarities and differences in their experiences of both power and oppression.

CASE EXAMPLE

A white female social work student was assessing a black male social work student as part of an assessment exercise. In attempting to bridge the gap in the way outlined, the two students shared experiences of their early lives. To their surprise and delight, they found that they both felt dislocated from large extended families in tightly knit small communities that were collapsing under economic pressures. These communities were located in a white, Lancashire context for the woman and a black African Caribbean context for the man, but they had more commonalties than differences in their experience of oppression.

Bridging the gap is still an unclear area of practice, with agencies tending to stress the need for professional boundaries and workers finding it difficult to be

truly empathic (White, 1995b). While personal disclosures that are not necessary for a true engagement with the service user are inappropriate, if there is to
be a moral dialogue leading to an appreciation of the other's world view and
values, and an understanding of their perceptions and attributions, then social
workers have to acknowledge at least their lack of cultural sameness and their
need to be helped by the other to understand. For example, in understanding
an ultra-orthodox Jewish family's threat to '*sit shiva*' for a daughter who plans
to marry outside her faith, it would be necessary for most non-Jewish social
workers to invite the family to explain their profound distress, which is based
on their regarding their daughter as dead. We are not saying that it is possible
to close the enormous gaps of race, gender, class and ethnicity, only that we can
acknowledge and reach across them, inviting the other person to reach across to
us, and hopefully making real human contact that will be accepting, respectful
and mutually empowering.

Black writers (see for example hooks, 1993) stress that black people need
to tell their story, to set their own frame of reference, to have their values and
spirituality appreciated, to be assertive, if they are to ensure continued growth
despite centuries of being deliberately crushed (Spence, 1995). Our position
as social workers who purport to empower service users demands that we be
aware of our own social construction of knowledge and of the influences of our
roles and agencies. Social workers' values interact with the very essence of their
work in constructing accounts of people's lives and in making judgements on
the basis of these accounts. As social workers encourage people to give their
own accounts of their lives, they also have to take account of their own lives
(Clifford, 1994). They need to be aware of the consequences of their theoretical maps and to seek to move from a 'reproductive' approach towards an
'abductive' one in which collaborative accounts draw more on the concepts and
meanings of service users. In their places of work, they also need to own up to
their deficits of experiences and knowledge of particular groups, seek to establish community links with groups whose experience and insights are useful to
their work, and work towards maximizing the range of experience within their
staff group. Tamasese and Waldegrave (1996) refer to this as *just therapy*, countering both individual and institutional discrimination through making one's
work accountable to subjugated groups by consulting always with local communities or colleagues who have more similarity with the service user. Epston
(1998) recommends that the worker is also active in assisting service users to
develop *communities of concern* from which they can not only gain confidence
and strength but also provide a forum for education, and Yuen and White
(2007) look at gender, culture and violence in narrative practice.

Similarities and differences

We argue throughout this book for assessing social workers to remain open
to the idea that there are multiple interpretations of each person-in-a-situation
and to ensure that their assessments are underpinned by the principles of anti-
oppressive practice. This is far from simple, requiring much more than the
acquisition of a list of anti-discriminatory tips or how to respond to people who

seem 'different' and the development of a 'correct' attitude towards challenging the various 'isms'. As current criticisms of political correctness demonstrate, there is the danger of dogmatism and further stereotyping of service users when dominant narratives are subscribed to wholeheartedly; for example:

> I believe there are some times when totalisation is absolutely necessary. It would be self-indulgent and morally unacceptable not to support the anti-racist forces that are attempting to unite black people, and a white person has no right to tell black people how to organise their resistance. However, I believe that solidarity with anti-racism should not be equated with an uncritical and knee-jerk acceptance of . . . antidiscriminatory orthodoxy. (Katz, 1996, p. 213)

CASE EXAMPLE

Such antidiscriminatory orthodoxy was evident in the response of a group of residential staff to the young female residents being targeted by pimps and drug-pushers. The home accommodated mainly white young people but was located in a predominantly Asian community. Staff had received antiracism training and subsequently developed good working relationships with the local community. Although both staff and residents were being seriously harassed by a small group of adults, supported by up to thirty youths, when they refused to allow the adults access to the young women, they felt powerless to do anything about what had become nightly abuse (mooning, banging on doors and windows, bricks being thrown). This was because the 'abusers' were Asian and the (white) staff feared being accused of racism – and undermining their relationships with the local community. This 'knee-jerk acceptance' of antidiscriminatory orthodoxy ignored the fact that there were three groups of people at risk whose needs were not being met: the staff, the young white women targeted, and the young Asian men who were being drawn into criminal activity by the adult pimps and pushers.

Acknowledging the ethnicity of the youths was an important factor in constructing a safety plan; they lived in an area of educational and economic disadvantage, and were additionally disadvantaged by their racial positioning in a shrinking job market. While they should not be pathologized on the grounds of ethnicity, to be colour blind to their racial disadvantage is equally racist (see for example Ahmad, 1990). An assessment was undertaken via a group meeting of residents, staff, senior management, local police, and local members of the community, advised by two Asian social workers. This meeting thus brought together all concerned parties, creating a 'community of concern' (Epston, 1998). It became clear that members of the local community already had plans in hand to deal with their identified concerns about youths being drawn into crime through disaffection with their career opportunities. Equally they, too, were worried about the danger of the female residents being drawn into prostitution and drug use and appalled at what the staff and residents were suffering each evening. Enabling minority groups to have their voices heard in this way is much more important than assuming that to intervene would be potentially racist.

In complex situations involving several people, some oppressors, some oppressed, some service users, some unwilling users and others with no social work involvement, the systems ideas of Pincus and Minahan (1973) can be useful in planning the work, reconsidering values, and coordinating efforts. They describe four systems:

1. The *change agent* system, which is made up of workers, colleagues, assistants and so on.
2. The *client* system, which includes those who are willing to engage with the social workers and who expect to benefit.
3. The *target* system, which is made up of those people that the social worker decides to change or recruit in some way – so-called 'unwilling' clients, relatives, other staff, or even the media.
4. The *action* system, which is made up of all those who help with what needs to be done, the social worker and those recruited from the target system.

While the traditional values of social work apply to work with the client system, work with the target system can involve different values. For example, dealing with a powerful, unjust landlord who is exploiting tenants may be characterized by forms of persuasion, such as exposure in the press, that would be inappropriate with others in the system. So we can locate the people in the above scenario into the four systems as shown in Figure 2.1.

Note that the client system is not always the system that most needs to change. Problems in the client system often result from the oppressions of others, including some members of the change agent system. In some situations, the social worker may invoke the power of the legal system against abusers of power. Also, one person may be a client in respect of one goal and a target in respect of another. This approach has the advantage of encouraging social workers to see that they do not need to work alone; if they build action systems they will empower themselves. In situations of risk, this is particularly important

The change agent system	The client system
Home manager, Home staff, Homes advisor, Ethnic advisors, Asian social workers.	Residents and staff (expecting to be rid of harassment and fear), the community, the state and the courts.
The target system	The action system
The abusers and the youths (change their abusive behaviour), some Home staff (to change their approach), some residents (to move them to the client system, to stop drug use), community leaders (to get their support), the youths (to move then to the client system, to address their disadvantage), the police (to get them involved)	Home manager and some staff. (The aim would be to recruit some people from the target system to this system, and then to maintain it as a system until the goal is reached.)

Figure 2.1 Systems of anti-discriminatory practice in a young people's home

so that the social worker is empowered to take some actions whether a person agrees or not.

To return to individual assessment, even in less obviously complex situations, the person the assessing social worker meets will have been entered into a story by the referrer; and may also have entered themselves into a story, so the various 'isms' can be highlighted or hidden in many and complex ways.

CASE STUDY: THEORY INTO PRACTICE

Both Karla and Andy were 15 years old, each of them the eldest child in a single-mother family living in conditions of moderate economic hardship. Both had statements of special educational needs which meant that they were seriously behind their peers academically and found the classroom a constantly humiliating experience. They had both been permanently excluded from school for extreme violence to other pupils at break times. The permanent exclusions followed a series of fixed-term exclusions despite remedial teaching (which had resulted in improved reading and writing skills) and attendance on 'anger management' programmes (which had little effect). They both ascribed their fighting to retaliation to racist taunts about which they said the school did nothing; a factor about which they were considerably aggrieved. Karla however was the daughter of a white mother and black father, living in a predominantly white, rural area. The school from which she was excluded contained mostly upper working-class, white pupils, with a substantial minority of middle-class pupils; the majority of ethnic minority pupils belonged to this group. Andy, on the other hand, was a white child, attending an urban school with predominantly Asian pupils. This school had a well-developed support system for pupils with special educational needs and an explicit antiracist policy. Although pupils tended to make marked *progress* at this school it ranked much lower in terms of academic *achievement* than Karla's school.

- What would be the 'correct' attitude for the assessing social worker to take in these two instances? (Karla's experience of racism might well be more readily sympathized with than Andy's, although racial tensions in his area were high; the area being on the boundaries of a city where BNP involvement had sparked off racial fighting.

- Should Andy be challenged when he expressed overt racial hatred and should Karla be free from challenging?

- Were either of them victims or offenders, or both?

- And was the oppression they subjectively experienced predominantly personal, cultural or structural – or a combination?

Of course neither Karla nor Andy were passive recipients of their secondary socialization processes. They had actively constructed their own identities. By asking them to elaborate on their initial accounts, it became clear that gender was the more significant element in their different identities. Both reacted to frustration and humiliation at school by 'getting into a temper' both at home and at school, but Karla was not comfortable with an identity of a 'fighting' girl. Racism turned out not to be her major issue (although it had been at her junior school) and she actively wanted to change her behaviour. Andy, on the other hand, coped with humiliation in the classroom (where his masculine identity was a subordinate one) by developing an oppositional masculinity in his social world. He was not only violent at home and school, but had also further developed his racist behaviour by entering shops owned by Asian people and instigating fights. His oppositional masculinity also had sexist overtones – he refused to undertake any chores in the home on the grounds that that was 'what women are for', at the same time as taking considerable pride in not hitting women 'that's no fun, they can't fight back'. His mother had difficulty in accommodating his masculine identity as he was now becoming too large and dangerous to his younger sibs for her to construct him as subordinated owing to his special educational needs. The day-to-day reality of him being at home all day owing to the school exclusion led to her tentatively reconstructing him as 'threatening'.

Assessment, therefore, demands a sophisticated analysis of gender, particularly as regards the way in which boys can develop different masculinities simultaneously (Messerschmidt, 2000).

As suggested earlier, there is more that joins men than separates them (Cordery and Whitehead, 1992); Cockburn (1991) maintains that there is a danger in the idea of 'multiple masculinities' in that it deflects attention from the consistency in men's domination of women and children at systemic and organizational levels: 'Troubled' masculinity may be, but male power is defending itself systematically and ferociously' (Cockburn, 1991, p. 216). Masculinity does not fall from the heavens, however, but is constructed by masculinizing practices, and there is evidence that the way in which men construct 'men-ness' affects masculinities as well as femininities (Connell, 1987). Not all men are dominant; not all dominate. Mackinnon (1987) says that men can be raped, feminized, even 'unmanned': 'they may even be de-gendered... for as women differ in their status, so do men in their power' (Mackinnon, cited in Evans, 1995, p. 150). For example, small boys and disabled, old and homosexual men are 'feminized' in that they are not considered 'real men' (see for example Marshall, 1981; Arber and Ginn, 1991; Mac an Ghaill, 1996). The process of construction of black masculinity is more complex and reversed, with black men being 'overgendered' and exoticized, and their physicality unduly emphasized (see for example Westwood, 1996; Denney, 1992). This construction of men as 'real men' or 'female men' or 'ultra-men' supports the claim of Sampson *et al.* (1991) that while gender is only one among many sources of power, it is central. Men have the institutional power of patriarchy but, at the same time, often experience themselves as powerless in some contexts (Milner, 2004a).

> **CASE EXAMPLE**
>
> Annie is chairing a review meeting at which it is confirmed that Social Care's plan for Kelly and John's children is adoption. Towards the end of the meeting, contact arrangements are discussed, with the professionals commenting that the interaction between parents and children is good. Annie asks the parents if this is their view. John looks up from comforting Kelly, who is in floods of tears, and says 'Yes, love.' Annie responds with 'My name is Annie. Do not call me love.' John leaves the meeting also in tears, commenting 'I call everyone love. I didn't mean anything by it.'

Hamner and Statham (1998) set out a feminist approach that looks at the similarities and differences between female social workers and female service users. Where two women are involved, the *commonalities* include the shared experiences of life in a male-dominated society, double workloads (paid and domestic), living with men, often as subordinates, and caring for dependants. They frequently include the experience of poverty, connected perhaps with being divorced, separated, a lone parent or restricted to part-time employment. In social service departments, many women service users' problems are clearly caused or aggravated by the men with whom they live. Many women's resources are overstretched or inadequate because of responsibilities for children or other dependants, poor housing, less access to education, health problems, transport problems and low pay. In addition, their situation and hardship is often compounded by a lack of facilities such as day care, nurseries and formal and informal support networks.

Society places different value on men's and women's behaviour, and the expectations of caring and of service weigh more heavily on women: women are expected to cope with everything! Self-esteem is greatly affected by how men perceive women and treat them as inferior. As Richards (1980) puts it, women suffer from systematic social injustice because of their sex. However, Evans (1995) holds that women can possess a superior and more accurate knowing derived from their experience of subordination, active parenting and nurturing responsibilities. We would argue that this is true also of 'unmanned' men such as disabled, elderly or homosexual men.

In making assessments, therefore, it may be helpful to ask some of the following questions of all potentially oppressed service users:

- What expectations do you feel you are not meeting?
- How do you feel you are coping?
- Do you expect too much of yourself?
- Are your burdens such that no one should be expected to do better than you?
- How good do you feel about who you are?
- How appreciated are you by others?

- Could your difficulties be due more to lack of resources than to lack of ability?
- What traditional supports are lacking for you in this day and age?
- What particular strengths have helped you to keep going?
- Where could we start building a network of support?

Equally, *diversities* need to be acknowledged (Thompson, 2003a, 2006). Differences in status, power, role, lifestyle, race, culture, sexuality, religion, education, work possibilities, access to community resources, degree of stigma and hope are elements of the differentiation of social worker from service user. This also applies to male and female social workers with male service users. These differences create the gap we were discussing earlier, and a dialogue is required that will result in at least a touching of minds across the divide. In may be, for example, that one woman's experience of living with a man has been abject humiliation, and another's enrichment and growth; the latter needs to learn of the pain of the former, what self-nurturance was possible, and what strengths and strategies enabled survival or escape. In the case of black women, the extended family was historically a source of support, 'combating depression, stress and loneliness and thus reducing the impact of those factors on mental health' (Spence, 1995). The reduction of this support in the lives of many black women in Britain today has a devastating effect on their wellbeing; they push themselves so hard that they are exposed to excessive stress, and when they do achieve, they still may lack any real sense of entitlement. They often do not feel understood by social workers who must reach across to them, make humble human contact and invite them to 'put us in the picture'. Devore and Schlesinger (1991) make the useful point that while white workers need to be aware of service users' possible fear of racist or prejudiced treatment, black social workers need to avoid the 'stance that says "I've made it, why can't you"' (p. 191), expecting black service users to 'shape up' and not let the side down. The gap between middle-class (often) female social workers and white male members of the so-called 'underclass' can be just as wide.

CASE EXAMPLE

Alan noticed that his mother, aged 90 and suffering from a stroke, was being neglected by the nursing home. He found another home where he felt sure standards were better, but the home in which she was residing called in a social worker because they felt that the resident did not wish to move, despite the fact that she had told her son that she did. The social worker interviewed the mother and agreed she did want to move but failed to confirm this to the other home, who were waiting for this approval before they could receive the resident. In the meantime, due to this delay, the bed at the second home was taken by someone else. The man met with the social worker and her manager to complain, but he felt they were not interested in his problem, denied that his mother wanted to move and would not answer his questions about their earlier acknowledgement that she had so wished.

> He came away from the meeting having had no sense of engaging with the workers; he said he 'might as well be talking to folk from space; snobs who couldn't give a monkey's curse for my sort; wouldn't listen to me, so I gave 'em hell'.

Ignoring class differences between social workers and service users involves lack of respect. Blair's (1996) study of black pupils excluded from school showed that both pupils and their parents saw class as an important determinant of teachers' treatment of them. What emerged from the study was a 'complex picture of personal and institutional factors which highlighted the relationship between gender, "race", class and age' (Blair, 1996, p. 21).

Critical comment

The interplay between social divisions is both complex and fluid; thus 'correct' anti-oppressive practice is continually contested. The major proponents of anti-oppressive practice sidestep important philosophical and conceptual issues in their anxiety to prescribe ways of promoting empowerment and emancipation. For example, Thompson (2003a, p. 10) admits that we are a long way from an adequate theoretical understanding of the intricacies and subtleties of promoting equality. It is problematic to prescribe ways of addressing inequalities and promoting social justice without a definition of equality. Similarly, Dalrymple and Burke (1995) equate inequalities with inequalities of opportunity. This is but one strand of the equality debate. Turner (1986) lists four types of equality:

- *Ontological equality*: the fundamental equality of persons as human beings; for example, equality before God.
- *Equality of opportunity* to achieve desirable ends.
- *Equality of conditions of life*: people starting at the same point (no advantages from cultural capital).
- *Equality of outcomes*: positive discrimination to compensate for significant inequalities of condition.

Turner argues that equality is not feasible unless there is massive social and political regulation, although critics of government attempts to promote equality of condition and outcome (for example, threatened financial restrictions on Oxbridge universities unless targets for increasing the number of places offered to disadvantaged young people are met) would argue that we are in the throes of massive regulation. Turner also argues that such regulation is also not feasible in the long term, as human beings are resistant to totalitarian regimes. In this sense, promoting equality will always be difficult to achieve. Baker *et al.* (2004) suggest that equality and inequality are so complex that we should perhaps be more interested in people's wellbeing or welfare. This would involve equality being regarded as equality of:

- Respect and recognition.
- Resources.
- Love, care and solidarity.
- Power.
- Working and learning.

This is remarkably similar to the desirable outcomes listed in *Every Child Matters* and, as such, provides a coherent basis for antioppressive practice. There is a difficulty here though; government guidance detailing the way these outcomes should be met uses an existing knowledge base that militates against diversity. This knowledge base has been developed to improve professionals' understanding of human behaviour (and to identify risk) and, as such, categorizes people and provides a common language through which professionals can share perspectives. Both these processes exclude the 'categorized' and therefore reduce the potential for active partnership in the assessment process. There is danger here of social workers operating what Jenkins (1996) refers to as a therapeutic tyranny. For example it is insufficient to challenge violent men 'elegantly' and with compassion (Thompson, 2003a; Gondolf, 2007) on the grounds that feminist research and theorizing shows them to be in need of educating about their (assumed) misuse of patriarchal power. Effective anti-oppressive practice would not dismiss their stories as cognitive distortions but rather would listen to them and reflect critically on what this means in terms of practice (see for example Healy, 2005).

An emphasis on inequalities at the expense of developing an adequate theory of equality also neglects the fact that inequalities are fluid. It is interesting to reflect on Hugman's 1991 statement on the inadequacy of the concept of rights; the Human Rights Act not only has had the effect of drawing attention to abuses of human rights but also has highlighted the complexity of competing rights and the need for a recognition of human responsibilities. This will influence the future development of anti-oppressive practice. This is not simply about empowering individuals within a linear social-worker-to-service-user relationship; there needs to be respect for all the people in each social work situation being assessed, and acknowledgement of their responsibilities towards each other at individual, family, agency and community levels: 'a restored belief in the role of the social worker at the level of *practice* can then provide the basis for a renewal of confidence in social workers' ability to impact on the other levels' (Lymbery, 2001, p. 382).

Outcomes

The anti-oppressive literature is singularly lacking in research measures into the effectiveness of anti-oppressive assessment practice. Partly, this reflects a gap in the research literature generally; outcome research has tended to focus on the outcomes of interventions, and, by implication, service user satisfaction with services provided. These studies indicate that effective anti-oppressive practice is as yet underdeveloped. For example, the Netton *et al.* (2004) study of service users' experiences of home care services found that while 60 percent of respondents were very or extremely satisfied with the help they receive, better perceptions of home care were significantly associated with the user being white, male and younger. Black and ethnic minority users expressed lower levels of satisfaction. Similarly, the Cleaver and Walker (2004) study showed that where parents reported being involved in the assessment and planning process, this was mainly where the focus was on families in need. Satisfaction levels were lower in child protection cases and there was little evidence of children being consulted. These findings are discussed in greater detail in later chapters.

A major reason for the lack of outcome research into anti-oppressive practice is, however, the very real difficulties of constructing a research study into a concept that is so complex and fluid. As Dominelli (2002) points out, the term has been developed conceptually in a number of different directions (p. 19). And the practice that is required to respond sensitively to oppressions may flounder as various oppressions and values compete with each other, as can be seen in the following case:

CASE STUDY: THEORY INTO PRACTICE

Robert is a 50-year-old Rastafarian whose partner has left him following a long period of the drink-fuelled couple's fighting. He is caring for their three children, Tyrone (12 years), Carly (9 years) and Omari (3 years). Tyrone's head of year became concerned after Robert visited the school to discuss Tyrone's disruptive behaviour in class as Robert said that he would give Tyrone 'a licking' when he got home. She has reported this to social services, who visited Robert at home to assess his care of the children. They have advised Robert on constructive ways of disciplining children but Robert has become disputational with them. He argues that doing well at school is the key to achievement for his children and that his older children from an earlier relationship have all done well in life, so he isn't going to change his ideas now. He is also scornful of the social worker's views on parenting on the grounds that she is young and has no children of her own. He says that he only drinks when the children are not there and that he separated from their mum because it was not good for them to see their parents fighting. His physical care of the children is excellent and his house is clean and tidy with many toys and books.

- How would you respond to Robert?
- What else would you need to do to gain a fair assessment of his parenting?

(Note: Government guidance for the 2004 Children Act states that, while it has long been recognized that a parent may use reasonable punishment or chastisement to correct a child, 'battery' (unwanted application of force to the body – commonly called 'assault') cannot be justified.

Respectfulness is, we suggest, a more useful starting point for antioppressive practice than attending separately to the various 'isms'. We have only occasionally heard service users complain of insensitivity which could be located within an 'ism'. Much more frequently they complain about being treated disrespectfully in more general terms of courtesy: social workers always being late, calling without making appointments, coming 'in numbers', writing things down about them but not sharing this with them, not being open and honest, not listening to them, and 'treating us like children'. At the same time, service users are held accountable should they behave in the same way; for example, 'If I'm late for a meeting, it goes down in the minutes. It counts against me. If they're late, and they always are, no one says a thing.'. Thoughtless disrespectfulness of this sort creates a new 'ism", namely being a service user whose time and privacy are not important. We invite the reader, therefore, to become reflexive researchers into their own anti-oppressive practice.

A primary value in recent government publications, and enshrined in the law, is that of *partnership*. While this entails respect in every sense, it also needs to be shown (in records and in fact) by providing good explanations for our work and our assessments, providing people with copies, fully engaging them in care planning, reviewing progress jointly with them and ascertaining their wishes and views. This emphasis on partnership is most welcome. We hope it will be conscientiously considered in all areas of practice and it is good that records are required to show how it is being done.

We suggest a possible questionnaire format to be completed by service users at the conclusion of your initial assessments, although you can probably improve on it:

1. How satisfied were you with the way the first contact was made with you?
2. Did your social worker explain fully the reasons for the assessment?
3. Did your social worker explain what was involved in making the assessment?
4. Were assessment interviews held at a place where you felt comfortable?
5. Were appointments arranged that were convenient to you?
6. Did your social worker arrive on time?
7. Did your social worker listen to your views?
8. Did your social worker encourage open and honest discussion?
9. Were you satisfied with how your social worker handled disagreements about the assessment?
10. Did your social worker show that s/he understood your difficulties?
11. Was your social worker respectful towards to you?
12. Did you get to see the assessment report in draft form and comment on it?
13. What questions would you have liked to be asked that your social worker didn't ask?
14. Have you any important qualities that your social worker missed?

15. How satisfied are you that the plan will meet your needs?

16. What could your social worker have done better?

17. From your experience of being assessed what is the most important message you would like to pass on to the social work team that would help them improve services?

SUMMARY

- Power, abused, is the main oppression; unequal power is at the root of injustice. Power concedes nothing until it has to.

- Powerlessness is linked to learned helplessness and is then all the more devastating.

- Oppressed people can have superior knowledge of the human condition.

- The isms are frequently interrelated and competing.

- Anti-oppressive practice dictates that social workers acknowledge and seek to bridge the gaps between themselves and service users in order to facilitate a negotiating of perceptions in each situation.

- To avoid being oppressive, social workers need to listen to people, validate their experiences and work collaboratively to seek out competence and promote a sense of personal agency.

- A focus on human rights, putting people's wellbeing first, showing respect and working in partnership, will go some way towards achieving the beginning of equality for service users.

FURTHER LEARNING ACTIVITIES

1. List your own values in order of priority.

2. Compare them with those of others in your study group.

3. Do they contradict or complement each other?

4. List what you can do to avoid being oppressive.

FURTHER READING

Healy, K. (2005) *Social Work Theories in Context: Creating Frameworks for Practice.* Basingstoke: Palgrave Macmillan.

Thompson, N. (2006) *Anti-Discriminatory Practice*, 4th edn. Basingstoke: Palgrave Macmillan.

Payne, G. (ed.) (2006) *Social Divisions*. Basingstoke: Palgrave Macmillan.

NATIONAL OCCUPATIONAL STANDARDS

For students working with the British National Occupation Standards for Social Work (see Appendix):

- This chapter relates to *practice* elements 1.1; 5.1; 11.1–4; 18.1–3.
- With which of the *knowledge* requirements in the Appendix does this chapter help you?

CHAPTER 3

Effective Assessment Processes

What this chapter is about

This chapter examines the effectiveness of the Common Assessment Framework and Single Assessment Process in meeting the outcomes set out in *Every Child Matters* and *Our Health, Our Care, Our Say*. (In Scotland there is the Integrated Assessment Framework and in Wales the Unified Assessment Framework.) The adequacy of the performance indicators used in social care inspections is questioned. There follows a discussion of different types of assessment before a framework for assessment utilizing the reflexivity of social research methodology is proposed. The chapter concludes with an outline of the stages of assessment.

MAIN POINTS

> ➤ Wider policy perspectives: assessment frameworks, monitoring assessments, performance indicators.
>
> ➤ Assessment as a process or an event.
>
> ➤ Approaches to assessment – three models.
>
> ➤ A framework for assessment.
>
> ➤ The stages of assessment.

Wider policy perspectives

Assessment frameworks

Following publication of the document *Modernising Social Services* (Cm. 4169, 1998), assessment frameworks were devised to improve interagency cooperation, involve service users more fully, and provide the basis for achieving the outcomes to be set out in *Every Child Matters* and *Our Health, Our Care, Our Say*. Good-quality assessment is vital if service users are to be provided with the services they want and need, and which effect positive change in terms of the outcomes set out in the government documents. To this end, the Common Assessment Framework (for children and their families) and the Single

Assessment Process (for adults and older people) have been designed to promote more effective identification of additional needs by:

- Coordinating the collation of information by workers from different agencies.
- Avoiding service users giving personal details several times.
- Identifying a lead professional with overall responsibility for the assessment and subsequent intervention.
- Listening to the views of all family members and discussing differences of perspectives.
- Giving as much weight to family perspectives as agency requirements.
- Focusing on solutions that all parties can agree on.
- Using evidence that is observable rather than speculation.
- Being open about why information is being recorded and what will be done with it, and giving families copies of assessments and care plans.
- Delivering on actions.
- Keeping an eye on progress and regularly reviewing the initial assessment.

Monitoring assessments

The acid test of an effective assessment is satisfaction with subsequent decisions and actions on the part of services users and service providers, with evidence that the outcomes set out in *Every Child Matters* and *Our Health, Our Care, Our Say* are being met. Formal monitoring of the effectiveness of assessment processes has as yet to be established, although the PSSRU is investigating how changes to the single assessment process can improve the efficiency and effectiveness of services (Clarkson *et al.*, 2007), and the work of Cleaver and Walker (2004) provides preliminary evidence of the effectiveness of the Common Assessment Framework, confirming the problems highlighted earlier by Sinclair *et al.* (1995). There have, however, been few attempts made to evaluate the effectiveness of the new assessment formats in terms of service delivery. User satisfaction tools are being piloted in several statutory and voluntary organizations but other monitoring depends largely on social care inspections, which examine selected indicators and compare units of organization with national standards.

The outcomes being assessed are: be healthy, stay safe, enjoy and achieve, make a positive contribution, and achieve economic wellbeing (*Every Child Matters*), and improved quality of life, making a positive contribution, increased choice and control, freedom from discrimination and harassment, economic wellbeing, and maintaining personal dignity (*Our Health, Our Care, Our Say*). The selection of appropriate performance indicators for assessing whether or not people get the services they want and need, based on the outcomes listed in *Our Health, Our Care, Our Say* and *Every Child Matters*, is problematic. It is clear from the Commission for Social Care Inspection (2006a, 2006b) that these performance indicators are inadequate on several levels. First, there are no performance indicators at all for some of the outcomes. For example, for adults and older people, *making a positive contribution* and *economic wellbeing* simply isn't measured, and for children *being healthy* is evaluated on progress made towards a comprehensive CAMHS (Child and Adolescent Mental Health Service) on the grounds that this is 'a key area of service improvement', thus 'it is intended to be included for two years pending its replacement by another, more outcome focussed [sic] measure' (CSCI, 2006a, p. 35). Equally, it is difficult to see how *freedom from discrimination and harassment* can be measured at all.

Second, many of the performance indicators measure specific services, regardless of whether or not they are the services either needed or wanted. For example, the performance indicator for *maintaining personal dignity* is the number of single rooms in residential care. This performance indicator cannot evaluate whether or not the adult wanted to be in care, neither does it accommodate maintaining personal dignity through home care services. Similarly, the performance indicator for evaluating the outcomes of children in terms of *making a positive contribution* is the number of looked-after children aged 10 and over who participated in their reviews; this largely ignores all other children being assessed as at risk or in need – other than children likely to become looked-after, as measured by the number of children aged 10 or over who have received a final warning, reprimand or conviction.

Third, and possibly most significantly, the Commission for Social Care Inspection has adopted a practice established by the Home Office for measuring the effectiveness of programmes aimed at reducing offending. Here, completion rates (outputs) rather than recidivism rates (outcomes) are used as performance indicators (for a critical analysis, see for example Falshaw *et al.*, 2004). Confusion between inputs (what services are provided), outputs (the number of people receiving a service), and outcomes (measurable changes) is evident throughout. Thus, *staying safe* is measured by the number of child protection reviews held at the time they should be held, the rationale being that 'reviews are a key element in the delivery of the child protection plan and effective reviews should ensure the provision of good quality interventions' (CSCI, 2006a, p. 55). This indicator is totally inadequate in measuring the *quality* of the child protection plan.

Fourth, evaluating service user satisfaction with the services they want and need is similarly underdeveloped. There are only two performance indicators for evaluating whether or not adults receive the services they want: the number of carers receiving specific carers' services as a percentage of people receiving community-based services, and the percentage of adults receiving a statement of needs and how they will be met. There are rather more performance indicators for evaluating whether or not adults and older people receive the services they need, but only one actually asks services users about their satisfaction with the help they receive (Netton *et al.*, 2004). The others depend upon output measures – for example, the number of reviews held and the percentage of assessments which led to a service being provided. Unless they are looked after, children's views and progress are not considered at all; for example, although looked-after children's educational achievement is monitored through the number of GCSE passes at A grade, the educational achievements of children subject to a protection plan are not monitored at all. There are no performance indicators for families' experiences of assessment, although there is much in the research literature that indicates a substantial degree of dissatisfaction; see, for example, the research into gay adoption experiences (Hicks, 2005); Brandon *et al.* (2007) on parental involvement in the Common Assessment Framework; Bowey and McGlaughlin's study of older carers of adults with a learning disability (2007); and Read's (2000) research into the contradictory demands that successive assessments make on the mothers of disabled children.

PLACEMENT THINKING POINT

1. Choose an assessment you have made where you have been pleased with the outcomes.
2. Using the performance indicators listed in one of the Commission for Social Care Inspection (CSCI, 2006a, 2006b), how satisfactorily do these measure the quality of your work?
3. What performance indicators would better measure the quality of your work?

Evaluating service user satisfaction with the decisions arising from what are often lengthy and carefully undertaken assessments is also fraught with difficulty because the service user is only one person to whom the social worker is accountable. Davies (1997) suggests that accountability is a complex concept in social work because the worker has to balance service user needs with agency requirements, often underpinned by a legal mandate. This is the source of the tension between risk, needs and resources which bedevils all social work assessments. Additionally, this balance also needs to have some sort of match with the assessing social worker's own ideals or sense of personal duty which brought them into social work in the first place. These ideals, and skills, can easily become eroded by agency requirements, especially the demands of adhering to local protocols which emphasize case management at the expense of direct practice with service users. What is clear from the research is that not only is there a high level of service user dissatisfaction but also social workers are disillusioned at all levels of service delivery (see for example ADSS, 2005; NISCC, 2006; Scottish Executive, 2006).

Assessment as process or event

Whatever the service user group, it seems generally accepted that assessment is more than a one-off event. However, outcomes research shows that this is largely a myth. Social workers almost invariably seek to confirm their original hypotheses (see for example Sinclair *et al.*, 1995; Kelly and Milner, 1996a; Scott, 1998). This poor practice can sustain prejudice and make anti-oppressive practice difficult to achieve. Scott's Australian study of hospital and community child protection social workers (1998) provides the most detailed evidence of this tendency. Prior to the new assessment formats, social workers used a framework of assessment that gave salience to a narrower range of factors than that specified in agency guidelines, being influenced most heavily by risk factors (see for example Challis *et al.*, 1990). They tended not to consider situational and interpersonal conflicts, although these are the main reasons for elderly people being admitted to residential care in this country. After risk factors, resource limitations had the most influence, with the result that needs factors were largely ignored. As yet, the new assessment frameworks have not changed this practice for adults (Clarkson *et al*,. 2007), and environmental factors are not receiving more consideration in the assessment of children and their families (Jack and Gill, 2003).

To support a hypothesis developed at the initial assessment conducted within this constricting framework, Scott (1989) found that social workers sought confirming data rather than disconfirming data and that their reasoning was not supported by hypothesis development or exploration. Kelly and Milner (1996b) also found this tendency towards verification of an initial assessment, which meant not only that there was no re-evaluation of the assessment, but also that the social workers' range of options was reduced until they were left with no option but to close a case. They also found that social workers used self-justification to support the initial hypothesis. This most commonly took the form of persisting with the care plan, on the grounds that it needed time to work – despite clear evidence that the plan was ineffective (see also Turnell and Essex, 2006).

PLACEMENT THINKING POINT

Check your assumptions

- Select a case where you consider the service user to be uncooperative.
- List the points that you and the service user disagree on.
- What confirming data do you have to support your point of view?
- What theory/hypothesis underpins your analysis of this data?
- What other theory/hypothesis would disconfirm your hypothesis?
- Have you explored this disconfirming knowledge thoroughly and fairly?

Sheldon (1995) similarly found that social workers used their interviewing techniques to 'shape' assessment data until they fitted a favourite theoretical model. Equally, he found that after one-off assessment, new information simply built up haphazardly on files, statements purporting to sum up problems and guide further actions being no more than lists of alleged factors loosely thrown together with little information on where they had come from or how they interacted.

While it is easy to sympathize with the resource and risk factors that constrain social work assessments, it is important to recognize that an initial assessment is the most influential determinant in the subsequent management of service user problems. Despite social worker complaints about feelings of powerlessness in the multi-agency arena, their assessments provide the frame available to the case conference and influence its decisions. We will discuss this process in more detail later, but here we wish to make the point that there is no evidence that assessment is an ongoing process that is improved by the involvement of a formal multi-agency group. It is largely an important, single event in which the assessing social worker is the lead professional.

Three approaches to assessment work

Smale and Tuson (1993) identify three different models of assessment, which appear to be closely linked to the salience given by social workers to risk, resources or needs factors:

1. *The questioning model.* Here, the social worker holds the expertise and follows a format of questions, listening to and *processing* answers. This process reflects the social worker's agenda and corresponds to the assessment style noted by Sheldon (1995) in which the data are 'shaped' to fit the social worker's theories about the nature of people. These theories are most likely to be psychodynamic or Cognitive-behavioural in nature.

2. *The procedural model.* In this, the social worker fulfils agency function by gathering information to see whether the subject fits the criteria for services. Little judgement is required, and it is likely that checklists will be used.

3. *The exchange model.* All people are viewed as experts on their own problems, with an emphasis on exchanging information. The social workers follow or track what other people are saying rather than interpreting what they think is meant, seek to identify internal resources and potential, and consider how best to help service users mobilize their internal and external resources in order to reach goals defined by them on their terms. This model fits with task-centred, solution-focused and narrative assessments.

Smale *et al.* (1994) make it plain that they consider the exchange model the desirable one: 'Routine, service-led "assessments" are the antithesis of an empowering approach to assessment and care management' (Smale *et al.*, 1994, p. 68). This, however, is not to say that there are not helpful questions that can deepen understanding, and these questions will flow from some theoretical map, as will be clear in later chapters.

We would suggest that the questioning model is most likely to be used when risk factors provide the main emphasis of the assessment, the procedural model fits the assessment subject to resource constraints and the exchange model comes nearest to meeting a needs-led assessment. The questioning and procedural models are often found in combination, while the exchange model embraces the principles outlined in government guidance. It is the only model which has the clear potential to lead to re-evaluation.

Smale *et al.* (1994) provide a daunting list of the skills and values that would be involved in such endeavours. These include:

- Joining with people yet developing a neutral perspective.
- Adopting the central skills of authenticity, empathy and respect.
- Empowering workers and service users so that essential decisions are located with the people who know most about the problems.
- Reinventing practice, being creative.
- Addressing social problems as a failure of a network of people.
- Testing the fallibility of existing theory and knowledge in each new situation.

We hope that this book will provide some practical guidance, some useful tools and a choice of theoretical maps from which to develop more understanding, without causing workers overload and confusion.

There are obvious difficulties that must be addressed if assessing social workers are to balance risks, needs and resources within an exchange model. These three aspects cannot be totally separated – a major need is often the restoration of the person's own problem-solving potential and the mobilization of his/her inner resources. There can never be a truly neutral perspective, although there can be explicitness. Service users prefer social workers to be explicit even where they do not agree with the perspective. Explicitness aids authenticity, but empathy and respect are more problematic than the social work literature admits. For example, a study of women social workers and women service users found that 'commonality with service users, beyond the experience of intermittent empathic feelings was regarded as either impossible or deeply problematic' (White, 1995b, p. 150). And it is difficult to show respect when social workers themselves are so little respected by service users and the general public. Neither social workers nor service users are likely to be empowered to the point where they will be entrusted with essential decisions. It is also difficult to be creative and reinvent practice when you are subject to criticism much more frequently than praise and when your best efforts are undervalued.

Addressing social problems in terms of a malfunctioning of networks of people is perhaps the most useful starting-point for improving social work assessments. Smale and Tuson (1993) consider it naïve to assume that local supportive networks exist 'in nature', and this is perhaps the major difficulty in actualizing the values and principles outlined in government guidance. Jordan (1990) refers to effective informal supportive networks as welfare with a small 'w', and it is individuals who lack this sort of welfare who require Welfare with a capital 'W'. The purpose of social work, we propose, is, first, the provision of a formal network of Welfare and, second, the development of an informal network of welfare – attention to the environmental dimension of the common assessment framework will show that many service users lack effective informal networks, or that their networks are either unsafe or inappropriate to constructive care and change. This purpose would underpin all assessment work, subsuming the principles of empowerment, participation, cultural sensitivity, multi-agency cooperation and value for money. We suggest an overarching framework below.

A framework for assessment

Although we recognize that it is extremely difficult to undertake a thorough assessment in a political climate that emphasizes risk assessment at the same time as it limits resources and does not take need seriously, we do not think that social workers should accept these implicit constraints at the first point of assessment. As Chapman and Hough (2001) comment, effectiveness-led practice helps both practitioners and managers target their energies, time and scarce resources, confirms the impact of their work with individuals, and provides greater job satisfaction.

We were struck by how the difficulties and deficiencies of social work assessments mirror early criticisms of social research efforts that attempted to move away from strictly quantitative, 'objective' research in order to achieve a better depth of understanding of human realities by using 'grounded' theory (Glaser and Strauss, 1969). Here, social researchers made no attempt to avoid the 'subjectivity' of the individuals and groups studied, allowing their subjects to tell their own stories, with themes and theories subsequently emerging from the data. This research method has obvious similarities with the exchange model of assessment proposed by Smale *et al.* (1994) in that it is founded on the basis of 'joining with people'; and it is supported in the new assessment frameworks' emphasis on listening to people and discussing differences of perspective openly.

THINKING POINT

Recall someone you know who has difficulty communicating through of lack of speech, learning difficulty or dementia. Then read:

Iveson, C. (1990) *Whose Life? Community Care of Older People and Their Families.* London: Brief Therapy Press, pp. 81–3. Or

Brewster, S. J. (2004) 'Putting words into their mouths? Interviewing people with learning disabilities and little/no speech', *British Journal of Learning Disability*, 32; 166–9.

How can you adapt these ideas to assist you in assessing the needs and wishes of your service user?

This type of research suffers from the same problems as social work assessments in that no matter how one tries to allow the theory to flow from the data, researchers do (however unconsciously) hold theories about the nature of people, and there is always the danger that data will be 'shaped' to fit these theories: 'Researchers cannot have "empty heads" in the way that inductivism proposes; nor is it possible that theory is untainted by material experiences in the heads of theoreticians' (Stanley and Wise, 1991, p. 22). However, this potential problem has been much better addressed by social researchers, and the qualitative methodologies developed have much to offer in the development of improved assessment processes.

Social work training devotes a great deal of time to the 'values' considered important in social work practice, but we have found that while students can talk intelligently about values, they find it difficult to demonstrate how they can be held accountable for values in action. They seem to think that appropriate action will necessarily flow if they have the 'right' attitude. For example, in our hypothetical scenario, we would expect social workers to be able to understand that Mrs Edwards, as a black woman, experiences double and perhaps conflicting oppression, and feel sympathy for this, but we would doubt that they could explain to her how this would actively affect their assessment (see p. 14). They would probably – and we would suggest, fruitlessly – attempt to empathize with her. While empathy is necessary for joining with her, it is not sufficient.

Social researchers are much clearer about how they will be held accountable for their value stance because they will have prepared a statement of intent that is quite clear about relevant ethical issues – what they are, how they influence the research and how the researcher will 'behave' rather than just 'think' or 'feel'. For example, researchers in this field are very much aware of the sensitive nature of their research (Renzetti and Lee, 1993), particularly the fact that they are 'joining with people' who are less powerful than themselves – what Walford (1994) refers to as 'researching down'. Therefore, they give careful thought to how they can protect their subjects from harm as a result of their endeavours *before* they begin the data collection phase. Social workers could give more consideration to the possibility that they may do harm as well as good. Their interviewing skills are so well developed that they may elicit disclosures that have little direct bearing on the referral they have received (what service users describe as 'digging'; Scourfield, 2003), and which could also put service users at risk – particularly where there is potential violence in the family. It simply requires the social worker to decide what the boundaries are and clearly state the purpose of the assessment. Sainsbury (1970) maintained that the purpose of making assessments was primarily to represent the individual or family in its struggle for resources, but it should include drawing attention to any form of inequity that may be operating, as well as an understanding of the individual or family dynamics. He added that assessments need to include some consideration of why the situation is described as a problem and how far the agency is responsible for dealing with it. This recognition of the nature of one's agency function is part of every assessment and includes considering whether the user in question is able to use the help that the agency can give.

Additionally, it means thinking about possible interview schedules at an early stage and deciding how free-ranging any interviews can be. The 'open' interview proposed is recognized as particularly problematic in social research (Robson, 2002) and may leave vital areas unexplored. It is most likely that a semi-structured interview format will be the most appropriate one, and social work assessors could do well to consider the careful design of these in social research (see for example Bryman, 2004). Focus group research methods are also particularly effective in generating a rich understanding of participants' experiences and beliefs (Morgan 1998).

In social research, this phase is accompanied by the drawing up of a plan to identify the key informants – the people, the documents and the agencies with the data needed for the assessment. This has the advantage of both broadening the range of data collected and setting limits on its potentially inexhaustible source (Coulshed and Orme, 2006). Social researchers also give thought at this stage to how data derived from verbal and written sources will be compared and evaluated (Jones, 1994), and how the data will be checked for authenticity (Forster, 1994).

PLACEMENT THINKING POINT

Read through a case file where you have made a recent assessment.

1. What are the main sources of information that led to your initial hypothesis?

2. Are there any sources of information you have neglected to follow up?

3. What questions did you fail to ask the service user? (Check this with that person.)

Possible explanations will exist at this stage in both social research and social work assessments, but, in the former, they are more likely to be explicit and contain details of how they will be checked. Intuition may be accurate but should be testable. Even where there is only a single explanation, disproof is as important a consideration as proof. This means that when the data collection is complete, not only will themes emerge, but also data that do not 'fit' easily with these explanations will not be discarded. Interpretations can then be extended and evaluated (Jones, 1994), and all the data will be checked for authenticity (Forster, 1994) and multiple hypotheses can be developed. This process could be usefully incorporated into social work assessments to guard against the tendency of social workers to be heavily influenced by the first item of data collection and the resulting premature hypothesis development. Subsequent government guidance provides basic checklists to aid this process, but these checklists need to be more systematically used, developed and refined.

Utilizing this approach in assessment activity would enable social workers to cope with the 'cognitive dissonance' that Scott (1998) noted was regularly avoided and to fulfil Smale *et al.*'s (1994) exhortations to reinvent practice and be creative in each new situation.

Social researchers are also more careful than social workers in recording and handling data. Huberman and Miles (1994) refer to this as the 'orderliness' of sound qualitative research via good data display. This can take the form of verbatim transcripts, but, rather than remind social workers of their experiences of verbatim recording during training, we suggest that other forms of data display would be equally effective. These include 'memos' (Field and Morse, 1985), flip charts and working diagrams. Memos are particularly useful for storing data that do not seem to 'fit', retaining them for later consideration, while flip chart displays are useful in supervision sessions to ensure that discussion does not centre on one factor to the exclusion of others. Working diagrams such as well-developed genograms and ecomaps are valuable items of data display at this stage of the assessment. All forms of data display can be created with families.

Clear data display aids the next step of social research – the identification of emerging themes. These are noted in the first instance and then 'collapsed' into categories (Burnard, 1991). Only after this process has been carefully undertaken are decisions made about the priority of emergent themes. The social researcher has to demonstrate how interpretation and analysis of data is as free from bias as possible. This is done by what is known as 'reflexivity'.

Reflexivity is a term that is understood in various ways, depending on the writer, and it can become confused with 'reflection' and 'critical reflection' or 'relational reflexivity', so let us briefly state what we mean by these words:

- We use *'reflection'* to mean thinking about an action or a choice afterwards, looking back on it and perhaps learning from a mistake. This however leaves the action unchanged.

- We take *'reflexivity'* to mean reflecting during an action and thereby changing what we are doing – reflection *in* doing, rather than *after* doing.

- We consider *'critical reflection'* to have two meanings: (1) questioning given knowledge or practice in the light of wider issues, changes, world views, outcomes; (2) the same as reflexivity, so the context should indicate which meaning is being used.

- We use *'relational reflexivity'* to mean being reflexive along with a service user, for example asking service users 'Is this a useful question for you?' or questioning with them one's ideas about them, to mobilize their resources or possibilities.

(For a full discussion see D'Cruz *et al.*, 2007.)

Reflexivity is a broader and potentially more useful way of checking assumptions than is the usual one-to-one supervision between line manager and practitioner. The role of line manager is a difficult one as it involves facing both ways within agency structures, and it may not encourage creativity. Reflexivity involves checking one's interpretations of the data with people who do not necessarily have a vested interest – colleagues and/or long-arm supervision – and, of course, checking with informants. The aim is not to establish 'truth'; there will be many truths and many realities that require various ways of knowing and being in order to appreciate the full diversity of meanings and understandings that exist. More simply, what is needed is a clear formulation of the situation that 'fits' with a range of other people's perceptions and is 'testable in practice' (Sheldon, 1995, p. 114). The case conference (we explain the problems of group pressures on consensus in detail in a later chapter) is not the most effective forum for good reflexive practice, but acquiring multi-agency views separately and then attempting to make sense of the possibly conflicting results will assist in getting more depth into the assessment and a formulation of possible problems and solutions that have broad agreement among key informants.

Reflexivity in a group of colleagues is enhanced if it is carried out in two stages. The first is the *how to* stage. This consists of the group listing hypotheses that flow from the heading 'In this situation it is really a question of *how to* ...'. For example, in assessing a situation in which a seriously abused and neglected child has been thriving well with foster parents for 4 years, but the birth mother wants the child, now 10 years old, to return to her, and the child wants to live with her and her abusive partner, it could be a question of how to:

- Collect evidence to oppose the application.
- Assess what support the birth mother would need to be able adequately and safely to mother the child.
- Find ways of making the birth mother's home safe.
- Use the law to remove the dangerous partner.
- Find ways of maintaining residence with the foster parents *and* a relationship with the birth mother.

Only when the key worker decides (usually in consultation with a senior colleague) which of these (or other) directions to take does the second stage begin, namely that of '*go and* ...'. This is a second brainstormed list of suggestions or options from which the worker can select, picking out what would be the most immediately useful to *go and* do. This process helps to counter the *group think* tendency noted in case conference decision-making (this is discussed in more detail in Chapter 10).

The process of gaining depth of understanding of data begins with looking at the question 'In what ways is the problem a problem, and for whom?' It involves weighing up the situation, tentatively patterning the data, finding theoretical ideas that illuminate and help to interpret the story and make sense of it, then applying some of the theoretical maps to gain analyses, understandings or new accounts, drawing inferences (reasoning from the known to the unknown) and finally considering how to test the interpretations and recommendations. This process may go on after the meeting with the user(s) and it may be necessary to re-interview to check out ideas and share insights. Then there is the consideration of what resources are needed and what resources can be mobilized. This should always include the user's own internal and external resources and what intervention would be needed to mobilize these, so that, ideally, it is not just about meeting need now, but meeting it in such a way that the individual's and family's resources are strengthened for coping for the future. Sainsbury (1970) adds that we should always consider whether it is necessary to intervene at all and whether there are any negative consequences from doing or not doing so.

By depth, we do not mean that social workers must know everything about their subject from cradle to grave. A preoccupation with past events has been a positive hindrance in social work assessments – and it runs on the unrealistic assumption that social workers can change people completely. Rather, 'depth' means reaching helpful explanations or analyses of what is happening and how things could be improved – being more rigorous and systematic. Thorough exploration of data from a number of sources means not only that social workers will have a wider range of alternatives, thus preventing 'stuckness', but also that we will become clearer about our practice theory. There is nothing wrong with checking whether data fits our existing theory as long as we actually know what it is and can explain it to people; we recognize when the data do *not* fit our theory, and we are prepared to revise and expand our theory and consider other analyses. This does not mean that we have to explain to service users that we are using, say, a social skills training or a psychodynamic approach, but it does mean that we should be able to explain to service users what views we hold on how key social roles work and what explanations we have for their malfunctioning, being explicit about our views on the nature of people.

PLACEMENT THINKING POINT

1. Read through an assessment or an assignment you have written.

2. Identify any words used in the document that have specific meaning to social workers (for example attachment, boundaries, failure to protect, proactive).

3. With a colleague, practice explaining in simple English exactly what these words mean to you, and how you might explain them to service users.

As distinct practice theories are difficult for many social workers to articulate clearly – students usually say that they are eclectic (we will present an explanation of the main ones used in social work practice in subsequent chapters) – we will not only outline the theories, but also include the implications for assessment of each theory. We do not offer them as prescriptive guides but rather regard them as a series of potentially useful maps to consult once one has identified the territory it is wished to cover.

If a social work assessment is undertaken with the same methodological rigour as sound qualitative research, it will necessarily include:

- A clear statement of intent which also demonstrates how one can be held accountable for one's values.
- A systematic approach to data collection from an identified range of sources which is carefully checked for authenticity and which identifies gaps in information.
- The development of more than one hypothesis about the nature of the problems and solutions.
- A clear statement on how the final judgement can be tested in terms of demonstrable outcomes.

As we emphasized earlier, the acid test of the assessment is satisfaction with subsequent decisions and action on the part of service users (empowerment in practice) and service providers (evidence of change for the better). There should also be social workers' own satisfaction at not being 'stuck'. We present below the stages of such an assessment process in a linear model, although some parts of the sequence will overlap because re-evaluations will necessarily emerge during the process of checking the hypotheses.

The stages of assessment

(Note: This long list is not meant to be prescriptive, but only suggestive of various possible steps in various assessments.)

Preparation

- Make a list of key informants – people, documents, agencies. Keep this on file so that gaps in the information source are clearly visible.
- Prepare a schedule for collecting data from *all* key informants. Adapt agency checklists for this purpose.
- Decide on an interview schedule. If it is inappropriate to use an open interview format, make a list of essential questions to which answers are needed. Keep this on file, but give copies to the informants where this will be helpful.
- Prepare a statement of intent that includes purpose, what one is able to do, limits and how one will be accountable for one's values. Although this may be given verbally to potential service users, keep a copy on file.
- Make a note of early (tentative) explanations.

Data collection

- Prepare a contents page for the file, listing the documents and where they can be found.
- Store the data display on file, marking it clearly with details of who can have access to it. Store working diagrams, memos and so forth in a plastic folder at the back of the file.
- Check verbal data for authenticity by repeating, summarizing, and so on. Provide key informants with copies of ongoing summaries for further checks.
- Check written data for factual accuracy and mark unsubstantiated opinion clearly.
- Consider widening the data sources if the accuracy is doubtful or there are obvious gaps.
- Do not discount any data at this stage but note obvious incongruities or inconsistencies.

We use the term 'data' simply to signify factual information. Because facts do not always speak for themselves and there is an element of subjective interpretation in most information-gathering, a distinction is sometimes drawn between 'data', which are unprocessed and raw, and 'information', which is interpreted and integrated into other knowledge. However, we favour data collection with as open a mind as possible, an awareness of biases if possible, and 'weighing' and 'analysis' as separate as possible, allowing for the spiral of theory and data discussed in the next chapter.

Weighing the data

- Consider how serious the situation is or how well the client is functioning in the circumstances.
- Identify persistent themes or patterns emerging from the data and list them.
- Cluster the themes and begin ranking them in order of priority.
- Check priority ranking with the key informants.
- Identify gaps in the data.
- Identify a group of people who will help with reflexivity.
- List the people to be consulted, noting their comments on file.
- Weigh the risks involved.

Analysing the data

- Identify theoretical perspectives and use them to gain depth of analysis (see Chapters 5–9).
- Develop more then one hypothesis, especially around what the goal of intervention might be.
- Reach useful but tentative explanations for the situation.
- Test the explanations for possible theoretical 'fit' (also what language could have talked them into being).
- Check this with the key informants.
- Run a final check of all the data to guard against the selective use of information.
- Consult with the 'reflexive' group again, if necessary.
- Develop further explanations and list the ways in which they can be tested.

Utilizing the analysis

- What help is needed by the user? By others?
- List the outcomes one hopes to achieve and the consequences one hopes to avoid.
- Clearly explain how these outcomes can be measured.
- Prepare an intervention plan.
- Establish an independent mechanism to monitor outcomes. This could include supervision, a multi-agency group or service users.
- Prepare a draft report that lists sources of information, analysis and initial judgement (see Chapters 10 and 11, which will also address risk).
- Obtain feedback on the report and revise it, noting any disagreements with one's judgement and the reasons for them.

We have emphasized the need to develop more than one explanation for the data collected because this seems to provide the most effective counter-measure to the problem of 'shaping' the data noted earlier. Sheppard (1995) argues that this is one element in assessment that justifies the status of assessors as professionals, the others being the development of precision and clarity in the understanding of the use of concepts and theories, and becoming continually sensitive to disconfirming information (pp. 187–8). Additionally, a premature framing of the data has the effect of influencing the progress and outcome of a case regardless of the more usual checks such as supervision and interagency consultation. We will discuss framing effects in more detail in Chapter 10, but present an illustrative example here to show how developing multiple explanations improves the assessment process.

A probation officer presented the following scenario at her local risk assessment case conference with a view to deciding whether or not the service user should be registered as a potentially dangerous offender:

CASE EXAMPLE

Troy, a 44-year-old man, had collected his children for a contact visit and taken them to his club, where he became drunk. He took the children home early and discovered his wife having a meal with another man. There was an argument and Troy left. After brooding about the incident, Troy drank further and then returned to the family home, armed with a knife. A fight ensued during which the new man friend suffered a punctured lung, his wife was cut and bruised, and the children became very distressed. Troy was arrested and bailed. Six weeks later, immediately after the preliminary divorce hearing, he once again got drunk and returned to the family home, where he shouted insults and threw a milk bottle through the window. He was sentenced to 4 years' imprisonment for the wounding and 3 months for the criminal damage.

The probation officer put the following explanations to the risk assessment meeting:

1. This man is in serious danger of reoffending because:
   - He has a history of offending (housebreaking, stealing, taking without owner's consent, and drug offences).
   - Taking a knife indicated premeditation.
   - The assault had serious consequences.
   - The man cannot accept that his marriage is over.
   - He has little consideration for the effects of his behaviour on the children, the 5-year-old having to undergo counselling following the fight.
   - His drinking is uncontrolled.
   - He has little to do with his time since he was made redundant.

- His wife reports previous domestic violence following drinking. He denies this or suggests that he must have had 'blackouts' after drinking.

(Sources of information: the offender, his wife and police records.)

2. This man's behaviour was a 'one-off', atypical offence with little likelihood of reoffending because:

- Previous convictions were all in his youth, his middle years having been trouble-free.

- His barrister recommended plea-bargaining for a lesser charge, but he insisted on pleading guilty to avoid his wife having to give evidence, thus showing real remorse.

- He now shows concern about the effects of his behaviour on the children and has negotiated with his wife to see them in the presence of relatives to reduce their distress.

- He now accepts that his marriage is over.

- He has begun anger management and alcohol education programmes in prison, where he is reported to be cooperative.

(Sources of information: the offender and prison staff.)

3. This man is likely to reoffend in particular circumstances because:

- It is easy to be remorseful and reformed in prison where there is no access to alcohol.

- He is likely to 'coast' through his sentence.

- He remains angry about his wife's new, much younger man.

- He is unrealistic about how he will avoid arguments in the future.

- There are potential problems over his accommodation on release from prison because housing away from his wife will remove him from sources of support such as relatives and friends, and he resents losing his own home.

- Anger management and alcohol education programmes are untested in real-life situations.

(Sources of information: the prison staff and probation officer.)

No one explanation was decided upon as the most likely 'truth' at the risk assessment meeting, but the ability of the probation officer to propose multiple explanations rather than having to defend a single one meant that the risk assessment meeting members could engage in a helpful discussion. They decided that they needed to know:

- What additional data were needed to check possible explanations; for example, interviewing his wife and children on their own to find out what their needs, wishes and concerns were, and making arrangements for this to be discussed at a further meeting.

- What resources would be needed to reduce the potential for reoffending; for example, what support relatives could realistically offer this man, what programmes needed to be established to continue and monitor the anger management and alcohol education courses begun in prison, what housing and employment facilities were available in the neighbourhood where the man would live on release from prison and how the marital property could be harmoniously divided.

The main advantage of the probation officer being able to hold more than one explanation meant that she could focus on all three areas of assessment – risk, resources and needs – and thus was able to develop a management plan appropriate for all the people involved, which was well resourced, with tangible outcomes and capable of being monitored.

In conclusion, we are arguing unashamedly for the making of high-quality assessment. This entails demanding, thoughtful work rooted in clear theory, and acknowledges useful assessment to be a complex ongoing process. It would be highly understandable if social workers, faced with excessive workloads and many conflicting demands, regarded our framework as unrealistic, but the need in their case is for adequate resources in terms of staff and for supervisory support, rather than for short-cuts or shallow work that can so easily backfire or make matters worse.

Before outlining the assessment implications of the various theories informing social workers' understanding of the nature of people, in the following chapter we discuss how those theories can be made more explicit so that an improved decision about what theory will be used can be made.

SUMMARY

- Despite helpful government guidance on outcomes, when measured, especially in terms of service user satisfaction, assessment outcomes are largely unsatisfactory.

- Assessment is usually a one-off event with little evidence of re-evaluation.

- Assessing social workers seek to confirm rather than disconfirm their initial hypotheses.

- Assessing social workers often 'shape' data to fit their favourite theoretical models.

- Where risk is a factor, this predominates in assessments to the exclusion of need.

- A social worker's initial assessment is the key determinant to future action and outcomes. Social workers tend to use a questioning, procedural or exchange model of assessment depending upon whether risks, resource allocation or needs are the main factors.

- It is important to see assessment as a staged process and to remain reflexive throughout.

FURTHER LEARNING ACTIVITIES

At a seminar, identify the performance indicators most appropriate for the measurement of the effectiveness of assessments with one specific service user group.

FURTHER READING

Netton, A., Francis, J., Jones, K. and Bebbington, A. (2004) *Performance and Quality: User Experiences of Home Care Services. Final Report*. PSSRU Discussion Paper, 2104/3, www.PSSRU.ac.uk

D'Cruz, H., Gillingham, P. and Melendes, S. (2007) 'Reflexivity, its meaning and relevance for social work: a critical review of the literature', *British Journal of Social Work*, 37: 73–90.

Clarkson, P. *et al.* (2007) *Assessment, Performance Measurement and User Satisfaction in Older People's Services*. PSSRU@manchester.ac.uk

NATIONAL OCCUPATIONAL STANDARDS

For students working with the British National Occupation Standards for Social Work (see Appendix):

■ This chapter relates to *practice* elements 1.1; 5.1; 11.1–4; 18.1–3.

■ With which of the *knowledge* requirements in the Appendix does this chapter help you?

CHAPTER 4

Selecting a Map

What this chapter is about

We have outlined the issues and the process of making assessments, and we have addressed data collection. Before considering in detail the theoretical maps that guide social workers' *analyses* of problematic situations, we will first explore the array of social work knowledge with a view to improving how we *weight* data (stage 3 of the process) and then decide which map(s) to select for the purposes of *analysis* (stage 4 of the process).

We aim to provide a way through the thicket of concepts and theories of which social workers become aware in seeking helpful explanations for the nature of people and society, and to locate some signposts. We identify the ideas that will be most useful in making judgements about data and map selection, and address how theoretical maps and data collection are not entirely separate. Additionally, we look at the debate about 'finding the truth'.

MAIN POINTS

➤ The range and variety of theory.

➤ Competing theories.

➤ False certainty and developing hypotheses.

➤ Uncertainty and openmindedness.

➤ Map selection – 'fit' and 'location of problem'.

➤ How theory and data spiral around each other.

➤ Introduction to constructionist ideas.

➤ Naming the maps.

The theory thicket

Social workers are introduced to, and familiar with, a wide range of theory from the sociological (for an introduction see Cree, 2002; Haralambos and Holborn, 2004) to the psychological (for an introduction see Cross, 2007, or Nicholson *et al.*, 2006). There exists a plethora of research findings concerning specific aspects of people's lives, including psychological research findings relating to such aspects as attachment and loss (Bowlby, 1982; Rutter, 1981; Murray Parkes, 1986; Howe, 1995), stages of human development (Crawford and Walker, 2003; Hobart and Frankel, 2004), personality development theories (Schaffer, 1998), the hierarchy of human needs (Maslow, 1954), intellectual development (Piaget, 1977) and moral development (Kohlberg, 1968). Sociology offers theoretical insights into social strata, power and oppression (Jones, 2003; Payne, G., 2006), while social psychology looks at, for example, groups, decision-making and stereotyping (Ingleby, 2006). So the question the reader will probably ask is: '*How do all these fit together?*'

To answer this, we take the reader back to stage 3 of our initial overall framework – weighing the data (discussed in the last section of Chapter 3, 'The stages of assessment'). It is at this stage in the assessment process that the social worker makes judgements and evaluations on how well service users are doing in their particular circumstances. Are their strengths sufficient or are their limitations too great? Do their capacities and resources seem to be sufficient for coping? How does the difficulty or the particular situation compare with the norm? How much does it deviate from the culturally acceptable, the legal or the affordable? Are the risks acceptable? In other words, is there a problem? The making of these judgements is informed by a background knowledge of all the above theories, is also usually assisted by agency guidelines and procedures, and is underpinned by core social work values and skills, even though these are not often made explicit (for an overview see Trevithick, 2007).

Agency practice will vary according to whether the dominant purpose of the work is the control of deviance, the empowerment of needy and oppressed people, or ensuring people's quality of life and safety. However, how any worker uses theory is a matter of great uncertainty, which we hear most commonly expressed via metaphors such as 'once you learn to ride a bicycle, you do it without thinking'. It seems to us that in weighing up the gravity or need of a case, social workers' judgement is informed, and their beliefs bolstered, by the above-mentioned core theory. Most social workers would say this is useful and that they are using more than mere common sense.

The very existence of alternative and often competing theories of human behaviour and human problems does add considerable complexity to the task but we hope in this chapter to provide some assistance in explicit theory selection. It is not, however, the intention of this book to elaborate on all these areas of theory. We simply point to them as informing social work activity and show some key sources where they can be studied. They do connect, however, with the maps in that preference for a particular map will lead to more use of, or reliance on, particular aspects of the core theories of psychology, human development and sociology. One theory will fit better than another theory with individual social workers' views of people and difficulties, and with ideas on 'the nature of people' (Aggleton and Chalmers, 1986) implicit in any one chosen map.

THINKING POINT

1. Consider a new method/technique you have just learned about.

2. What are the theoretical underpinnings?

3. How does this fit with your existing theories about the nature of people?

We wish to emphasize that much of the theory can be used oppressively when social workers use it as if it were *the truth* for particular client situations. Most of it is culturally biased and presented as more 'certain' than it really is. For example, we rightly hesitate to describe any family as normal or abnormal, healthy or unhealthy, although we do need to have some idea of which families need help and which do not. Theories help us to develop *informed* opinions when they increase our understanding of the likely relationships between events in people's lives, the impact of personal history and social background and present needs and behaviours, and when they add to our awareness of the sources of distress, be they external, such as oppression, or internal, such as guilt. They can help us to understand the values implicit in policies, human motivation and the importance to people of their roles in life and their expectations.

The trouble with certainty

We would like to think that theories can usefully help us to consider how some solutions can make matters worse, how outcomes are often so uncertain that it is only at the end of our involvement that they can be verified, how all assessments are essentially tentative and how uncertainty can be positive.

No assessment should be 'once and for all' – it is a continuing process that is improved as intervention proceeds. It is also revised when work is formally reviewed and needs to be reconsidered when termination is being planned. It remains in focus as effectiveness is evaluated after the work has finished. However, it is never to be believed in to the exclusion of other possibilities. Hence we say that rather than seeking to 'prove' hypotheses, we seek to *improve* them – and 'proof' will come only when the work is evaluated. Ideally, we need to develop competing hypotheses and look for evidence to disprove them because along with uncertainty comes hope for change, or at least such an approach would reduce the risk of grave inaccuracy. Overreliance on theory conflicts with what Pozatek (1994, p. 397) calls 'the uncertainty principle' because the very act of observing changes what is being observed. This should prompt us to ask how we can tell that what we see is what was there before we saw it. Without realizing this difficulty, workers can disseminate information and 'initiate and maintain a pathologizing discourse' (Pozatek, 1994, p. 398) that is oppressive. By way of contrast, the constructionist approach is to work with service users in a way that is respectful of the unique complexity of each person's life and his/her understanding of it. This shift in perspective is necessary to 'account for the unpredictability and randomness that are part of every day life' (Pozatek, 1994, p. 398) in any particular culture. Assessments by professionals all too often get accorded the status of truth and, unchallenged, the resulting beliefs become accepted as true.

CASE EXAMPLE

Following the removal of children, Ann's social worker, Mary, has undertaken a comprehensive assessment, concluding that Ann has resolved many of her difficulties but remains vulnerable because of her lack of social support. Mary has also commissioned a psychological assessment. This assessment concludes:

> The results indicate that Ann has a poor self image, seeing herself as being of little value, inadequate and feeling a sense of hopelessness. There is a marked lack of self-confidence and a belief that she is not capable of doing things on her own. In essence there is a lack of a strong feeling of identity . . . Although her history was not discussed in detail, it is my view that her childhood experiences have played a significant role in the development of this personality style. There is an urgent need for her to address this area of functioning via extended counselling.

Ann is greatly distressed by the psychological findings: 'That's not me. He's twisted my personality. I couldn't answer the questions so I answered in the middle. He didn't discuss his opinions at all so I had no chance to disagree. It's so final, his word goes, like it or lump it. The Guardian ad Litem is going with that report, so Mary's panicking now. It's turned things round, and it's so late. I've no chance of proving I don't need that work.'

As this example shows, this is not only oppressive to service users, but also limits what social workers think can happen. Pozatek (1994) reports seeing many interventions unhelpful to service users that involved a high degree of worker certainty. Understanding people's experience is as important as understanding their behaviour. This requires a collaborative/partnership approach to interpreting meaning, an awareness of the power of the prevailing discourse, a willingness to co-construct shared understandings of situations by dialogue with service users, and adopting a stance of uncertainty that pushes us to try harder to grasp a service user experience. Assessments have to be more like qualitative than quantitative studies, and be 'making sense' activities rather than ones clinging to naïve realist epistemologies. Influenced by postmodern perspectives, we believe that no single theory can fully tell the truth and that there is anyway a plurality of truths. Truth can only be interpreted (Parton and Marshall, 1998) and certainty is illusory. We like the expression 'working truths'.

So we take an interpretist view, committed to understanding the *meanings* that service users use to make sense of their lives, meanings that are constructed by the language used in talking about life. Although we do acknowledge the existence of reality that we can 'bump into', we maintain that assessments never fully reproduce it. What we see and hear is evidence or data but we need reflexive checking of our assumptions and our plans for action in coming to an understanding of the *meaning* of the data. Therefore, while we need to be aware of what is known in the social sciences, and use theory to check our own prejudices as we make the initial judgement in stage 3 of an assessment, we need to welcome uncertainty in work where 'the perturbing agent can only serve to trigger an effect: it is the living being [the service user] who determines the outcome of the interaction' (Maturana and Varela, 1987, cited in Pozatek, 1994, p. 397). What separates the creative social worker from the mere technician is the capacity to shift from one perspective to another. Parton and Marshall (1998) put it well when they say this demands that we can make our minds up about what to do but still remain openminded. It will be clear to the reader that we are attracted to social constructionism in the way in which we view social and psychological theories; for an introduction to this approach, we recommend Burr (2003), Parton and O'Byrne (2000) and Taylor (2004).

Map selection

Stage 4 of the assessment framework involves analysis of the data, and this requires an application of one or more of the theoretical maps (derived from methods of intervention) in order to gain a useful depth of understanding that will guide plans for intervention. In our experience, many assessment reports simply describe problems from various subjective perspectives and then give a common-sense summary of the situation, perhaps adding some suggestions for what should be done. When we ask workers how they arrived at their recommendation, they may say that this is what they always do in these cases, or that's the way it is done in the particular agency. When asked whether other social workers might see the situation differently, they readily accept that they may well do so. The idea of selecting a theory to provide a particular analysis or explanation of how things have become as they are, or how they might be changed, is felt to be only adding to the workers' difficulties and a rather academic exercise in any case, but it is crucial that our theoretical models are made explicit if we aim to practice anti-oppressively. We need to be aware also of the consequences of using a particular map, with its underpinning philosophy, as this may not accord with service user experiences.

PLACEMENT THINKING POINT

1. Read an assessment.
2. Which theory underpins this assessment?
3. Does it lead logically to the interventions proposed?

There are many 'maps' from which to choose but none of the resulting analytic descriptions can reproduce reality; they can only propose helpful reunderstandings:

> It is now widely accepted that any statement that postulates meaning is interpretive – that these statements are the outcome of an enquiry that is determined by our maps or analogies or, as Goffman puts it, by 'our interpretive frameworks'. (White and Epston, 1990, p. 5)

Fit

In considering the factors that influence theory selection in social work practice, it is our impression that *fit* (in the sense that a metaphor can fit a situation) with the original data or type of problem is the greatest influence in theory selection. For example, family therapy ideas *fit* problems of family relationships, parenting problems *fit* with notions of skills training, a task-centred approach has particular ways of looking at interpersonal interactions, and behavioural problems *fit* with the behaviour modification approach. However, substance abuse could *fit* equally with a behavioural approach or with a solution-focused approach, and affective disorders such as depression *fit* with a cognitive analysis of difficulties or psychodynamic interpretations. We need to arrive at *fit* not only between data and analytic maps but also between our analyses *and those of service users themselves* – except when these are clearly in conflict with the needs or rights of others. The existence of adequate *fit* between original data and intervention should not, however, be seen as necessarily prescriptive. In assessments of need or risk, notions about capacity for self-care *fit* well in some situations, such as an older person living alone, but less well in situations such as a parent struggling to manage a child's temper tantrums. At the end of each of the following 'map' chapters, we will suggest some advantages and disadvantages in terms of outcomes that might be associated with that map and therefore possibly with its use in certain situations.

Perhaps the second greatest influence on assessment is the actual services that are available and the criteria for suitability of these, even when these lead only to fitting people into the best (least bad) alternative available (Wright *et al.*, 1994). The interventions that the worker can personally deliver and the worker's preferred explanation for problems influence theory selection. As the reader will discover, some maps claim to be useful for most situations, and most social workers will feel that they do not need to draw on all five maps.

'Locating' the problem

An alternative way of selecting the most useful map would include the following features. Having engaged with a potential service user and begun to establish trust, thus generating a flow of information or data to which one has listened attentively, one could begin to ask 'Where is the problem/need/solution mainly located, outside the service user, within the service user, or between the user and others?' In other words, is it extrapersonal, intrapersonal or interpersonal?

Frequently, a person's need/problem/solution is perceived by the individual or the family as being *both* internal and external.

Where the problem or solution is considered to be mainly outside the service user, it is for the most part not the service user who is the main target for change but the social system. Then it may be a matter of advocacy, or a needs and risks assessment and a survey of appropriate resources, or possible systems analysis as a preparation for systemic change.

If it is felt to be inside the person, the assessing social worker needs to ask whether it consists of a habit, in which case behavioural ideas may fit best. If it is a feeling, a psychodynamic approach or a cognitive approach might be considered, while cognitive theory strongly suggests itself for a self-defeating pattern of thinking. If it is most likely to be found between the person and others, task-centred theory, narrative ideas or cognitive theories may help.

Matching theories to types of problem is difficult. This difficulty arises from the fact that more than one theoretical approach may be helpful in any one case and various theories can tackle some problems equally well, depending on the skills of the worker. For example, if a service user is depressed, psychodynamic theory may provide useful insights, but cognitive theory also has its own way of helping with this problem, claiming that feeling is the result of dysfunctional thinking (NICE, 2007). If the cause of the depression is interpersonal, then solution-focused or narrative ideas could be indicated, whereas if the cause is external then tackling oppression and finding resources will be more important. Also, social workers' own preferences and abilities have to be taken into account, as long as they can show that they are effective in achieving service user satisfaction. Some social workers and writers claim that one method of assessment and intervention can suit all situations, an example being de Shazer (1993), who suggests that there are no contraindications for solution-focused work (see Milner, 2001, for a discussion of how solution-focused ideas are applied to a range of social work situations).

Of course, various ways of working may take a longer or shorter time, and since our premise is that assessment is more helpful if it matches the intended intervention, busy workers will favour ideas from brief therapy. We feel that there is little point in doing a thorough Freudian analysis if there is neither the time nor the expertise to carry out the related psychoanalytic intervention. Cost will be a further factor to consider, not that 'quickest and cheapest' is necessarily the best.

In some situations, the theory will immediately suggest itself because the intervention will be 'ready-made'. For example, if the problem is one of bed-wetting, most social workers will suggest a reward system such as a star chart, or a warning bell, both being based on behaviourist theory. So too is skills training for, perhaps, a man with underdeveloped fathering skills, and assertion training for those who have not learned to assert their needs appropriately and who may be either too aggressive or too passive. However, we cannot stress too strongly that assessors need always to look at the extrapersonal and the interpersonal before focusing on the intrapersonal because power is an ever-present issue. It is extremely rare in any case for any 'problem' to be entirely intrapersonal; people may be *in* the problem but they rarely *are* the problem.

In practice, the selection of a theoretical framework is usually not a clear-cut matter. Finding the *best fit* will, especially for new social workers, often entail consideration of more than one map and trying them for fit and usefulness, rather like finding which *metaphor* fits a particular situation best. In this process, one would be looking not only at aspects that fit well, but also at aspects that clash or misfit and then weighing up the positives and the negatives. By positives we mean those aspects of theory that shed light on the difficulty and how it might have started and, more importantly, on how it is maintained in existence and what might be helpful in its resolution. By adding together these positives and allowing for any negatives, social workers can compare different approaches for fit and usefulness. There is no reason why the service user should not be included in this process.

The spiral of data, theory and analysis

We now wish to address another aspect that can be confusing to assessing social workers: the overlap between theoretical analysis and data collection. This comes about because the particular theoretical approach that a social worker implicitly holds, or selects, influences the questions asked when reaching for depth of understanding. Furman and Ahola (1992) maintain that it is not the truth of a theory as established by research or some value system that matters but the usefulness of the questions that flow from it. They demonstrate this by using a totally fictitious theory and showing how it can lead to a useful analysis. The social worker begins by saying something like this:

> Come with me on an imaginary interview. This interview will take place in a dark, damp cave outside of town where lives a gremlin called 'The Jaahak', whose sole purpose in life is to get people to have problems like yours. Any steps to change these problems upset him very much, because his whole life is dedicated to making people suffer these problems, in your case substance misuse. Our job is to defeat The Jaahak and our first step is to work out what he likes you to do and what he hates to see you doing.

So, in this interview, the theory being used to explain the problem is that such problems are caused by a gremlin called The Jaahak. This being the case, the questions naturally include him – they lead to collecting new data that are linked to the theory – data about what The Jaahak likes and dislikes people to do. The questions could seek out a list of these likes and dislikes; for example, in the above scenario the service user discovers that The Jaahak likes him to:

- Associate with other users.
- Not bother about getting a job.
- Sleep during the day and 'hang out' at night.
- Steal money to feed the habit.
- Avoid treatment.

- Ignore warning literature.
- Squat.
- Be anti-police.
- Not talk to the family about the drugs.

As the service user completes this list, he could be asked if it includes many of the things currently done. Then he could be asked to begin a list of dislikes the Jaahak may have, such as:

- Returning home.
- Looking for a job.
- Discussing the problem with the family.
- Visiting a counselling service.
- Sleeping at night.

Or anything else the Jaahak would really hate, for example:

- Reading about drugs.
- Trying to change his/her friends.

> We could ask 'Which of these things could you start practising in order to begin to worry the Jaahak?'

Note that the Jaahak's likes and dislikes include both *interpersonal* and *extrapersonal* factors. It would not be difficult to include *intrapersonal* factors too.

These questions, driven by this fictitious map, can lead to a helpful analysis that helps the service user see what might be done to start developing a solution for the difficulty. The service user may begin to see that many of the behaviours now engaged in are ensuring the continuance of the problem, or at least are helping to maintain it, and make its resolution less likely. However, our purpose in presenting this 'theory' is to show how the theory shapes the questioning, which, in turn, leads to sets of data being produced because our very questions construct their own answers: 'New narratives yield new vocabulary, syntax and meaning in our accounts [and] they define what constitute the data of these accounts' (Bruner, 1986, p. 143).

CASE STUDY: THEORY INTO PRACTICE

Amy and Ali have had their children removed to foster care following a series of drunken fights in front of the children. At a meeting to consider what work needs to be undertaken before the children can return home, the social worker says that she wants the parents to understand the impact of their behaviour on the emotional wellbeing of the children, and for Ali to accept responsibility for his violence to Amy. Amy insists that she started all the fights, but that they are fine now she has stopped drinking. The social worker does not accept this and presses Ali further to take responsibility for his behaviour.

- What theory underpins the social worker's assumptions about the causes of domestic violence?
- How would Amy and Ali demonstrate that they understand the impact of their behaviour on the emotional wellbeing of the children?
- How could this be measured?

In beginning an assessment, therefore, after having engaged with the service user, it is a matter of collecting initial data by listening to the stories of the potential service users and others. These data will point to a possible preferred theory in the mind of the worker and the resulting questions will provide their own data (service users' answers or information). This will lead in turn to an explanation of this service user's particular situation, the explicit use of more than one theory clearly being an important safeguard against bias. Data collection does not stop dead at the end of a checklist so that inference-making can begin with the use of a theory; rather, these aspects spiral around each other as the theory is drawn on to generate new data of its own. This will be true of any theory that may be selected.

Interventions follow from the assessment, which is based on the data, including needs, risks and resources, and on the inferences made. This is not the same as the methods-led assessments referred to in Chapter 3, nor is it the same as jumping to conclusions too soon and making the data fit one's theory. As we stressed in Chapter 3, social workers should have more than one hypothesis, and both hypotheses and questions are generated by theory. Because we cannot empty our heads, there is always some 'theory'. Thompson (1995) discusses 'the fallacy of theoryless practice' and shows how complex actions cannot be divorced from thought. He is referring not just to 'book theory' but also to the informal theory that underlies people's explanations of events. It is only when we acknowledge what ideas influence our actions that we are in a position to question them. Without such reflection, we risk becoming dogmatic. Because social workers ought to know why they are asking particular questions, they need to know and make explicit what 'theory' is driving their assessment questions.

PLACEMENT THINKING POINT

1. Read an assessment you have made.
2. How did you decide what questions to ask?
3. What theory/working hypothesis guided you to these particular questions?

Finding the truth – the road to constructionism

By now, the reader must be wondering how we can be placing equal value on different theories or even suggesting that a fictitious theory might be useful. Surely the truth about a situation is what counts? We do believe that there is such a thing as *the* truth about a situation, certainly in the collection of accurate data or the description of service users and the resources available to assist with their needs. However, we also believe that there are many, and often conflicting, truths about any one subject's situation. Since an analysis is a making sense of a set of 'facts' and it is possible to construct any number of accounts, we would argue that the most truthful analysis is the one that is the most *helpful*; the one that leads to the most useful understanding and to an intervention that achieves the service user's goals is the one that has the most utilitarian truth.

CASE STUDY: THEORY INTO PRACTICE

Sixteen-year-old Graeme's social workers view his physically abusive behaviour towards his grandparents as evidence that he has unresolved issues to do with his witnessing his father stabbing his mother to death six years previously. Graeme explains that he gets angry when his grandparents don't allow him to have an opinion. He adds that he copes with his mother's death by not thinking about it.

- Which explanation of Graeme's behaviour has the most utilitarian truth?

In the current state of the social sciences, it is not possible to prove that any helpful analysis is more or less true than another, and we know of no one who expects that it will ever be possible to reach one analysis universally accepted as the most true. Neither is it likely that we will be able to reach a deeper level of meaning beneath surface appearances that will rule out all other meanings. For constructionism, it is unlikely in social work that there will be one version of events that is true in the sense of making all others false. This can be attacked as leading to a relativism that puts the very premise of constructionism in doubt (Burr, 2003) but its strength is that, if accounts can be said to be neither true nor false, meaning can easily be mobilized in the social world in the interest of particular disadvantaged groups. We know that the powerful are skilled at using discourses ideologically and politically in their own interest.

Positivists felt that experts could acquire the necessary knowledge to explain and correct the world, to make continual progress and to know when they had found the truth of what was 'really' the matter. However, in this age of postmodernism, the subjective meanings of the individuals who are experiencing difficulties are being seen as central, and their 'stories' (accounts of their world view) are being seen as mattering a great deal. Their attributions and explanations are part of the reality and even create that reality. Because there is a scepticism that we can locate 'the truth', what matters is the currently operating created 'truth' of this person and how a thematic map might help us to co-construct with the person a more helpful and empowering account. It is interesting that, later in his life, Freud shifted the emphasis from historical truth to 'narrative truth'. Essentialists feel that truth is something external to the person and something the person can regard objectively, whereas constructionists see it as essentially something that is created by the ideas, thoughts, constructs, beliefs, communications, words and language of the knower. We 'author' our lives, and if they are unsatisfactory we can 're-author' them. Language does not simply represent reality; it makes it.

This approach, that one story is as true as another, can be attacked as an exaggeration. After all, a cat is not a dog. There has to be some fit or correspondence between external reality and what we construe. Except when we are deluded, we can usually tell the difference between fact and fantasy. In our daily lives, we rely on those ideas that are 'object-adequate' (Pocock, 1995, p. 161), that fit with the hard realities which we 'bump into' daily. Some stories are more testable than others, and some stories come to dominate our understanding from time to time. Pocock (1995) takes the view that we can have more confidence in some stories, so it is a matter of looking for the better story. A most useful theory represents the best story that can be written from a particular perspective to make sense of the uncertainties of life. Indeed, several stories can coexist, offering different layers of perspective. What we need to locate is the 'pragmatic truth' (Pocock, 1995, p. 160), which will be the most useful in facilitating change in any particular situation as long as the outcome is both ethically sound and useful. It is, therefore, important to hold to uncertainty, to develop more than one hypothesis and to compare alternative and competing understandings for usefulness.

In another sense, a theory can be seen as a story's plot, but we want to keep to the notion of map in this book. We hold to the postmodernist view and the belief that the narrative can create the reality in human difficulties, so substitution of the term 'map' is meant in the narrative sense, as a plot for a story, or as an analogy that makes sense of a situation and gives direction. In social work, the situation is usually a 'stuck' one, where life has become like one episode of a miserable soap opera repeated over and over again. The best map is the one that fits that current situation best and is the most useful in facilitating progress – the most pragmatically 'true' and the most positive and empowering for the service user.

We maintain that social work's search for one cohesive theory is misplaced. Social workers need a selection of practice principles and values, coupled with a range of theoretical models and methods, as a foundation from which they can respond creatively to the infinite range of situations they will meet. This creativity will enable them to be thinking, reflecting, responsive professionals. In the words of Milton Erickson:

Each person is a unique individual. Hence [work] should be formulated to meet the uniqueness of the individual's needs rather than tailoring the person to fit the Procrustean bed of a hypothetical theory of human behaviour. (Erickson, cited in Zeig, 1985, p. 8)

We must avoid being like Blaug's (1995) carpenter who, possessing only a hammer, tended to see every problem as a nail. Each theoretical approach has its own usefulness or domain in which it is helpful in some particular way. No one map has been proven to be more effective than another in all situations, nor is it likely that such a map will be found. Many writers (see for example Pinsof, 1994) maintain that it is, therefore, a matter of linking together more than one fitting map to maximize usefulness and reduce deficit. Pocock (1995) supports this pluralist approach, which gives the worker more positions from which to be helpful by selecting 'a highly congruent better fitting set of ideas' (p. 162).

CASE EXAMPLE

Poppy, aged eleven, was having severe tantrums over contact with her mother who, according to the father, had walked out and left them all. This father was distressed and angry, condemning his wife in the child's hearing. He repeatedly said of the child that she was 'disturbed' and 'It will take years to get her back to normal.' The mother was seeking contact with the child, but the child was refusing to cooperate. We worked with the couple, drawing on a divorce mediation map, and the father was able to agree that the child should be told that her mother had not left her, but that her mother and father would be living in two houses in future, and they both still loved her and would always be her only parents, and her father now wanted her to see her mother. To the father we said, 'Perhaps this child is not disturbed, perhaps she is playing a game, the game of being on her father's side and, as soon as she knows that seeing her mother is not disloyalty to her father, she may recover very quickly.' When they were seen a week later, the child was staying with her mother during the agreed times without difficulty. In this case, we had recounted a different plot from that developed by the family, using our knowledge of separating families and of mediation to develop a story that altered the meaning of the components of the problem and helped to bring about change.

Naming the maps

Suppose one were travelling from a small town in Scotland to a village on the south coast of England. One could buy various maps that might be useful depending on one's mode of transport, on one's needs for the journey or on how well developed were the roads or ways. Assessing a potential service user can feel like entering uncharted (or variously charted) territory as the worker searches for ways by which to 'arrive' at a 'conclusion'.

In the following chapters, we will be considering five theoretical approaches, which we have called maps of various kinds. We use the map metaphor derived from Bateson (1977) and subsequently developed by several writers in the family therapy field and by solution-focused writers such as Durrant (1993). This metaphor appeals to us because it helps to deal with the issue of truth.

Our traveller from Scotland has quite a choice of maps. She could get a motorway map, which would show junctions and service stations. As she passes each of these, she will know how far she has travelled, whether it is in the right direction and what else she has to do to arrive at her destination. However, she may need a detailed road map to help her find her way when she is not on the motorway. If she wishes to walk, say to raise funds for a charity, she may prefer to take minor roads and footpaths, in which case another kind of map, such as an Ordnance Survey map, showing hills and valleys, might be more helpful to her. Likewise, if she were to travel by boat she would need a map of coastal waters. Perhaps maps also need to be understood by the person being met, or else the service user might not be waiting at the harbour! Maps should ideally have meaning and helpfulness for both parties and be in a language that both use.

Each of these maps could claim to be a map of Britain, and they all are true in what they represent. But none of them is truly Britain; the map is not the territory. On the other hand, if we consider the domain of 'the meaning of experience', we could say the map is the territory – that real meaning is simply that which we construct and narrate. We regard theories of human situations as maps to the understanding of problems, all different, all offering a different construction, yet all potentially useful and equally true. It is crucial that, when faced with the often pressing needs of service users, we avoid taking the 'naïve realist' view and that we are reflexive about the effects of the lenses we use. What matters is what gets the best outcome for all concerned.

Because Freudian ideas relate mainly to getting below the surface of the person and their feelings, we have named Chapter 5 'A Map of the Ocean'. On the other hand, Cognitive-behavioural work focuses on observable conduct and on the ups and downs of action, so in Chapter 6 we have named it 'An Ordnance Survey Map'. In Chapter 7, we have labelled task-centred work 'A Handy Tourist Map' for several reasons: it is popular with busy workers, offers relatively brief ways of working, is easy to explain to service users, and is an easily accessible guide to assessment that has a wide application. We have used the metaphor 'A Navigator's Map' in Chapter 8 for the solution-focused approach because this is a map specially prepared for locating and getting to a particular goal, as navigator and service user fly towards the constructed solution. Chapter 9 presents 'A Forecast Map', so called as it deals with oppressive climates and is also future-focused; it will address the narrative approach and the implications of the notion of 'story' (in the narrative sense) for assessment and intervention.

It will be clear that, at least in some instances, one map does not rule out another. Rather, they can complement each other (for example, the maps in Chapters 8 and 9 combine easily), adding a further layer of understanding and providing further indicators towards possible interventions to bring about change.

We hope in particular to show that several maps can apply in helping in any one situation and, to some extent, the choice that works best for one worker may be different from that which works best for another. In our view, social workers and service users should be encouraged to experiment and thus eventually devise their own most useful blend of ideas, although that cannot work if we seek to combine ideas that are not compatible. The really important point is that professionals ought constantly to review their effectiveness, seek out ways of increasing usefulness to users, and explain their 'maps' to service users. In this way, their array of maps can evolve over time in an atmosphere of research and evaluation, drawing especially on user feedback, but never claiming to have found the truth. This involves constantly checking for the advantages and limitations of each map, and for ways of making them more useful to the service users by helping to generate really helpful analyses of their difficulties and their solutions.

Finally, it may be helpful to look on the various 'maps' (or method theories) as differing *metaphors* for the same reality, as well as different ways of telling the story.

SUMMARY

- In developing a deeper *understanding* of difficulties, with a view to deciding on intervention, social workers can draw on a range of theoretical maps, based on the theories from which methods are derived.

- Differing hypotheses result from viewing situations with the aid of theoretic maps. This is healthy since no one map can claim to lead to a single truth, and because forming alternative understandings safeguards against bias.

- Pragmatic truth, that is the interpretation which is most helpful to both social workers and service users in developing solutions, is the most desirable, provided the work is firmly rooted in the values of respect and anti-oppressive practice.

- Social workers need more than one map or tool in order to avoid being likened to a carpenter who only has a hammer.

- Having more than one map helps us to retain uncertainty and open-mindedness, which is the beginning of hopefulness.

- Maps have been developed in three 'waves' since the middle of the twentieth century (see Figure 4.1).

Waves	Philosophical focus	Cause of problems	Methods/Maps
1. Pathology-based	The way it is(science)	Result of early life experiences	Psychodynamic – map of the ocean
2. Problem-based	The way it is done or seen	Behaviour and thought habits (learned)	Behavioural, cognitive, and task-centred maps
3. Solution-based	The way it can be (socially constructed)	It just happens, or there are invitations that constrain choice	Solution-focused and narrative maps

Figure 4.1 Waves and maps

FURTHER LEARNING ACTIVITIES

In a seminar group, everyone brings in a newspaper and reads the main story in each.

- Discuss how the papers constructed the issues of the day.
- How else could they be constructed?

FURTHER READING

Burr, V. (2003) *An Introduction to Social Constructionism*. London: Routledge.

Parton, N. and O'Byrne, P. (2000) *Constructive Social Work*. Basingstoke: Palgrave Macmillan.

Payne, Mm. (2005) *Modern Social Work Theory*. Basingstoke: Palgrave Macmillan, (chapter 8.)

NATIONAL OCCUPATIONAL STANDARDS

For students working with the British National Occupation Standards for Social Work (see Appendix):

- This chapter relates to *practice* elements 5.2–3; 9.1–3; 11.1–4; 17.1–4.
- With which of the *knowledge* requirements in the Appendix does this chapter help you?

CHAPTER 5

A Map of the Ocean: Psychodynamic Approaches

What this chapter is about

In this chapter, we will be considering various ideas associated with the psychoanalytical approach to understanding the nature of people. We are selective in our sources, limiting ourselves to the work of Erikson (1948, 1977), Hollis (1964), Berne (1978) and Bowlby (1982, 1988), who have built on and developed Freudian theories in ways which have proved particularly attractive in social work. Our description of the theory will reflect a synthesis of many people's ideas and insights, their terms and their language.

MAIN POINTS

➤ Wider theoretical issues: psychodynamic social work, ego psychology, transactional analysis.

➤ Implications of psychodynamic theory for assessments.

➤ Practice theory: attachment theory.

➤ Implications of attachment theory for assessments.

➤ Critical comments on the difficulties of using this theory and on the expression of feelings.

➤ Outcomes of this approach and of research into it.

Introduction

Social work theory can be said to have emerged in three main 'waves'. The earliest of these was rooted in the ideas of Freud (for example, 1937) and his successors; it was a medical model and therefore was pathology-based. Subsequent 'waves' have been described as characterized by problem-solving and by solution-building, and we will address them in subsequent 'maps'. Despite its medical origins and its purely psychological theory, the psychodynamic map remains the most used in social work. We have, however, stressed that since external problems become internal and the internal affects the external, looking at nothing other than psychological aspects is as inadequate as looking at nothing other than social aspects; we need to consider both. Also, the ideas in this and the next four chapters all need to be used alongside the 'climatic' ideas outlined in Chapter 2.

Wider theoretical perspectives

Psychodynamic social work developed from Freudian theory, particularly 'psychic determinism': viewing our actions as determined by inner forces that develop in early childhood. It places great store on a person's early childhood and on early parental relationships, the past influencing the present. Some Freudians go so far as to say it can even be tyrannical in its influence. Therefore, this approach can have a feel of digging down deep as an archaeologist would but, more so, it can have a feel of descending into the unconscious as if exploring in a submarine. Our chapter title comes from a comment by Hall (1954, p. 2) that the id is 'oceanic', in that it contains everything and recognises nothing outside of itself; if there is too much rough weather, it can turn nasty. We begin with a simplified diagrammatic presentation of the core ideas in this exploratory map (Figure 5.1). Bear in mind, however, that we are not discussing physical parts of a person but mental constructs that seek to explain people's functioning: '[T]he relationship between conscious and unconscious functions within the psyche can be more fully understood and appreciated if they can be seen as much as metaphors as literal statements' (Jacobs, 1999, p. 9).

Although the id might not be capable of recognizing anything outside itself, Freud certainly did recognize the outside world and its impact on the ego, so we have shown the world of reality on our version of this map and, as we shall show later, a large area of the map will deal with the interaction of the ego with reality.

Freud's earliest distinction was that between the conscious and unconscious mind, considering the latter as the greater part, consciousness being only the tip of the iceberg above the surface. In the 1920s, Freud developed the notions of ego, superego and id. While a large part of the ego, although by no means all of it, can be conscious, the vast majority of the superego and probably all of the id are unconscious. Freud also identified the 'pre-conscious' as that part of the unconscious that we can readily recall, that is just under the surface.

Mind		**World**
Unconscious	Conscience	(Other people and environment)
Superego ('parent') Id ('child')	Ego ('adult')	Reality

Figure 5.1 Mind and world

The superego develops through a process of internalization. The child internalizes the values, rules, prohibitions and wishes of the parent and of authority figures, but the process is one that magnifies these rules and records them in the raw, without editing, and laden with amplified feelings. So it is not just what a parent says to a child but all the emotion, perhaps terror, that was felt at being blamed, abandoned or hurt in various ways: the small child who breaks a cup can feel that s/he has destroyed everything. Admonitions and rules go straight into memory, carrying the weight of total truth, never to be erased from the tape. The research of Penfield (1952) and the work of Berne (1964) have helped to shape this view of the superego, and Berne (1964) later referred to it as the Parent (using a capital P to indicate that this is an internalised parent) part of the person, the part that tells and teaches. Even though the telling is long lost from consciousness, the recording remains active in the unconscious, shouting loudly.

The superego may be restrictive or permissive (Caplan, 1961). People riddled with guilt can be said to have an overrestrictive superego and people with too little guilt an overpermissive or weak superego. Those with no internal rules, no conscience about hurting others, are labelled sociopaths (commonly called psychopaths). Caplan (1961) talks of the superego as the condemning and prohibiting part of the mind that says 'Do not...', or 'I must not...', and distinguishes this from the ego-ideal, which says (of a desirable act), 'So as not to let myself down, I ought to do it because that would fit my ideal me.' So, some people's conscience tells them they have to strive for great heights of achievement and set themselves high standards, be thrifty, and so on. On the other hand, too rigid and dominating a superego could create difficulties by way of excessive guilt, leading to neurotic effects such as depression, phobias, obsessions, compulsions, neurotic anxiety and moral anxiety or shame. Reality anxiety (Hall, 1954), however, is seen as an ego reaction to the threat of loss.

The id is that aspect of the person which is primitive, the animal drive: it is the Child (again with a capital C in Berne's terms), full of feelings, capable of rage, operating on instinctual drives and urges, hungry to fill any voids that are felt. Like the superego, according to Harris (1970), the id is also shaped by early recordings of feelings of blame, fear and abandonment. Even those with a happy childhood will record Not OK feelings that can loom larger than all the OK feelings. We can all be said to have a Not OK Child in us. The child who feels unloved may seek to fill a sense of void by theft, sometimes impulsively, as in kleptomania. The id also feels hurt by rejection or oppression.

Berne (1978) distinguishes between two main id drives – *libido*, which is sexual impulse, desire and attraction, and *mortido*, which is the killing instinct, hating, attacking and hitting out violently. He suggests some people are more prone to one rather than the other, although these are close relatives born of the need to propagate and survive. They explain something of what some people are looking for, so the id is described as being governed by the 'pleasure principle'; the lack of sufficient pleasure leaves it hurting, demanding and wanting irrationally, sometimes leading to a chaotic life of acting out, living for 'kicks' or sending out cries for help, such as the abused person who shoplifts to attract attention to his/her plight, behaving in a way that could be interpreted as asking to be caught.

The third area is the *ego*, the I and Me, the self. Berne labelled this as the Adult (with a capital A) part of the mind, which thinks, decides, plans and relates to the world of *reality*. It is governed by the 'reality principle', exploring and testing, born of curiosity.

The ego is placed between the superego and the id in Figure 5.1 because it acts as a referee between them, struggling to keep a balance between the gratification of needs and impulses and the sacrifice of this gratification to the demands of reality. This is what 'psychodynamic' means – an interaction and tension between (a) the id drives (b) the superego, with its possibly guilt-ridden prohibitions, and (c) a tension between inner needs and outer realities, in an attempt to keep a balanced ego.

Defences

The ego lives under great pressure from three sides: the id, the superego and real threats in the world. Anna Freud (1936, 1968) itemized various mechanisms of defence used by the ego to help it cope with the instinctual drives of the id and, to a lesser extent, with the condemnations of the superego and the demands of reality: '[T]he infantile ego experiences the onslaught of instinctual and external stimuli at the same time; if it wishes to preserve its existence it must defend itself on both sides simultaneously' (Anna Freud, 1936, p. 191). She listed denial, repression, reaction formation, intellectualization, displacement and sublimation as the main defences. Repression gets rid of instinctual derivatives, just as external stimuli are abolished by denial. Reaction formation secures the ego against the return of the repressed impulses, while by fantasies, in which reality is reversed, denial sustains it against attack from outside. The ego uses sublimation to direct instinctual impulses from their sexual goals to higher aims, and reaction formation is the ego further draining itself of the capacity for reversal (p. 190). The existence of neurotic symptoms itself indicates that the ego has been overpowered and some plan of defence has miscarried (p. 193).

Post-Freudians have added to Anna Freud's defences, up to 44 such defences being mentioned in the literature. For example, Bibring (1961) suggests that there are dual aspects of defences: first, warding off anxiety in relation to unconscious conflict and, second, actively supporting adaptive functions of maturation, growth and mastery of the drives. They list 39 defences, 2 of which have 2 subdivisions and 1 of which has 4 subdivisions. These include asceticism, clowning, compliance, depersonalization, eating or drinking, falling ill, identification, reutilization and whistling in the dark. Most people use several of these, at least from time to time, and they can be helpful, or not, depending on the degree of usage and the particular circumstances. It is important to remember, however, that defences can be helpful or unhelpful, particularly in a crisis when the ego is under great stress. For example, intellectualization might helpfully involve making lists of tasks, or thinking through the traumatic event. On the other hand, defences can be unhelpful when they lead to ongoing denial of loss, or projection of cause onto others. We sometimes think that projection is the curse of contemporary life where there seems to be a growing tendency towards not accepting personal responsibility. Part of the task of assessment in psychodynamic social work is to decide which defences are being used and whether they are a help or a hindrance, and, if the latter, to consider how they can best be confronted.

In translating psychodynamic ideas into social work practice, Coulshed and Orme (1998) wrote that, in assessing people, we need to see whether the ego can tolerate self-scrutiny without becoming too anxious. In cases in which such scrutiny does not promise for change, we need to ask ourselves what level of support is needed to help the person cope with external pressures. Coulshed and Orme suggest that indications of such lack of promise might be anxiety, dependence, low intellectual capacity and distrust. They warn against 'laying bare' repressed feelings, or offering interpretations to that end, if the ego thereby risks being overwhelmed. An immature, weak ego needs defences to be strengthened, rather than torn down; ego supporting is to be preferred to ego modifying in such cases.

Wasserman (1974) points out that it takes a strong ego to be able to mourn, suffer, verbalize anger and even be depressed. So the absence of depression in some situations, while it might appear to be adaptive, might in fact be due to an overdefended ego and therefore be maladaptive. In psychodynamic assessments, social workers look not only at behaviour, but also at the situation and consider the stresses that may be operating, the degree to which the ego is pressed upon and the stresses with which the ego can or cannot cope. So, ego functioning is not only influenced by internal pressures from the superego and the id, but very much also by external stimuli. Social, cultural and economic factors, injustice and oppression, do not remain outside the person: they become internalized. Since practice is often concerned with efforts to influence adaptive capacities, assessments are more likely to be useful if they focus on the interface of the ego with the world: how the ego is learning, controlling and balancing with self-reliance and pride. This will mean that a social worker will not be concerned about intensive psychoanalytic techniques of free association, the recovery of the repressed, or the interpretation of dreams and breaking through resistance. Rather than a blank-screen approach, she will offer a relationship, listening and reflecting with the client, joining the resistance (Strean, 1968), so that they can get going with the problem-solving that needs to be done. This does not in every case require the reliving of past traumas.

CASE EXAMPLE

Thirteen-year-old Emily was receiving hourly psychotherapy sessions to explore her experiences of being sexually abused as a means of helping her understand her current physical and sexual abuse of peers. She protested that she did not want to talk about her own sexual abuse and, when this was ignored, she became silent. When this too was ignored, she began protesting more aggressively: writing 'slag' instead of doing the prescribed art work; telling her therapist that she was useless; and playing up in the car going home with her foster carer. The therapist saw this behaviour as evidence that she was engaging with therapy. Emily saw it as due to their refusal to listen to her protests.

Ego functions

We would now like to consider the *functions* of ego, another area that can offer useful possibilities for assessment, particularly of the strength of the ego. It is the function of the ego to provide stability, equilibrium and predictability in such a way that, once we get to know someone, we can say that in certain circumstances s/he is liable to react in a certain way that is 'true to character'. This makes for sound relationships. Bowlby (1982) explains this in terms of the child making stable internal representations that will depend upon attachment styles developed in infancy but persisting into adult ways of relating. (Note that the prediction of others' behaviour that makes people feel in control of social situations is explained in different ways in the psychological literature. See, for example, the discussion on attribution theory in Chapter 2.) The ego also manages cognitions, perceptions, planning and problem-solving. It makes judgements and decisions, adapts to reality and controls impulses, for example, not hitting out at someone being offensive who is bigger than oneself! The ego is responsible for personal growth, coping with stress, using skills and tolerating frustration, loss, pain and sadness. It is the ego that neutralizes pressures from the superego and urges from the id. It produces self-assertion, the ability to verbalize feelings rather than act them out, and finally directs our striving, our attempts to achieve and to care. To do all this the ego needs to be flexible, adaptable, resilient, reality-based, stable in the face of pressure and tolerant of anxiety and loss.

The ego, therefore, has a massive task to perform, which can make it feel overwhelmed and in need of defences. We all need some defences at times, but many clients may particularly need us to strengthen or support their egos, not by breaking through defences with interpretations but by respecting and working with defences, acknowledging the threats they face and discussing the implications and confusion of their ambivalent feelings, or considering their unfinished emotional business, providing support perhaps through a corrective relationship that provides an emotional re-education, so that the client can move on to be an independent, coping person. This can, though, be slow work.

Women often have no other choice; they dread failing to cope and are likely to suffer serious consequences if they do. For example, women tolerate much domestic violence rather than risk losing their children, and put up with accusations that they have failed as mothers to protect their children (Kelly, 1994; Scourfield, 2003). Worse still, a black woman is stereotyped as being expected to cope with 'all kinds of hardship and material and emotional deprivation, as though she had no feelings or needs at all' (Lawrence, 1992; hooks, 1991 and 1993). Thus, we need to consider how reality is structurally more difficult for some people due to the oppressions of society, sexism and racism and other forms of discrimination:

> Following the early work of Richmond, psychosocial casework does promote indirect or environmental interventions as well as direct clinical work, but even today it retains a narrow understanding of what constitutes 'the environment', resulting in social interventions which usually seek little more than to mobilise or modify existing community resources. (Barber, 1991, pp. 16–17)

The terms 'independence' and 'separation', so central in psychodynamic explanations of 'healthy' personality development, have difficult connotations in that, because society is fundamentally patriarchal, women are more likely to have feelings of vulnerability, weakness, helplessness and dependency (Miller, 1973) or, on the other hand, to have learned from their mothers that they must orientate themselves 'towards meeting the needs of others' and 'to be a carer and not to expect to be cared for' (Lawrence, 1992). For an alternative view of ego development see Mead (1934).

Transactional analysis

Harris (1970), and later Berne (1978), developed the idea of transactional analysis (TA) in order to look at the relationship between any two people, not just parents and their children. They describe the transactions as taking place between the Parent, or the Adult or the Child of one person and the Parent, or the Adult or the Child of another. Hayes (2000) states that the main concept in TA is that of ego-states. Jacobs (1999) says that the model describes the related behaviours, thoughts and feelings that are manifested in one's personality and that have both internal and external functions, while Steward and Joines (1999) stress how the interacting states are constantly overriding each other in positive and negative ways. This is shown diagrammatically in Figure 5.2.

If person A is being irresponsible, sulky or childish, this behaviour is likely to provoke the Parent of person B. This transaction is shown by the line x, and y is a complementary reaction from B; it is expected and appropriate. Other obviously complementary interactions are Parent–Parent, Adult–Adult and Child–Child. However, if the transactions are crossed, there can be trouble, for example if A's Adult addresses B's Adult but B's response is from B's Parent (telling A off, perhaps), as shown by lines p and q.

For Berne (1978), the transaction, 'the unit of social intercourse', is the key unit of study. Transactions will vary, depending, for example, on whether the service user is relating to her social worker, to a partner, to a friend or to her own children. In some situations, she may find that she may need to be helped to practise using her reasonable, reasoning, grown-up Adult more. If

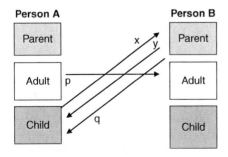

Figure 5.2 Parent–Adult–Child

practice makes no difference, she may need to be encouraged to get in touch with feelings from the past which, because they are presently out of consciousness, are dominant in certain circumstances. Events and people in our lives can 'hook' our Parent or our Child, which can appear to 'take over' for a while. This often operates in situations of conflict. Berne further developed notions of 'life scripts', laid down in childhood and often followed later.

Parent–Adult–Child contamination is another interesting idea from Harris (1970). Parent contamination (of the Adult) is when the Adult is holding to unreasonable, taught ideas, such as a strong prejudice against a certain group. This may be accompanied by a 'blocked-off' Child, making it difficult for the person to play or have fun. Child contamination of the Adult is when feelings from the Child are being inappropriately externalized/exhibited in the Adult, for example as delusions. This may be accompanied by a 'blocked-off' Parent, leaving a risk of a weakened conscience, a low sense of guilt or responsibility, and a lack of social control, remorse or embarrassment.

Harris (1970) further expands the Parent–Adult–Child metaphor to describe a manic person as one whose Parent is applauding the Child, and a depressed person as one whose Parent is 'beating on the Child' (p. 105). In both of these, there is Parent–Child contamination, and Harris suggests that such people are probably brought up 'under the shadow of great inconsistency' (p. 105). It may help here to 'recap' and show an ego gram of a particular service user, Miss O, aged 70, based on the work of Berne (1978) (Figure 5.3).

This can be seen as a graph of the 'family within' Miss O, who had become quite depressed when relatives were 'nasty' towards her because she would not give them a loan. It is based on conversations with her, listening to her memories of her responsibilities as the eldest child, her impressions of her parents as strict and stern, and her assessment of herself as being afraid to have fun but planning little deceptions to help her cope. Her Parent (the capital indicates that this is the internalized version of a real parent) is therefore represented as highly critical and not very nurturing. What nurturing there is is more rescuing than encouraging. Her Child, on the other hand, is not very free, being fearful of the critical Parent. It is, however, fairly well adapted, meaning that it has found a good deal of (possibly 'naughty') ways of making do. Meanwhile, her Adult

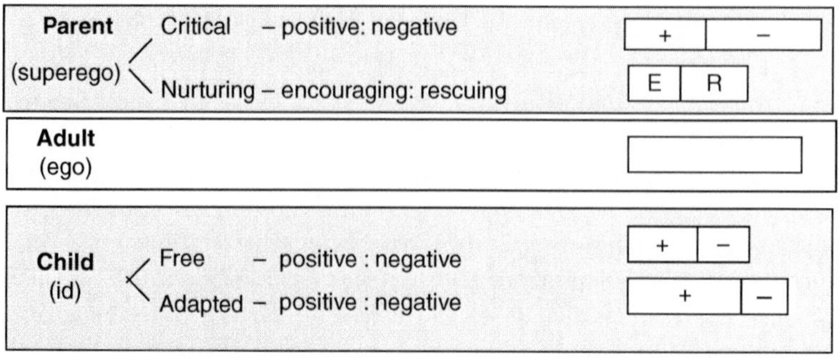

Figure 5.3 Ego gram

(ego) is reasonably strong, but she still has some growing to do. The critical Parent and the adapted Child are both difficult to manage. Much depends on what level of stress is caused by the world, especially the world of relationships. If this proves to be too bleak and stormy a place, this ego will need quite a lot of support and luck.

Implications of a psychodynamic approach for assessment

Whatever criticisms exist of this approach (and there are many, as we will shortly discuss), it remains a useful way of attempting to understand seemingly irrational behaviour. This is pertinent when service users' difficulties appear to reside inside themselves rather than at the interface of the client and structural inequalities. The notion of defence mechanisms can be a useful consideration in the assessment of people who have difficulty expressing their emotions and transactional analysis provides a simple and accessible way of looking at clients' interpersonal relationships. It acknowledges the influence of past events and helps to create a healthy suspicion about surface behaviour.

Insight can empower people to understand what is going on within themselves and between themselves and the outside world. Despite the assumption that psychosocial work is lengthy, it is possible to use the approach briefly in the course of assessment.

CASE EXAMPLE

The father of a boy who was not doing well at school was 'in a state', trying to cope with his anger at the teachers while trying to maintain his son's enthusiasm for education. The social worker asked the father whether he had been keen on education when he was at school. He said he had not, and he had a very negative experience of teachers. When it was suggested that perhaps he was still addressing his own past school issues, rather than his son's, this insight helped him to rehearse his meeting with the school so that when it took place he was better able to focus on his son's situation, behaviour and needs in a rational and helpful manner.

Supporters of this model suggest that it is useful for situations in which long-term work with a neurotic person is indicated. Cases of compulsions, hysteria, excessive dependence and people unable to face an emotion (loss, for example) may also fit this approach. One needs to understand the process of transference in order to keep the therapeutic relationship reality focused. Although transference is not strictly a defence, more an example of the past manifesting itself in the present, it is a process that takes place when a person transfers feelings relating to one person, for example a parent, onto the social worker. Thus, the social worker needs to privately consider whether the client is really referring to the social worker or perhaps to some early parental figure.

This approach has also influenced a listening, accepting attitude in social workers that avoids overdirectiveness and can be useful in informing the earliest stages of assessment: deciding on the interview format and helping to focus on specific parts of the analysis. All maps lead to a set of questions that can be considered by an assessor, although these are not directly put to the subject. This map suggests the following questions, but rather than developing an interrogation, they ought to be considered as directing a conversation, using the values of exchange and narrative, so that the answers to them emerge:

- Which developmental stage is reflected in the behaviour?
- Is the superego (conscience) overly rigid or overly permissive?
- Is there anxiety? How severe is it? What 'indirect' support might be helpful?
- How dependent or independent is the person?
- Are there signs of ego breakdown?
- What ego defence mechanisms are being employed, or are implicit, in the person's behaviour?
- Which ego defences need supporting or strengthening?
- Or are they strong enough to allow some insight work?
- What threat is the person experiencing? External (social) or internal (psychological)?
- What ambivalences are present?
- Are there some repetitive themes?
- Have there been past unsatisfactory relationships that need a corrective relationship?
- Which ego coping functions are working or not working for this person?
- What are transactions with others like?
- What 'contamination' is there?
- Does the person know what they should do and yet repeatedly not do it?
- Has the person had a figure with whom they have been able to identify?
- Have I considered the gender difference implications, especially in terms of coping and independence?

Attachment theory

Psychodynamic theory sees people as developing in a sequence of stages, each one dependent upon the successful negotiation of the earlier one for its own success. Freud's interest in the early stages of child development, particularly sexual development, was extended across the life span by Erikson (1948, 1977), while Klein's object relations theory (1988) and Bowlby's attachment theory (1963, 1979, 1982) focused more on the social and emotional interactions of this period. We focus here on attachment theory as it is used more frequently in assessment than are the theories of Klein and Erikson.

Bowlby agrees with one of Klein's main hypotheses: that childhood experiences of mourning link to ways of responding to loss in later life, but considers that the vulnerable period extends over a number of years of childhood and that the significant object is the mother (and sometimes the father) rather than the breast. The primary loss of a parent gives rise not only to separation anxiety but also to processes of mourning in which aggression plays a major part. Attachment theory also claims predictive power, making it a useful theory for those who have to assess risk. Whereas psychoanalytic theory and practice (particularly the work of Goldstein *et al.*, 1973, 1979, 1985) influenced the emphasis on the welfare of the child in the Children Act 1989 and, at the same time, in court decision-making (Mr Justice Thorpe, 1997), attachment theory has been particularly influential in shaping subsequent child protection policy and practice. It has long been the dominant theory in assessment guidance: of a list of 23 texts that social workers undertaking a comprehensive assessment of children at risk were recommended to read (Department of Health, 1988), 10 were by attachments theorists (BAAF, 1996; Bowlby, 1982, 1979; Fahlberg, 1981a, 1981b, 1982, 1984, 1988a; Fraiberg, 1980; Winnicott, 1964, 1971). Although later guidance on assessment (Department of Health, 2000) considers a broader range of factors in the assessment of risk, attachment theory predominates as both explanation and prediction. Attachment theory has, therefore, become the official discourse of child protection work, *the* way of talking about it. It has also been invoked as an explanation for dysfunctional behaviour in all forms of interpersonal violence: marital disharmony (Weiss, 1982, 1991); poor relationships between elderly parents and their children (Cicirelli, 1991; Yan and Tang, 2003); dysfunctional family systems (Byng-Hall, 1985; Marvin and Stewart, 1990); and adult bullying (Randall, 1997).

Attachment theory is an ethological theory of interpersonal relationships that emphasizes the evolutionary significance of intimate relationships, also referred to by Bowlby as *affectional bonds*, particularly those in early childhood. Bowlby believed that people possess an inborn need for close attachments to significant others that serve a survival function. Throughout childhood and adolescence, people develop expectations regarding the availability, or otherwise, of attachments through specific attachments in the first instance (usually the mother, but sometimes the father), and then through multiple attachment relationships. Each relationship builds on the previous one and contributes to the construction of what Bowlby called the 'internal working model', a characteristic way of thinking about and responding to others in relationships. As the person matures, these models become more stable and part of the personality, serving as an interpreter for new information regarding attachment relationships, and thus influencing behaviour. Attachment patterns not only persist but they also self-perpetuate; for example, a securely attached child is happier and more rewarding to care for than an anxious ambivalent child, who is apt to be clingy and whiny, or an anxious avoidant child, who will be distant and prone to bully other children (Bowlby, 1988).

The terms 'secure', 'anxious' and 'anxious attachment style' derive from the research findings of Ainsworth and colleagues (Ainsworth *et al.*, 1978; Bretherton and Waters, 1985), who researched mother – toddler relationship styles by means of a 20-minute miniature drama known as a 'strange situation'. They observed toddlers' behaviour in a sequence of three situations. First, the toddler was left with the mother in a small room with toys. The mother was then joined by an unfamiliar woman who played with the toddler while the mother briefly left the room. A second separation ensued, during which the toddler was left alone before the mother finally returned. The researchers were interested in the reunion behaviour between the mother and toddler.

They found that the toddlers exhibited three basic relationship patterns. These were those with non-expressive, indifferent or hostile relationships, in which the toddlers devised a strategy whereby maximum closeness to the mother was obtained without fear of rebuff; those with strong, positive feelings towards the mother, where the toddler looked for the mother, but played freely; and those with markedly ambivalent relationships, characterized by the toddler being clingy and angry. The researchers labelled these reactions as types A, B and C; type C was later subdivided into two related types (for an overview see Bretherton, 1992). Type B was the normative response among the white, middle-class sample. Although the researchers reported that they did not impute that any one type of response was better than another, these attachments styles soon developed labels which imply healthy or unhealthy psychological development. Type A became known as insecure-avoidant; type B secure; type C was subdivided into anxious-ambivalent; and anxious-disorganized. Although similar research in Germany found that type A relationship styles were the dominant pattern (Grossman *et al.*, 1985), and Type C more frequent than anticipated in Israeli kibbutzim (Sagi *et al.*, 1985) and Japan (Myake *et al.*, 1985), a secure attachment style has been translated into the desirable style in child protection work:

All children need secure attachments if they are to flourish and develop their potential. In any assessment of children, therefore, it is important to get to know the details of the current and past attachment figures in a child's life (Department of Health, 1998, p. 38).

Ainsworth *et al.* (1978) found that the toddlers' behaviour in the *strange situation* could be explained by the behaviour of their mothers. For example, secure children had mothers who were sensitive to their emotional signals, while insecure children had mothers who could be observed to be insensitive, rejecting or unpredictable. This does not mean, says Bowlby, that mothers should be blamed for treating their children in a way that is a major cause of mental ill health: '[T]he misguided behaviour of parents is no more than the product of their own difficult and unhappy childhood' (Bowlby, 1988, p. 145); this is seen as pointing to an intergenerational effect. Main and colleagues (Main and Weston, 1981; Main *et al.*, 1985) found a strong correlation between how a mother describes her relationships with her parents during her childhood and the pattern of attachment her child now has with her. Her interviews have been developed into an 'adult attachment interview', in which a person is invited to talk openly and at length about childhood experiences and memories that may be quite painful, and then analysed for style and manner in which the story is told rather than content (see also Hesse, 1999), Whereas the mother of a secure child is able to talk freely and with feeling about her childhood, the mother of an insecure child is not. Four types of attachment style were identified; these are similar to the categories used in the strange situation research:

- *Secure-autonomous*. The mother's story is coherent, consistent and objective. She is able to collaborate with the interviewer.

- *Dismissing*. The story is not coherent. Although she claims in a generalized, matter of fact way that she had a happy childhood, she has no supporting detail and may say that she can remember nothing of her childhood.

- *Preoccupied*. The story is incoherent and will describe an unhappy relationship with her mother about which she is still clearly disturbed.

- *Unresolved disorganized*. This is similar to dismissing or preoccupied styles but may include long silences or overtly erroneous statements.

Main also identified an exceptional category of mothers; those who had unhappy experiences but had incorporated these with happy ones, and had securely attached children. She hypothesized that these women seemed to have come to terms with their experiences.

Bowlby (1979) makes the important point that because affectional bonds, such as those between mother and child or husband and wife, are subjective states of strong emotion, the threat of loss arouses (separation) anxiety, which in turn arouses anger in various degrees. It is the situation that signals an *increase* of risk that creates a fear response, he says, therefore threats of abandonment are terrifying. These threats create intense anxiety, and they also arouse anger, often also of intense degree. For Bowlby, anxiety and anger as responses to the risk of loss go hand in hand, thus attachment theory explains all interpersonal violence.

CASE STUDY: THEORY INTO PRACTICE

Emma and Aktar's children (Mark 7 years and Mohammed 3 years) have been made the subject of a care order following the discovery that Aktar had beaten Emma badly after drunken rows. Specialist psychological assessment of the children indicates that Mark has an idealized, anxious attachment to Emma, an avoidant attachment to his father, and a distant one to Mohammed. It also suggests that Emma is significantly depressed and suffering low self-esteem related to her early experiences of physical and emotional abuse at the hands of her mother. The foster carers report that the boys get on extremely well with each other and look forward to their parents' visits. During your assessment interview Emma talks freely about her unhappy childhood experiences. Aktar talks about a happy childhood and continuing close relationships with his family.

- In what way does attachment theory help you to understand the relational dynamics of this family?

How attachment theory informs assessment

The links between the attachment patterns of children and adults who are violent or neglectful and their parents is the subject of research aimed at predicting which specific attachment patterns are the most likely to precipitate people to behave violently or neglectfully to their children, partners and peers. Parents who abuse their children have been demonstrated to have experienced poor childhood experiences themselves (for an overview see Howe, 1995), although there is some disagreement over which parental attachment pattern is the more damaging for children. Crittenden (1988) and Finkelhor (1983) suggest that anxious-ambivalent and anxious-disturbed attachment patterns, which lead to emotional abuse and neglect, have more serious consequences for children than an avoidant attachment style, which leads to physical abuse. Browne and Hamilton (1998), however, found that a smaller percentage of their respondents who reported emotional maltreatment were violent compared with those who reported either physical or sexual maltreatment. Bowlby also highlights the damaging effect of physical abuse, citing research that shows physically abused children were not only more likely to assault other children but were also notable for a 'particularly disagreeable type of aggression, termed "harassment"...malicious behaviour that appears to have the sole intent of making the victim show distress' (1988, p. 91).

A link between poor childhood experiences and men assaulting their partners has also been a recurring finding in the research into violence and attachment style; a particularly large study (8629 participants) found correlations between adult violence and childhood physical or sexual abuse or witnessing domestic violence (Whitfield *et al.*, 2003). Hazan and Shaver (1987) add to Bowlby's analysis of male violence; they found that men with avoidant attachment styles had relationships that were characterized by fear and extreme jealousy, and anxious-ambivalent individuals' relationships were characterized by emotional highs and lows, accompanied by obsessive thoughts concerning the other and a strong desire for union with others. Later research (Bartholomew and Horowitz, 1991) reconceptualized avoidant attachment styles in adulthood as dismissing and fearful, the latter category being significantly related to measures of anger, jealousy and verbal abuse, which Dutton *et al.* (1994) describe as an *angry attachment style*. They found that couples with different attachment styles may actually antagonize each other, escalating aggression with violence. Kesner and McKenry's (1998) research adds detail to this finding: not only did they find that attachment factors are unique predictors of male violence towards a female partner, but that these partners were more likely to have insecure adult attachment styles. With refinements to the adult attachment interview, more distinctions have been made about the form violence may take: *dismissing husbands* have been found to be the most controlling and distancing, their violence being related to instrumental violence to assert their authority and control; *preoccupied husbands* tended only to precipitate violence when their partners threatened withdrawal, their emotional and physical violence being related to expressive violence in response to abandonment fears (Babcock *et al.*, 2000). Attachment patterns are also predictive of elder abuse;

these links between poor childhood experiences and poor relationships between elderly parents and their children were established by Cicirelli (1991).

Caution in applying attachment theories

A word of caution is necessary. The Babcock *et al.* study (2000) makes an important point that although 74 per cent of the violent husbands (out of a sample size of only 23) were likely to be classified into one of the insecure categories on the adult attachment interview, there were 6 violent husbands who were classified as secure. As the authors comment:

> Clearly not all men who engage in repeated physical aggression against their wives have attachment patterns that differ from other men. It is likely that there are many different pathways to becoming maritally violent and a route involving insecure attachments and dysregulated affect is *only one* of them. (Babcock *et al.*, 2000, our emphasis).

The reader also needs to bear in mind that the correlation between abusive parents and insecure attachment style is not the only correlation revealed. For example, the abusing mothers in the Crittenden study (1988) were also those who had the least education, were likely to be unsupported by either partner or extended family and contained the largest number of women with learning difficulties. Crittenden (1999) argues that these disadvantages were a result of their own childhood experiences resulting in them having severe difficulties in sustaining interpersonal relationships. Equally Fraiberg (1980) suggests that insecure attachments are detrimental to cognitive functioning, but it is dangerous to dismiss the effects of hardship on effective parenting (see for example Howe, 1995).

Belsky and Nezworski (1998) maintain that although the association between poor-quality, insecure relationships in childhood and later social and behavioural difficulties is not inevitable, it is probabilistic. But by no means do all parents with poor childhood experiences go on to become abusing parents. Our experience of working with adults who have been sexually abused as children is that they are incensed when their abusers claim their own childhood abuse as a mitigating factor.

Sound assessments logically lead to appropriate interventions, but as McLeod (2003) points out, Bowlby's ideas on attachment have not resulted in the creation of an 'attachment therapy', although it could perhaps be argued that Fahlberg (1988b) has come close to doing so. The central feature of psychodynamic social work with people who have relationship problems is helping them to recognize that their internal working models of relationships may not be appropriate to their present and future; that is, 'to modify old representational patterns, to change old inner working models of self and its relationship with other people' (Howe, 1995, p. 220). To accomplish this, the practitioner needs to provide a *secure base* in which it is 'safe enough for members of the family to reconnect with old memories that are resonating with current themes' (Byng-Hall, 1985, p. 211), or enhance and support secure relationships with non-abusive care-givers. Fonagy (2001) argues that it is the capacity to learn how to reflect on experiences that lies at the heart of effective therapy, helping individuals develop the ability to think about and talk about painful past events. Kennedy (1997) divides assessment of outcome in his work with violent parents into hopeful, doubtful and hopeless, dependent largely on parents' capacity for self-reflection. Those who can reflect on their own abuse and show evidence of change in their parenting capabilities are most likely to be classified as 'hopeful'.

Critical comment

A practical difficulty in using psychodynamic theory as a base for assessment is that the theory is top heavy in content (Butt, 2003); that is, it provides an explanation for the causes of relationship difficulties but it is less successful in developing interventions that are effective in terms of either costs or user friend-liness. Psychodynamic social work interventions have been demonstrated to be consistently unpopular with adults who are violent (see for example Mayer and Timms, 1970; Davies, 1999; Scourfield, 2003; Milner, 2004), mainly because service users become frustrated with a focus on the past when they locate their concerns in the present. Gallwey acknowledges, for instance, that when parents lose a child following a child protection assessment, 'it may well be that they become paranoid and persecutory and it can be very unfair to pick up the projection and suggest that these are necessarily long-term psychological problems' (1997, p. 139). Neither is denial necessarily a psychological response; people often have sound social reasons (loss of a job, friends, family) for denying responsibility for many problem behaviours (Turnell and Essex, 2006; Milner and Myers 2007). And it is important to bear in mind that 'resistance' does not necessarily prove what is being resisted. It can simply be resistance.

Despite this, psychodynamic hypotheses have become part and parcel of folk psychology. Butt makes the point that psychological expertise and therapeutic potency have become magnified with theories being selectively 'raided' for those components that seem to explain the phenomena under scrutiny: 'The lesson that seems to have been taken from a century of therapy, rightly or wrongly, is that emotions are better out than in' (2003, p.164). This echoes only part of Bowlby's claim about effective therapy: 'that a patient not only talks about his memories, his ideas and dreams, his hopes and desires, but also *expresses his feelings*' (1988, p. 156, our emphasis). Storr (1966) cautioned that express-ing feelings is only one valuable feature of the psychoanalytic process; that many people do *not* show an improvement as a result of expressing feelings. Encouraging people who are violent to express their feelings is positively dan-gerous as catharsis (and, by implication, uncovering work) actually makes people more aggressive (Bushman *et al.*, 1999). Sadly, this sometimes is interpreted as evidence that the 'uncovering' therapy is working.

It is also worth noting that how people express their feelings varies from cul-ture to culture and age to age. As Butt (2003) points out, being 'in touch with one's feelings' is a relatively recent construction in the United Kingdom. Storr (1966, p. 66) states that the idea of cure in psychoanalysis raises fundamental problems of philosophy, such as what constitutes human happiness and what sort of person one should be. This argument has been taken up by feminist psychotherapists, who redefine relational bonds in terms of mutuality between mothers and daughters (Jordan, 1997), and view dependency as being able to count on the help of others rather than a pathological state (Stiver, 1991).

The second main working hypothesis that has emerged from attachment theory – that the past inevitably influences the present and the future and may need to be modified (see, for example, Howe, 1995, p.190) – has become axiomatic in a wide range of professional interventions, despite it not being particularly well supported by the literature (see, for example, Dogra *et al.*, 2002), or by prominent psychoanalysts. As Rycroft commented, the idea that children should be treated lovingly and humanely does not require any psychological backing; loving is not an activity that can be easily engaged in on mere advice, since its essence is sincerity and spontaneity; and much of the trauma and suffering endured by children is inevitable (1966, p.16). In the same volume, Gorer (1966, p. 32) argues that psychologically tinged explanations are invoked for failures, not for successes, so the research base of attachment theory is necessarily skewed. More recently, Kennedy (1997) suggests it is counter-productive to focus on the negative aspects of behaviour.

Outcomes

Most meta-studies of social work outcomes place psychodynamic and psychosocial work as the least effective approaches to practice (see for example Thyer's comprehensive review of outcomes (1998, 2002). Research into this approach is troublesome in any case since the approach places more store on process rather than on results. A study by Hilsenroth *et al.* (2001) showed that, after nine sessions, while 59 per cent of service users felt some improvement in subjective wellbeing, only 25 per cent showed reliable improvement in symptomatic distress as measured on the GARF (the Global Assessment of Relational Functioning scale used by psychologists). They report that some rapid improvement happens early in the process and is followed by a 'negatively accelerating positive growth curve' – improvement diminishes as the number of sessions increase. It took 6 months to a year to get 75 per cent improvement. In the early phase, the subjective experience of wellbeing precipitated a reduction of symptoms.

SUMMARY

- We have explained briefly the ideas of Freud and the post-Freudians, with some emphasis on 'defences' and ego-psychology.
- The main functions of the ego have been outlined, and the application of ego strengths in assessment explained.
- TA (transactional analysis), a popular version of Freudianism, has been presented, as well as its application in assessment.

- Attachment theories were described and discussed, with notes of caution about their application.

- Outcomes were briefly mentioned, showing that this approach usually requires a great deal of time if good outcomes are to be achieved, although brief versions can be used during assessment.

FURTHER LEARNING ACTIVITIES

Twenty-nine-year-old Samantha divorced her violent husband after finding out that he had been unfaithful to her. School have reported major concerns about her care of her two boys (Luke 6 years and Jaiden 5 years). Both boys have special learning needs requiring one-to-one teaching support for their behaviour. The boys are invariably late for school and sometimes are absent for days at a time. Jaiden has told his support worker in school that 'mummy drinks and doesn't wake up to take them to school'. Samantha also leaves the boys with her mother at weekends. Her mother finds the boys difficult to handle and also says she has had 'nothing but violent men in her life'. Samantha complains that she cannot control the boys at all and responds to their behaviour by withdrawing emotionally.

- Using attachment theory as a base for your initial hypothesis about the relational dynamics of this family, what interventions would such an assessment imply?

FURTHER READING

Bowlby, J. (1988) *A Secure Base: Clinical Implications of Attachment Theory*. London: Routledge.

Howe, D. (1995) *Attachment Theory for Social Work*. Basingstoke: Macmillan

Howe, D. (2000) 'Attachment', in J. Horwath (ed.) *The Child's World. Assessing Children in Need*. London: DoH/NSPCC/University of Sheffield.

NATIONAL OCCUPATIONAL STANDARDS

For students working with the British National Occupation Standards for Social Work (see Appendix):

- This chapter relates to *practice* elements 1.1; 5.1; 11.1–4; 18.1–3.

- With which of the *knowledge* requirements in the Appendix does this chapter help you?

CHAPTER 6

An Ordnance Survey Map: Behavioural Approaches

What this chapter is about

As with psychodynamic social work, the application of learning theory to social work was taken initially from clinical psychology and then adapted to a wide range of social work situations. We will identify two main strands of learning theory in this chapter: traditional behaviourism, consisting of three types of learning based on the work of Pavlov (1960), Skinner (1958) and Bandura (1969, 1977), and cognitive behaviour modification, consisting of four types based on Beck (1967), Ellis (1962), Seligman (1992) and Ward and Mann (2004), Ward et al. (2007). The cognitive part of the map looks at how habitual ways of thinking can be considered as habitual behaviour, with an emphasis on how unhelpful thinking can be replaced by learning and practising more helpful thinking, and on how these ideas develop useful assessments that can accommodate both quantitative and qualitative aspects of change.

MAIN POINTS

> ➤ Wider theoretical perspectives: respondent and operant conditioning, social learning theory.
>
> ➤ Implications of these theories for assessments.
>
> ➤ Rational emotive therapy, cognitive-behavioural therapy, learned helplessness, Good Lives model.
>
> ➤ Implications of these theories for assessments.
>
> ➤ Critical comments on the psychological reductionism, values and assumptions of this theory.
>
> ➤ Outcomes of this approach in working with certain service users.

Introduction

We now turn to the first of the 'second-wave' (problem-based) chapters, where problematic behaviour and thinking is seen as learned. This takes a less essentialist psychological perspective than the psychodynamic approach in that there is less a sense of a 'given' reality within people and more a sense that people learn to be what they are. Therefore they can learn to be different and behavioural disorders can be changed through the application of learning theory principles. Behavioural social work emphasizes the assessment process on the grounds that, without a behaviour baseline, intervention cannot be judged (Barber, 1991). This involves a detailed examination of specific behaviours to establish how they have been acquired and maintained as habitual ways or paths that people 'walk', day in, day out, step by step, so we describe this map as an Ordnance Survey map.

WIDER THEORETICAL PERSPECTIVES

Traditional behaviour modification

Traditional behavioural practice is based on three types of learning: respondent conditioning, operant conditioning and social learning theory. We will address these in turn.

Respondent (classical) conditioning

We first consider *respondent* (classical) conditioning, which is mainly based on the work of Ivan Pavlov, a Russian physiologist working in 1911. Any basic text in psychology will tell the story of how Pavlov conditioned dogs to salivate at the sound of a bell by associating the sound of the bell with the arrival of food. This was described in the language of experimental psychology: the bell being said to be a stimulus (S) and salivation a response (R). This is known as classical conditioning, with a stimulus always preceding a response:

$$S \rightarrow R$$

Responses are not only learned, but can also be unlearned or become extinguished; for example, if food did not follow the stimulus of a bell, Pavlov's dogs ceased to salivate after a while. Probably the most common application in clinical psychology of respondent learning is in dealing with phobias. Here the assessment involves the development of a hierarchy of responses to the feared object before the sufferer is gradually helped to relax and is then presented with the item at the bottom of the hierarchy. More greatly feared items are not presented until each step has been successfully achieved. This process is called 'systematic desensitization'. In other words, the person's reflex responses to the fear such as increased heart rate are gradually removed. The S-R sequence of learning, however, explains only a narrow range of learning opportunities that involve reflex actions.

Operant conditioning

Operant conditioning explains a more extensive form of learning. It has a very wide application in addressing a range of human behaviours in which reflex actions are not necessarily present. This part of the theory also derives from animal experiments. For example, Skinner (1953) demonstrated how pigeons could learn to peck at a set of levers to obtain corn. The reward of food followed their effort, reinforcing the behaviour. In operant conditioning it is the person's actions that operate on the environment; any one act is still labelled a response (R) and the consequence a stimulus (S), even though in operant conditioning responses precede stimuli. The stimulus then elicits a stronger response (R2):

$$R \rightarrow S \rightarrow R2$$

This clumsy use of jargon terms may seem confusing, but as Hudson and Macdonald say:

> [D]o not be exercised over it, simply think of them as different animals, having a familiar meaning in the respondent paradigm (stimulus eliciting response) and an unfamiliar one in the operant paradigm (the association of a behaviour with a consequence). (1986, p. 28)

Operant conditioning is often referred to as the ABC approach. A stands for Antecedents, that cue in the start of the behaviour; B stands for the Behaviour itself; and C stands for the Consequence, which reinforces. Stuart (1974) gives considerable attention to antecedents as a key focus for intervention. He distinguishes between three types of antecedent:

1. *Material and competence antecedents.* These are the tools and skills without which the behaviour cannot occur. For example, a student needs ability, books and other materials.
2. *Instructional antecedents.* These are rules, requests and expectations, not always explicit, set by others. For example, parents often unfairly criticize children for not doing what they were not asked to do, saying they should have known it was expected.
3. *Potentiating antecedents.* These consist of a setup in which the rewarding impact of the consequence is increased. This can happen in three ways:
   - By restricting the consequence so that it follows only when the desired behaviour has happened. For example, no television viewing until after an assignment has been completed.
   - By providing a sample of the consequence for a person who has never experienced it, for example the excitement of using a computer.
   - By offering a person a choice of consequence from a menu of options, for example going out for a burger, or playing pool.

In assessing problematic behaviour, therefore, it is essential to begin by examining its antecedents and considering how their effect could be either increased or reduced. The behaviour itself (B) must also be mapped out in detail. Sheldon (1982) says that a behavioural assessment takes place independently of the definitions and labels that others place on problems. For example, a behavioural assessment would not state that a person is deluded, but rather it would state precisely what behaviours were involved.

The consequences of behaviour (C) in operant conditioning strengthen or weaken subsequent behaviour. Rewarding consequences, or reinforcers, make it more likely that a behaviour will occur. Positive reinforcers strengthen (reward) behaviour by gaining/giving a wanted/positive consequence, for example money; whereas negative reinforcers strengthen (reward) behaviour by removing an unwanted/negative consequence, for example pain. The unwanted consequence may be present, for example, a twisted arm, in which case the required behaviour enables the subject to escape the pain; or it may be threatened, for example 'You will be grounded unless you behave well from now until 3.00 p.m.,' in which case the subject avoids the unpleasant consequence by behaving well for that period.

Confusion, however, is common here. Because avoiding threatened sanctions is a negative reinforcer, we are apt to think punishment is the same as negative reinforcement. While punishment is usually unwanted or aversive, it does not necessarily remove or reduce behaviour; often it encourages endurance or the avoidance of being observed in the behaviour. This adds to the confusion in that punishment can be said to be either positive (giving unwanted pain) or negative (taking away a want, for example money). Figure 6.1 may help to clarify matters.

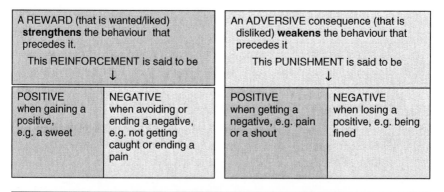

Figure 6.1 Reinforcement and punishment

There are no absolute examples of positive and negative reinforcers because what is perceived by one person as negative or bad may be considered by another as desirable, and vice versa. Something unpleasant or painful would probably be considered negative by most people, but others may enjoy it or see it as a proof of macho strength, for example. Thus the terms positive and negative (like good and bad) must always be seen *as perceived by the service user*.

A vital part of a behavioural assessment, therefore, is establishing what is or is not rewarding for the particular service user: 'It is a good general rule that the "customer knows best" ' (Sheldon, 1982, p. 113). When making behavioural assessments, social workers can expect to find both positive and negative reinforcements operating with unwanted behaviour being reinforced. They may be part of this learning process. For example, the social worker who rushes round to the foster home each time a child exhibits unwanted behaviour and never visits at times when the behaviour is acceptable may be unconsciously reinforcing unwanted behaviour.

Reinforcement is more effective the nearer in time it is to the behaviour and when it is consistent, although there are different schedules of reinforcement; for example, continuous or intermittent. Intermittent reinforcements have a more lasting effect on behaviour. Schedules of intermittent reinforcement may be 'fixed ratio', like pay for piecework, or 'fixed interval', like a weekly wage. There are also variable ratios in which the number of performances of the behaviour is varied before the reward is given, and variable intervals where the time between rewards is varied. These variable schedules provide the most lasting effects on behaviour.

CASE STUDY: THEORY INTO PRACTICE

Julie has two children aged 8 and 10 years. A neighbour has reported much shouting in the home and the children crying a lot and being distressed. Her husband works long hours and gets upset with her when faced with repeated complaints about the children and how they pay no attention to her requests even when she shouts at them. They occasionally respond by crying and shouting back at her, each making allegations about the other.

When the social worker visited she asked Julie for more detail about how she attempts to manage the children's behaviour.

Julie explained that because the children don't seem to take her seriously, she loses her temper and threatens them with dire consequences when their father gets home. She has even told them that he will 'bl...y kill them this time', and 'Now you've done it – he will flog the living daylights out of you.' This makes them cry and 'they start hating each other more than ever.' She says she can't understand what is happening to them as both she and her husband are really quiet and pleasant people. Her husband has never, and would never, hit any of them.

- What sorts of conditioning or learning are taking place in this family?
- What type of behavioural intervention might help them?

Social learning theory

The third type of traditional behaviourism is based on Bandura's (1977) social learning theory, or vicarious learning (modelling). Very briefly, the theory says that we learn by observing and imitating others. We observe, we think about what we see or experience and we copy what the 'model' has done. These models give advance information about the likely consequences of behaviour, and social learning theorists claim that this is a more efficient way of learning than is classical or operant conditioning. Here learning is further facilitated if the observer sees the model's behaviour being rewarded, if the model is reasonably like the observer (which aids identification), if the model is popular or of high status, for example a professional sportsperson or a television personality (the 'wannabe' syndrome), and if the observer can practise the behaviour immediately and gain reinforcement.

Implications for assessment

In using the traditional part of this Ordnance Survey map, assessment begins after a 'get to know you' phase, with a detailed description of the target behaviour(s) or required behaviour(s) in precise terms. This requires the direct observation of current behaviour, by either the social worker, the service user or a third party, who counts the frequency of certain behaviours in certain circumstances, listing antecedents, behaviours and consequences. A log may be useful here, for example that suggested by Schwartz and Goldiamond (1975), as adapted in Figure 6.2.

Time	Activity	Where	Who was there	What you wanted	What happened
7.00					
8.00					
9.00					
10.00					
11.00					
and so on until bedtime					

Figure 6.2 Record of behaviour

The behaviour modification approach promotes several techniques that are useful for reducing unwanted behaviour and strengthening wanted behaviour. Social workers may wish to check through a list of these ideas and consider which might be the most effective for the removal of a particular problem. In general, operant techniques are appropriate for operant behaviour problems and respondent techniques for respondent problems (Fisher and Goceros, 1975).

Persistence with behaviour despite distressing consequences suggests that such behaviour might be the result of limited-choice alternatives, given the history and circumstances of the person involved. The task is, therefore, to help construct new ways of producing positive consequences that might be accompanied by less distress.

- A traditional behavioural assessment would attempt to establish a baseline of behaviour using points in the following sequence:

1. Decide on the goals with the client in strict behavioural terms, that is those which are not only clear to the client but also capable of measurement.
2. Where, when and how often is the new behaviour required?
3. How would the service user measure success?
4. What will other people notice about the behaviour when this happens? This could be at home, at work or at leisure.
5. How will this differ from what is happening *now*?
6. What areas of life will be changed for the better?
7. Has there been any condition under which the problem was not a problem?

- Next, set a *baseline* for the current behaviours (wanted and/or unwanted), showing how often they occur, hourly or daily, over a period of a week or two. Then decide whether the problem is one of an excess of unwanted behaviour or the lack of wanted behaviour, using the following questions:

1. What behaviours are in excess and what behaviours deficient?
2. What behaviours need to be increased or decreased?
3. What behaviours are occurring in the wrong place and at the wrong time?
4. If it is a matter of removing unwanted behaviour, how is it being maintained or reinforced?
5. Is the consequence one of positive reinforcement or negative reinforcement?
6. Can these reinforcers be removed?
7. What alternative behaviour could be put in its place? This needs to be carefully considered because behavioural change techniques have been shown to have more power in strengthening than weakening responses, so 'no deceleration technique should ever be used unless alternative behaviours are positively reinforced' (Stuart, 1974, p. 411).
8. What are the antecedents or cues –
   - Material/competency?
   - Instructional antecedents?
   - Potentiating antecedents?
9. If the behaviour is acquired by modelling, can contact with the model be discontinued?
10. If it is a matter of needing to develop wanted behaviour, ascertain:
    - What new behaviour could be desirable.
    - What antecedents are missing and need to be put in place.
    - What is considered by the client to be rewarding.
    - What reinforcers are available or could be gained.

- Because reinforcers need to be administered immediately and consistently, who would be available to do this.
- Whether the new behaviour could be acquired by modelling; and if so, whether an appropriate is model available.

11. If it is a matter of strengthening current behaviour, check out:
    - What the antecedents are.
    - What the consequences are.
    - How more rewarding consequences can be achieved and by whom.
    - What schedule or reinforcement would be most efficient.

The answers to these questions should be used to build up a baseline.

CASE EXAMPLE

A student has a problem with doing college assignments on time.

Next goal: Wants to get next essay finished on time.

- This requires a considerable amount of reading and note-taking.
- If he read a chapter an evening and made notes on it, he could be better prepared.
- This could be done in the bedroom, away from distractions.
- A daily log of chapters read could be kept.
- This will be better than wasting time watching television.
- Change is needed now because of college deadlines.
- Unless dealt with, the problem will continue until the course is passed.

The student's difficulty could be seen as an excess of unwanted behaviour (watching TV) or as a deficit of wanted behaviour (study). Because it is easier to strengthen weak behaviour, he decided to look for ways to strengthen studying, choosing the bedroom as the best location for study.

The consequences (in the longer term) of more effective studying are passing the course and avoiding the embarrassment of failing. Since negative reinforcement is more powerful, the student asks his partner to remind him of this consequence. There is also something (a certain crunchy chocolate confection) that he finds very rewarding, so his partner acquires some of this and shares it when a chapter has been read. The rewards of watching TV cannot easily be removed, and this is a further reason for concentrating on rewarding the study behaviour. However, modelling can be assisted by the partner also reading instead of watching TV at study time. The emphasis, in the short term, is on the pleasant consequences of having the chocolate following a period of study. The student knows that this work will avoid dreaded failure in the long term. He drew up the baseline and progress record (x = reading for 1 hour) shown in Figure 6.3.

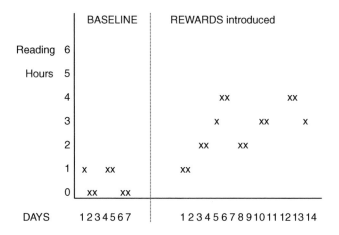

Figure 6.3 Behavioural baseline and response to rewards

In the previous case example, Julie did not realize that making threats which are not carried out is a strong reinforcement of the behaviour that preceded the threat. The children escape the threat each time and the bigger the threat the stronger the reinforcement. This negative reinforcement can be stronger than positive reinforcement. The social worker asked her:

- To not make any threat that she was not certain she could carry out.
- To plan in advance her sanctions for bad behaviour, calmly tell the children what the consequences will be and impose them as soon as they misbehave.
- To try to catch the children being pleasant and reward this behaviour as often as possible for a few weeks.

Julie shared these suggestions with her husband and, despite some slip-ups, they achieved a reasonable measure of peace and began to have more fun together. This outcome had a major impact on the assessment of Julie and her family.

Cognitive-behavioural theory

The cognitive dimension of behavioural approaches looks at thoughts as if they were behaviours where unhelpful habits may be learned. This is the most widely used of all therapeutic interventions. It suggests that behaviour is mediated through thought processes just as much as through a series of responses to stimuli. As Cigno (1998) explains, the focus is therefore on current causes, here and now, on the basis that people are not just responding to stimuli but also *interpreting and construing* them in various ways that maintain problematic behaviours and states such as depression; for example through self-blaming. This is particularly relevant to social work, which seeks to individualize service user behaviour but does not always find this easy; insight does not necessarily change behaviour, nor does traditional behaviour modification always prove effective.

Indeed, although the latter seems scientific, logical and accessible, each human situation contains so many variables that even Skinner commented in his novel *Walden Two* that predicting behaviour is rather like making a weather forecast. On the other hand, as the term implies, the cognitive dimension considers 'how behaviour is guided by the perceptions and analysis of what we see' and how 'irrational thoughts or disturbances in perception lead us to process our view of the world incorrectly' (Sheldon, 1995, pp. 184–5).

Within this cognitive model, there are numerous variations, but we will confine ourselves in this brief outline to four categories, as follows:

- Rational emotive behaviour therapy (sometimes known as REBT), based on the ideas of Ellis (1962, 2005).
- Cognitive behaviour therapy (sometimes known as CBT), based on Beck and Beck (2005) and Beck and Tomkin (1989).
- Learned helplessness, based on Seligman (1992).
- The Good Lives model (GLM), based on the work of Ward and others (2004, 2007).

The work of Ellis has been further developed by Dryden and Yankma (1993) and by Ellis and Dryden (2007). The work of Beck and of Ellis has been further developed by Burns (1999).

A cognitive approach had been implicit in the ego psychology of the 1940s, but Ellis and Beck redefined *emotions* as clearly cognitive in essence, Ellis (1962) describing them as *a strongly evaluative kind of thinking resulting from what he termed self-talk, internalized sentences and self-verbalization* (Ellis had built his ideas partly on the work of Adler, who had parted company with Freud on cognitive issues) – all aspects that could be un-learned. Emotion, in this approach, 'is a feeling a person experiences after estimating [in an unreasonably negative way] what an event *means* to him' (Werner, 1970, p. 254, our parenthesis), inferring that people must be confronted with the disparities between their perception and reality and be offered alternatives to inaccurate perception, as the discrepancies between stated goals and actual behaviour are being addressed. Behaviour is shaped neither by unconscious inner drives nor by externally conditioned habits but by a third force, cognition, the self-determination of the individual who *uses* both internal forces and the external environment. 'Action is not completed unless conscious thought processes support it' (Werner, 1970, p. 252).

Werner saw choosing goals, evaluating events and self, and solving problems as the three conscious cognitive processes intimately associated with personality development. For Werner, change in the three elements just listed results in changes in personality. For example, a person whose personality is characterised by withdrawn behaviour is not necessarily seen as fixated at one stage of development. Instead, this is seen as probably due to frequent failure to attain desired goals, and a 'personality change' can be effected if that person experiences success in goal achievement. In assessment work, this leads to asking questions about perceptions of goals, of expectations, of self and of difficulties (in general about one's private logic).

In the case of the student mentioned earlier, these questions discovered that, while his goals were constructive and realistic, there is a possible opponent factor in that his children did not understand or agree with them; the family atmosphere was rather indulgent but also reasonably competitive. A private logic of 'Do I really have to be so hard on myself?' operated, and there were early recollections of being sent to the bedroom as a punishment, so there is quite a mix of emotions and perceptions, the clarification of which was helpful, both as an understanding of the difficulty and as providing signposts towards change.

In this approach, behavioural change involves recognizing thought patterns and practising new ones (see, for example, Milner and Myers, 2007). In recognizing the role of cognition, it is a move on from traditional behaviour modification practice. It also underpins work such as assertion training and skills training in general.

Rational emotive behaviour therapy

Ellis (1962) was primarily interested in anxiety and depression states and how these were caused or maintained by thoughts. He developed an *ABC alternative* to that of operant conditioning. For Ellis, A is the Activating event, such as loss of employment; B is the Beliefs one has about that event, such as 'My whole life is ruined'; and C is the emotional Consequence. For Ellis, those consequences are mostly feelings of depression.. He suggests that cognitive processes (especially negative interpretations or high expectations), rather than simple reinforcements, influence behaviour, with people usually blaming the Activating event for the Consequential emotion. Ellis seeks to *break this A–C connection* and show the service user that the emotion follows from the Beliefs (B) about the event rather than from the event itself (A). This explains why different people react differently to the same event. Ellis would say that A–C thinking is a distortion and needs to be replaced by B–C thinking. It is *what we make of events* that leads to problems.

Ellis (1962) outlined a set of 'irrational beliefs', the most common being that people oppress themselves by believing they *must* do, or have, or achieve certain things. He coined the word 'musterbation' to challenge this process in the application of cognitive therapy. For him, 'musts' and 'shoulds' were irrational demands of self and others that lay behind many difficulties. He wrote that the main dysfunctional 'musts' were 'I must do well', 'You must treat me well' and 'Life must be easy', whereas the reality is that we are all imperfect, we are all capable of 'acting like jerks'. So we need to ease up on ourselves and others, and get away from slogans like 'Good enough is not enough.' He also coined the word 'awfulizing', the process whereby merely unpleasant or uncomfortable experiences are described as awful, horrendous: 'It has totally ruined my life – things will never be the same again,' that is, it is worse than 100 per cent bad. For example, when the bus is late, some people will refer to this as 'terrible' or 'disgusting'. Burns (1999) has added to the following list of common damaging distortions:

- *All-or-nothing thinking*: what is short of perfect is a total failure.
- *Overgeneralization*: a single failure is a never-ending pattern of failure.

- *Mental filter*: selecting and dwelling only on the negatives.
- *Disqualifying positives*: rejecting them as not counting.
- *Jumping to conclusions*: making negative judgements on little evidence and also mind-reading that ascribes negative rather than positive intent.
- *Magnification/minimization*: exaggerating one's faults or another's strengths, or shrinking one's own strengths (also known as reversed binocular vision).
- *Emotional reasoning*: 'I feel it, so it must be true.'
- *'Should' statements*: by which one whips and punishes oneself before one can be expected to do something. Additionally, 'should' statements directed at others lead to anger and frustration.
- *Labelling/mislabelling*: 'I am a loser,' 'He is a dirty rat.'
- *Personalization*: seeing oneself as the cause of negative events.

In REBT, Ellis (1962) takes a prescriptive approach, strongly debating with, confronting and challenging people to correct their distortions and replace them with more rational reasoning. Such rational reasoning is supported by (behavioural) rewards in the first instance until the service user achieves the self-rewarding effect of attaining an agreed goal.

Cognitive-behaviour therapy

Beck (1993, 2005) has a more gentle style that leads people to reconsider their beliefs and is, perhaps, more rigorous in the assessment stage of therapy. He developed a system of identifying negative automatic thoughts, for example, 'I can't make real friends,' 'I'm stupid,' 'I always say the wrong thing,' 'Everyone knows how disorganized I am,' 'I'm no good.' So Beck used to set about 'cognitive restructuring' – examining how a service user is interpreting a situation, perhaps employing 'cognitive distortions' that lead to miserable emotional states, and then replacing this thinking with more reasonable interpretations. Burns suggests the keeping of a daily log to identify the details of both the behaviour and the accompanying cognitive processes, which might look something like Figure 6.4.

An automatic thought will usually be a form of self-criticism, whereas a rational response will be a self-defence or a rebuttal of an automatic thought. For

Date/ time	Situation	Emotion	Automatic thought	Rational alternative thought	Outcome

Figure 6.4 Response record

example, parents experiencing problems with their children may catch themselves thinking 'Where did I go wrong?', while a more rational response might be: 'I am not a bad parent; I do try; I cannot control all that goes on in my children's lives.'

Keeping an assessment record such as that shown above becomes the therapy in that the service user comes to appreciate the improved emotional and relational outcomes of more rational responses. Burns (1999) provides a selection of checklists and self-evaluation instruments that a service user could complete. These facilitate data collection and diagnostic analysis because they include many of the assessment questions a social worker needs to consider.

Cognitive approaches have their own specialized therapeutic offshoots, such as the Institute for Rational-Emotive Therapy, which suggests that service users list irrational beliefs, then dispute them, before putting 'effective rational beliefs' in their place (see for example Dryden and Mytton, 1999). An example of an irrational belief is: 'I can't stand it when he...' or 'I can't stand it when I do not have the drug', an effective rational alternative being 'It's unpleasant and uncomfortable, but I can stand it.' Equally, the irrational belief 'I cannot be happy unless I have someone to love me' could be replaced by a rational response such as 'As an independent person I can love myself, so I can always be loved, and this will make me more attractive to others.' Yapko (1988) suggests some further examples of distorted thinking that may lead to depression: 'It's me;' 'It will always be this way and it affects everything I do;' 'It can only be this way;' 'Life always has been bad, therefore it will always be bad;' 'The whole thing is ruined.'

Implications for assessment

This approach leads to the following questions during the assessment phase:

- What cognitive distortions can be heard in the client's story?
- What automatic thoughts enter the mind when things are not right?
- How is the person putting him/herself down?
- How can these irrational beliefs be disputed?
- How can rational beliefs be developed?

Social workers can design their own assessment instrument to fit with the language and situation of the service user. We have seen some interesting examples of this:

> CASE EXAMPLE
>
> Kath had three failed relationships, the first with a man who beat her and the other two with men who humiliated her and emotionally abused her in various other ways. She has two children, both of whom insult her and have little respect for her. The younger child has come to the attention of the social care team with reports that he is out of control.

Kath says she thinks that it's true what they say to her: 'They can't all be wrong,' and 'It must be true that I am no good as a mother.'

The social worker asked Kath to catch herself thinking negative thoughts about herself, and said: 'Because these are *not true*, replace them with true thoughts in column 3.' She gave Kath some examples and ensured that she understood the exercise. Kath agreed to do this for a week.

Table 6.1 is the *self-esteem table* that was designed during the session.

Table 6.1 Self-esteem table

Negative thoughts that arose	Score negative feeling. (Score out of 10: 0 = very bad 10 = very good)	Positive (TRUE) thoughts you replaced them with	How did that feel? (Score out of 10 0 = very bad 10 = very good)
1.			
2.			

CASE EXAMPLE

A different log was used for Sam.

Sam had acquired a police record for assaults on family members and their friends. He said he feels provoked on these occasions and feels that he cannot control the urge to hit those who annoy him. He becomes verbally abusive and sometimes, as others become verbally abusive to him, he 'loses it'.

The social worker invited him to practise replacing feelings with *thoughts* for a week and record the results.

The *anger log* shown in Table 6.2 was designed for him.

Table 6.2 Anger log

Situations when I FELT provoked to be annoyed or angry	THOUGHTS I used to gain control of my words and actions.	My success (Score out of 10)

Learned helplessness

Cognitive theorists are also interested in the concept of *learned helplessness* (Seligman, 1992). This is a state that results from repeated exposure to unpleasant events that are beyond the control of the individual so that whatever a person does has no predictable effect one way or another. An example of this is a woman who sometimes gets battered when she does something, and sometimes gets battered when she does not do the same thing. This information about the lack of connection between effort and outcome grows into an expectation or belief that responding to one's situation is futile, that all future efforts will fail in the same way and that it will always be so.

CASE STUDY: THEORY INTO PRACTICE

A social worker arrived at a home to find a woman being beaten violently by her husband. She hurried the woman and her four children into her car but was amazed at the woman's behaviour. This woman had become so accustomed to the futility of any action on her part during violent episodes that she sat perfectly still in the car, apparently calm, while her husband beat the car with a spade.

- What are the main features of learned helplessness?
- If she has a good day, will this end the helplessness? Why/why not?
- To what is she likely to attribute good days? Of what is she likely to see them as proof?

The key features of learned helplessness, lack of energy, negative mood, self-condemnation and withdrawal, are similar to those of depression, so Sheldon (1995) maintains that depressive and anxious people attribute success to good luck or the task being easy, while attributing failure to lack of effort or poor ability, adding that irresponsible people do the opposite. This means that even when action could be taken, a person who has learned helplessness is unlikely to try anything and it is important not to label this as 'unmotivated' or 'lazy'. Barber (1991) describes this as a psychology of powerlessness, which explains the passivity of many recipients of social work services – single mothers on income support, disabled persons dependent on others, victims of child abuse and domestic violence.

Implications for assessment

Learned helplessness highlights the need for social workers to combine psychological and sociological factors – not only to attend to external resources but also to mobilize internal resources, considering the dispositional factors within each person. Additionally, it may be more immediately helpful and empowering for the service user in the short term if accessible dispositional factors are changed while situational factors are addressed as part of a long-term strategy. It is important to bear in mind that attributions are not just the product of an individual's mind but are also influenced by culture. When internal attributions are addressed, the service user may then be empowered to make more appropriate external attributions. In assessing learned helplessness, Barber (1991) suggests using the following questions:

- How long have things been bad?
- What efforts have you made to change things?
- How much success have you had?
- How much good times have you had compared with bad times?
- What do you put your good times down to?
- What do you put your bad times down to?
- If attributed to internal causes, do you put it down to effort or ability? (Effort is easily improved.)

If attributed to external causes, do you put it down to luck or task difficulty? (Real luck is totally outside our control but, since there is an element of one making one's luck by planning and effort, some so-called luck can be self-made).

The Good Lives model

This model has been developed in the decade beginning 2000, mainly for work with offending behaviours – see for example Ward (2002), Ward and Stewart (2003), Ward and Mann (2004), Ward *et al.* (2007). As with all developments, it has drawn on other approaches that we outline in this book and has been applied mainly to violent behaviour, criminal activity and sexual abuse. Its main contribution is the way in which it applies 'positive psychology' (the study of human happiness and mental wellbeing) to problematic behaviour. It also provides a different orientation between worker and service user. The following assumptions underpin the approach:

Human wellbeing requires the achievement of eight 'primary goods':

- LIFE – optimal functioning physically, sexually, mentally and socially.
- KNOWLEDGE
- EXCELLENCE – a level of mastery/agency at play and work (autonomy and self-directedness).
- INNER PEACE – free of turmoil, stress and conflict.
- RELATEDNESS/FRIENDSHIP – belonging, being intimate, family and community.
- SPIRITUALITY – in the broad sense of finding meaning and purpose in life.
- HAPPINESS
- CREATIVITY

This list of primary goods does not claim to be exhaustive and others may wish to subdivide some of the items. A primary good is something sought (not necessarily consciously) as an end in itself, whereas secondary goods are sought as a means to a primary good. The primary goods are the foundation of human wellbeing and of a clear sense of identity and therefore are in the best interest of the individual and the community.

The theory suggests that all human behaviour is in the pursuit of these goods and, in a sense therefore, can be said to be for a good purpose. What we all hope to achieve is a Good Life – one that optimizes our sense of wellbeing. The problem is that some people want to gain 'goods' by the 'direct route' (short-cuts) like theft or sexual assault – routes that are usually dangerous to another person or that infringe their rights. While the pursuit of primary goods is to be supported, *the means* have to be socially acceptable, and unacceptable, disrespectful and unsafe means are to be challenged, especially *the beliefs and ideas that support offending behaviour* (as we do in other cognitive approaches). The pursuit of self-interest is supported so long as it is done in a satisfying way for all concerned.

The challenges to beliefs and means however are not confrontational, for the style of the approach is *supportive of the person*, looking at their strengths and abilities, examining in some detail how they go about achieving other primary goods. So a holistic view is sought, strengths are mobilized and built on and the pursuit of a good life is encouraged throughout. Negative language is avoided as much as possible – words such as 'distortion', 'irrational' and 'deviant' are replaced with 'change of life', 'new approach', 'self-management', 'intimacy-building' and 'healthy functioning'.

The focus on the service user's best interests and good intentions means that it is easier to avoid moral condemnation of *the person*, because it is undesirable/harmful *means* rather than intentions that are being challenged, and so an empathic working relationship is maintained. It is claimed that this accounts for greater motivation on the part of service users and more persistence with the work. The past and its meaning are explored to understand its influence and the obstacles it placed in the person's way.

Implications for assessment

In this approach assessment starts with the present situation but soon broadens out to look at the person's pursuit of primary goods as a whole. It establishes:

- What is important to the person, what their priorities are for the attainment of wellbeing.
- What lacks or influences tempted them to take the unsatisfactory direct routes or shortcuts?

Risk to others, need and responsibility are explored as the service user is invited to draw his/her own conclusions during a joint investigative conversation. Strengths and life achievements are underlined. How can the person become more fulfilled? What goals would promote this? In this process it is recommended that workers avoid using a list of the primary goods to be taken in turn as in a questionnaire. Such a form-filling approach is considered to cause the person to feel they are doing a test, whereas the aim is to get them to examine themselves. The intentions and rationale of the worker are to be transparent, namely to work out how to get the person to achieve a fulfilling life, as this is seen as the best safeguard for the future. The link between the offending behaviour and a specific good is examined, as well as the details of daily living and how this might be relating to other goods, or not, as a picture of the person's relationships and environment emerges, and in particular how they see themselves *vis-à-vis* various primary and secondary goods:

- What is important to them and how do they go about getting it?
- What else do they hope to achieve in the future? Are there cognitive processes that need to be changed?
- Is there an overarching good or value that sums up the person?
- Could that be a focus to begin with? Where to start? Tasks? A plan?

In conclusion, the traditional behavioural approach can be used on its own, as can the cognitive dimension, but added together they provide a more powerful analysis of a wide range of troubled situations, examining what precedes and follows behaviour environmentally, and also what thoughts and resultant feelings precede, accompany and follow from the behaviour, giving clear indications of which interventions are most likely to be helpful. In the cognitive approaches the assessment process begins by assessing the consequent emotional problem (C) – how problematic it is it? Does the service user want to change it? What goal can be agreed? What are the activating events (A)? How does the person perceive the activating events – what beliefs are held about them (B)? Having taught the B–C connection, B is assessed for rationality/helpfulness, or the opposite. In the Good Lives approach the support of the pursuit of primary goods is key, along with an examination of the means of attaining them.

Critical comment

Behavioural approaches have considerable appeal for social workers because they offer a systematic, scientific approach that makes it possible to structure the work: 'The objective is spelt out clearly, the method predefined, and the end product always measurable' (Davies, 1981, p. 54). The initial stages of assessment are given prominence in this approach and the production of behaviour baselines aids data display. Additionally, a strict behavioural approach has the advantage of going some way towards meeting the values of social work in that client participation is encouraged, labelling discouraged and accountability made evident. Sheldon (1982) argues that a behavioural assessment has the advantage over other approaches of not 'squeezing out' the client's story or shaping the evidence to fit a favourite theory, so this careful attention to detail is particularly useful in 'blowing up' aspects of client situations so that all variables can be explored. When the ideas about learned helplessness are taken on board, this has the potential to bridge the gap between psychological and sociological explanations of behaviour and maintain the focus on social as well as individual factors. O'Hagan and Dillenburger (1995) maintain that a functional behavioural approach offers a thorough, non-abusive approach to childcare work.

However, despite the claims of behavioural social workers that the approach is value-free and client-friendly, it remains in practice largely psychologically reductionist. Although the cognitive-behavioural approach can improve people's responses to inequality, it is no substitute for addressing social problems. In residential work, for example, usually it is only the immediate environment of the service user that is examined; even with behavioural group-work, it tends to yield little more in the way of solutions than the establishment of token economy regimes. Whatever the value of these, they do not take into account the realities of, for example, children's experiences in residential care where homes are understaffed, underfunded and, in some cases, abusive.

Also, the approach is not as value-free as it claims. For example, Ellis's (1962, 2006) rational therapy is really about appropriate white, masculine assertiveness. It would be difficult to challenge many women's 'irrational' beliefs as they may well be embedded in the 'rational' context of patriarchal relations. Renzetti (1992), for example, suggests that many lesbian women remain in violent relationships because of 'learned optimism'.

The scientific nature of traditional behavioural assessment rests on modernist assumptions about certainty and, in practice, assessments need to include the cognitive aspects. Even then, there often appears to be a tendency to go for a rushed solution after a limited assessment; see, for example, the modified and limited use of social skills training in group work. One is left with the same basic criticism we made of psychodynamic approaches: it is usually easier to bend the theory so that the assessment suggests an intervention that changes how an individual accommodates their lot, rather than actually look at whether that 'lot' should be changed. This is, of course, the perennial problem of social work, as it always seems easier to change an individual than challenge the status quo.

Outcomes

Research into the outcomes of behavioural social work (Sheldon, 1995) suggests that a combination of traditional behavioural approaches and cognitive approaches produces better results, and the cognitive dimension is being increasingly applied to a wider range of problems. Vennard *et al.* (1997) found that the use of cognitive-behavioural work was more effective than psychosocial approaches for reducing antisocial behaviour in both adults and juvenile offenders, and Buchanan (1999) found it the single most effective (problem-focused) approach for children with emotional behavioural problems, as did Kasdin (1997). Concerning work with children, Sutton (2000, p. 4) concludes that

> [T]here is abundant evidence that when practitioners develop a warm, empathic and respectful therapeutic alliance with family members and can help them to employ principles and concepts drawn from cognitive-behavioural theory, they have been able to help thousands of children with a variety of problems.

However, even though other studies found that cognitive-behavioural work produces the most positive outcomes, the meta-analysis of Gorey *et al.* (1998) did not find evidence to support this and it probably has not been compared with constructionist approaches.

The Department of Health (2001) *Evidence-Based Clinical Practice Guidelines* considers CBT to be well supported by the Cochrane-registered reviews (the Cochrane Library, Oxford) and other high-quality reviews from 1990 to 1998. It is reported to have the best record of effectiveness in the treatment of depressive disorders. McLeod (1998) comments that 'the effectiveness of cognitive behavioural therapy for a wide range of conditions is amply confirmed in the research literature' (p. 80). However, Mair (2004) argues that it is wise to treat any early apparent successes with caution given the incrementally disappointing reconviction rates indicators that have emerged over time. For example, the Mid-Glamorgan STOP initiative and the initial research into pre-accredited cognitive skills programme, which revealed 14 per cent lower reconviction rates than comparison groups (Friendship *et al.*, 2002), have not been echoed by subsequent research findings. An evaluation of accredited cognitive skills programmes for adult prisoners found no differences in reconviction rates (Falshaw *et al.*, 2003), neither were there any differences between reconviction rates of adult men and young offenders who started custodially based cognitive skills programmes (Cann *et al.*, 2003). What works better seems to be community- based supervision where support can be offered to increase desistance by helping overcome problems such as family problems, employment and so on (Farrall, 2004). That suggests a move away from Cognitive-behavioural therapy programmes to customized, relationship-oriented practice.

SUMMARY

- Behavioural approaches offer a detailed and thorough method for the analysis of problems, suggesting useful techniques to aid assessment.

- These approaches are most effective in developing strategies to *strengthen* behaviour.

- Despite the advantage of rigour in the assessment of behavioural problems, the traditional behaviourist approach is little used by social workers.

- Cognitive-behavioural approaches, in that they emphasize the role of thought processes in behaviour, offer a more acceptable approach to assessment and intervention for many social workers because they help them to understand the emotional component of behaviour difficulties.

- The emphasis on learned helplessness gives behavioural approaches the potential to deal with anti-oppressive practice issues, and Barber's questions can be useful in analysing helplessness and in starting empowerment and increasing self confidence.

FURTHER LEARNING ACTIVITIES

- Consider (or discuss) which of the various behavioural approaches, considering your own values and style of working, is the most attractive to you?
- In what circumstances might you consider using an alternative?

FURTHER READING

Payne, Mm. (2005) *Modern Social Work Theory*. Basingstoke: Palgrave Macmillan.
Milner, J. and Myers, S. (2007) *Working with Violence*. Basingstoke: Palgrave Macmillan.
The classic works of Beck and of Ellis – numerous new reprints available cheaply on the internet.

NATIONAL OCCUPATIONAL STANDARDS

For students working with the British National Occupation Standards for Social Work (see Appendix):

- This chapter relates to *practice* elements 1.1; 5.1; 11.1–4; 18.1–3.
- With which of the *knowledge* requirements in the Appendix does this chapter help you?

CHAPTER 7

A Handy Tourist Map: The Task-Centred Approach

What this chapter is about

The map presented in this chapter is also from the 'second wave' of social work theory. It too is problem-focused, having much in common with the cognitive element in the previous map, but it moves further towards social construction-ism and also towards acknowledging and dealing with external social factors in human difficulties.

This chapter addresses the task-centred approach to social work assessment and intervention – probably the most used approach of the past 20 years after psychosocial casework. This theoretical map differs from those in preceding chapters in that, while it is implicitly behaviourist and cognitivist, it did not originate in clinical psychology but is based on research into social work prac-tice and written specifically for social workers. We refer to it as a handy tourist map because it involves no elaborate or complex theory, its principles could fit on a folded card and social workers use many of its elements, perhaps without naming them, as a guide to where they need to get to in much of their work.

MAIN POINTS

> Wider theoretical issues: assumptions about problem classification and causation.

> Techniques: goal setting, from wants to goals, task selection.

> Implications for assessment: task review, assessment questions, obstacles.

> Critical comments on the usefulness of this approach and on task selection and performance.

> Outcomes of research studies of this approach and on its social dimension.

Wider theoretical issues

The task-centred approach arose from disenchantment in the 1960s with the existing open-ended and long-term ways of working. William J. Reid's dissertation published by the Columbia University in 1963 was the first state-ment of the ideas, which were subsequently developed by Reid and Shyne (1969), Reid and Epstein (1972), Reid (1978) and Epstein (1988). The main British publications are those of Doel and Marsh (1992) and Marsh and Doel (2005). Most texts on social work interventions now include the task-centred approach (see for example Coulshed and Orme, 2006).

There are certain assumptions underlying this approach, many of them drawn from the (cognitive) philosophical writings of Goldman (1970) and from the crisis intervention ideas of Parad (1965). Briefly these are:

- The usual and best way to get what you want is to take action.
- Action is guided by beliefs about the world and self, and these are the basis for plans of action.
- Many psychosocial problems reflect only a temporary breakdown in coping.
- Time limits help to motivate service users, before the edge of discomfort becomes blunted with time.
- One positive problem-solving experience improves one's ability to cope with the next difficulty.
- 'Normal life consists of one damn thing after another,' said Dorothy L. Sayers's character Lord Peter Wimsey. Difficulties are mostly normal; they become problems only when they become 'the same damn thing over and over' (O'Hanlon, 1995) as a person becomes stuck.
- We are what we do, and feelings flow from behaviour.
- Feelings can be viewed as beliefs about wants.

The approach is mainly cognitive in that emotions become translated into beliefs, as we shall see when we address causation, and people's capacity to think is utilized to solve their problems. It concentrates mainly on 'exposed prob-lems' (Payne, 2005, p. 100), which it classifies in defined categories although, as Payne mentions, emotional problems can be helped by success in performing tasks. It is suitable for a very broad range of problems, even problems in care management and service systems (Ford and Postle, 2000). It is mainly con-cerned with problems that can be solved by tasks performed by the service user and the social worker. It sees the worker in a collaborative role with the service user, puzzling out together what to do.

Problem classification

Reid (1978) classifies problems into eight types:

1. *Interpersonal conflict*: interactions with others are presenting difficulties: 'We don't get along.' The problem is in a relationship be it marital, parental, school or work conflict.

2. *Dissatisfaction with social relationships*: 'I am not assertive; I get picked on.' The problem here is more general, within the individual rather than between them and others.

3. *Problems with formal organizations*, such as housing, schools, hospitals and state benefits systems.

4. *Difficulty in role performance*, such as parent, spouse, worker or student.

5. *Problems with decisions.*

6. *Reactive emotional distress*, such as depression or anxiety resulting from a situation.

7. *Inadequate resources*, such as money, food, work or housing.

8. *Others*, not included in the above, such as behavioural problems associated with addictive or compulsive patterns, substance abuse, crime and gambling.

In the assessment stage of task-centred work, it is also important to seek out how various problems are *interconnected*. This can arise in two ways. First, actual problems in different categories can be interconnected, such as drinking, unemployment and lack of money. Having identified these connections, the potential service user together with the social worker can consider which would be the most useful to tackle first – as, in dealing with that problem, other problems may take care of themselves. The second way in which interconnectedness can arise is in the problems of different people, for example two parents where the problem of one is maintaining the problem of the other in each of their cases. We find that service users find it helpful to be given a scale, setting out the eight types in a way such that they can write in the problems and score them at the beginning of work and again at the end (Figure 7.1).

Problem type(s)	Nil	Low	Some	A lot	Serious
Interpersonal: [Add some detail]					
Social relations:					
Formal organizations:					
Roles:					
Decisions:					
Emotional distress:					
Resources:					
Others					

Figure 7.1 Problem scale

Problem causation

Next, there is an analysis of the *cause(s)* of the problem. This is where there is a major shift of thinking from earlier approaches to assessment in social work. In this approach there is no question of seeking out the original cause of a problem. Even where a prior event, for example a loss, is recognized as starting the problem, it is what the service user is making of that loss here and now that matters. The event cannot be changed, but the person can be helped to grieve, to accept the reality and to plan a new life without the lost person or status. Of problems, it is said that they simply happen. Rather than searching for complex 'original' causes, the assessing social worker looks for *obstacles* that are contributing to *maintaining* the problem in existence by preventing its resolution. It is those *'causes' of the problem continuing to be* that really matter. The removal of these obstacles will allow the change to happen. The focus, therefore, is mainly on the here and now, with perhaps some attention to the recent past, because irrespective of the original cause that started the problem off, the cause that counts is the cause that is 'blocking' the resolution of the problem in the present. These are current things that the service user and worker can do something about – we can do nothing about changing history. It is important in this approach not to interpret service users' behaviour or explain it in terms of irrational behaviour, resistance or defence mechanisms. Doel and Marsh (1992) refer to this as 'shooting the reflective parrot' that sits on the shoulders of many social workers trained in essentially psychosocial approaches.

In a task-centred assessment, 'cause' equals *obstacle* preventing the problem from being moved. There are four main obstacles:

1. *The social system.* This could be the family, extended family, community, formal or informal networks, or society at large (as in the case of many oppressions). Here the task-centred approach is clearly saying that the cause of problems can be outside the individual. Where that is the case, to see it anywhere else would be to pathologize the service user unjustly. However, obstacles are frequently complex and can include both internal and external elements.

2. *Beliefs or constructs* about the world, life, self and the problem. Beliefs can be factual or evaluative, and their accuracy or consistency can be challenged.

3. *Emotions,* which are translated into beliefs about wants. For example 'What I want is lost or unobtainable' = depression; 'What I want is wrong' = guilt. Moving feelings to an explicit cognitive level makes them easier to deal with, since the underlying beliefs can be disputed. For example, a person feeling guilty about being sexually abused can be helped to see that it was not they who initiated the behaviour.

4. *Attempted solutions,* or actions being taken, that are making matters worse. There are three main types of attempted solution that can become obstacles:

   ■ Seeking utopian goals, or aiming too high, such as wanting children to be 'angels'.

- Trying too hard to do what can only be spontaneous, for example trying to get to sleep or trying to get a stepchild to love you.
- Seeking to change attitudes when the service user could settle for behaviour, or wanting someone to want something they do not want.

Examples of these attempted solutions include challenging children for stomping up stairs because they do not think they should have to go to bed so early, or complaining that a child is not enthusiastic about going to school. In both cases not settling for the behaviour concerning going to bed and to school will turn a minor difficulty into a problem. If the 'attitude' were simply ignored, there would be a better chance that it would go away. Tasks can be designed to undo these unhelpful attempted solutions.

From wants to goals

Problems are defined by Reid (1978) as unmet or unsatisfied wants as perceived by the service user. These perceptions may often be unclear but, more importantly, an unmet want is often attributed to the potential service user by someone else. For example, person A may say 'My partner B has a drink problem – he needs to control his drinking.' This is the attribution of a problem by person A (the 'referrer') to person B. A is seeking help for B, so A's want/problem is really 'I have a problem with my drinking partner.' That is the only 'acknowledged' problem so far. B has not acknowledged any want; he is not an 'applicant', and it is mainly service users who are applicants in some way that concern us in the detailed use of this map.

Of course, in statutory agencies especially, many of the people we work with are 'referrals' rather than 'applicants'. They are the unwilling people whom courts, child protection panels, schools, parents and families refer to us. These people may say they have no unmet want with which they wish us to help. In these situations, task-centred work does not move forward unless, and until, some want is acknowledged, even if it is only 'I want you off my back.' Unwilling 'referrals' can be engaged by exploring how it is that others see them as having problems or as being problems, how the situation is affecting them, whether there is something they would like to see changed, and whether there is something they could do that would free them from interference in their lives. When they acknowledge some such want they become 'applicants'. In this approach, therefore, the first step in assessment is to establish whether this person has any want, that is 'Is there anything you want to change?', 'Do you want my help in achieving it?' Some people see themselves as confirmed failures in life and may not believe that any help will make a difference. They may need to consider the questions 'If effective help was available, what would you like it to tackle?' and 'Are any of the attributed problems real problems for you in any way?'

Fourteen-year-old Dean has been living in a residential care home for young men since it was discovered that he had sexually assaulted the 8-year-old friend of his sister. He refuses to go to school as he is afraid of reprisals from the girl's older brothers. Care staff complain that he is bullied by the other lads and spends much of his time in the home on his play station. He also raids the fridge in the night and has put on a great deal of weight.

Dean refuses to talk about his offence, except to say that he will never do anything like that again. He wants to return home to his mother and two younger sisters.

He currently visits them for two hours each week and these visits are supervised. The supervisor has no concerns about Dean's behaviour on these visits but she has expressed concerns about his mother often smelling of drink. His mother denies drinking excessively, saying she only has the occasional drink when she gets upset at local youths throwing things into the garden and chanting 'Nonce house!' She would like to move but is in arrears with her rent.

■ Using the problem scale (Figure 7.1), list the problems and wants for everyone in this situation. How might the wants translate into goals?

This approach takes nothing for granted and asks the most basic and obvious questions, respecting potential service users' states, seeking to start where they are and looking at life through their perception of it. Epstein (1988) describes this phase as the 'start up', in which the worker establishes whether there are acknowledged wants in the mind of those referred for help – she referred to them as 'up-front' problems.

The next step focuses on *wants*, to firm up *goals*, assessing whether they are specific and achievable and, if so, in how much time, particularly how short a time. This consideration of time-limited work is seen as crucial for motivation and clearly fits well with the current requirement that assessments should include the costing of interventions. Many potential service users will have more than one want; these are prioritized at the assessment stage and usually no more than three are targeted. Once agreed, these (three) problems become the basis of the goals of the work. Where, when and with whom these problems arise is explored, as are the consequences of behaviours, the meaning the problem has for the person and for significant others, and also the social context.

These considerations arise in clarifying *goals* at this point:

■ What needs to be done or changed?
■ What constraints make this difficult?
■ What tasks will be required of the service user and/or the worker, mainly the service user, in order to begin to improve matters?

NAME	What I want from them	My chances of getting it	What they want from me	Their chances of getting it from me
Dad				
Mum				
Rebecca				
Paul				

Figure 7.2 Want sheet

How long will it take? Discussing and agreeing time limits appears to greatly heighten motivation. We suggest that when in doubt about length, err on the side of brevity.

We also recommend the Want Sheet (Figure 7.2) designed by Masson and O'Byrne (1984), which is particularly useful where two or more people are involved, as in family conflicts. Instruments such as these help people to clarify wants or, often more importantly, to express wants. The vagueness arising from an inability to explain, clarify and express wants is often a further problem compounding the original problems.

> ### CASE STUDY: THEORY INTO PRACTICE
>
> Samantha is asking for help in dealing with her 15-year-old daughter, Rebecca. Rebecca gave her no cause for concern until her dad left the home after discovering that Samantha had been having an affair with a woman she met at work. He now lives with a new partner in the next town. Samantha reports that Rebecca has 'got in with the wrong crowd' and is staying out until all hours. She thinks she is taking drugs, and is concerned that Rebecca has also started cutting herself. Rebecca says that she only cut herself once or twice and this was only as a result of a craze for cutting at school. She doesn't see why she shouldn't stay out late with her friends as she can still get up for school. The conflict between Samantha and Rebecca has escalated to the point where they have 'screaming matches' every day. Samantha is also concerned about the effect of this on her younger son, Paul.
>
> ■ Complete the want sheet in Figure 7.2 for this family.

Goal clarification at the assessment stage is in itself also a major part of helping. The social worker will want to help or 'coach' service users in taking action to deal with the problem themselves. The service user, rather than the social worker, being the main agent of change in this approach, clarity and agreement are vital at this point. Each member of a family or group can be asked to complete a want sheet and then share them with one another, giving them an opportunity to challenge misconceptions about each other's expectations within the group. Such exchanges can give valuable information about the potential of the group for sorting out its problems through its own action. The approach therefore is essentially an empowering one with the social worker serving/servicing the user(s).

The meeting of a want is equivalent to reaching a goal. Every social work text will stress the need for clearly defined realistic goals that are salient to the service user; however, there may be a tendency among some social workers to busy themselves with tasks and miss out on the work of identifying goals, which in turn makes evaluation difficult. The task-centred approach sees the clarification of wants/goals as a crucial step in the assessment and helping processes.

Task selection

The next step is task selection, working out with the potential service user which tasks could be attempted to bring about change. A wide range of tasks is usually developed and these are discussed, the social worker and potential service user collaboratively assessing which would be the most useful, which are within the potential service user's repertoire and, if they are not immediately capable of being done, how much help, coaching and rehearsal the potential service user would need in order to be able to do them. If outside resources are needed, the assessment needs to consider what are they and who should get them.

In this step of the assessment process, decisions are made jointly with the potential service user, discussing the task options available and considering:

- The potential benefits of each.
- The work involved in carrying them out.
- Any factors that may make a task difficult.

The following are some of the options available in selecting tasks:

1. *Exploratory tasks.* These further examine the problem or challenge factual beliefs. A parent may say, 'My son is always disobedient', so the task could be to count up the occasions when he obeys or disobeys over the next week and set out to catch him being obedient as much as possible, or at least once.

2. *Interventive tasks.* These are used to make a change or move towards solving the difficulty or meeting the want, such as parents going out together more. Attempting such intervention by way of experiment provides valuable evidence for the assessment.

3. Tasks can be *simple* (one action) or *complex* (several actions or parts). However, simple tasks are preferred in this approach.

4. *Single* (done by one individual) *or reciprocal tasks* (someone does something and another person reciprocates).

5. *Physical or mental tasks.* It is recommended that mental tasks be made as physical as possible, for example by making *lists* of one's ideas or observations.

6. *Incremental tasks*, beginning with small steps and then increasing in difficulty as the client gains in confidence and skill.

7. *Pretend tasks*, such as pretending that something has changed, for example a depression having lifted, noting the difference or seeing if someone else notices anything different.

8. *Reversal tasks.* These entail doing the opposite of what the service user has been doing to tackle the problem. These are especially recommended where the attempted solution is the main cause of the problem being stuck.

9. *Paradoxical tasks.* These may be considered where straightforward tasks have failed and where they can be preceded by a positive reframe of the problem. These ask the service user to not change or to make the problem worse, and, unlike any of the above tasks which are negotiated with the service user and which hope for compliance, these are not negotiated or discussed. The hope is for refusal, the intention here being that the service user will recoil from the injunction and thereby change.

We then consider:

- What practice, rehearsal or guidance may be needed.
- The overall plan for carrying out the task.
- How and when progress will be reviewed.

THINKING POINT

Referring to this list, which sorts of tasks might you use in the early stages of your assessment of Samantha and her family above?

Whichever tasks are chosen, they work better when a brief *time limit* is set. Reid (1992) found that goals and tasks without time limits were less effective; he suggests that when longer work is required it be broken down into short periods for task work towards specific goals.

Implications for assessment

Task review

When reviewed, tasks provide useful information/evidence, not only about the problem but also about the most helpful way of addressing it, about the motivation and capacity of the service user and about the likely time and effort that will be required. The final step, therefore, is task review. If the tasks are carried out and some progress is found, the assessment is well on its way to completion; we already know what needs to be done – it is only a matter of estimating how long it will take to complete. If, however, the tasks are not done, or they have made no difference, we know that further analyses and changes are required. If the tasks are completed but ineffective, this is valuable information that will increase the likelihood that more effective tasks can be and will be designed. So the step of task selection is retaken.

The task review will not only seek to discover any reasons for tasks not being carried out but will also include supportive discussion, especially of any beliefs and anxieties that may be impeding progress. This is followed by the planning of more appropriate tasks or rehearsals for their performance. (The questions listed under Stage 7 below will apply.)

Assessment questions relating to the six stages of the process

Stage 1. Meeting the service user

- Is this case a matter of a referral or an application?
- Is the service user's want attributed or acknowledged?
- If attributed but not acknowledged, is there anything else wanted?
- If mandated by court to cooperate with the service, how does s/he want to proceed? What are his/her own wants?
- To sum up, do we have an applicant for anything? Do we have a service *user?*

Stage 2. Exploring the wants (unsatisfied want = problem)

- If referred, what is wanted by the referrers ?
- Does the service user want this? Or is that a problem for the service user?
- What does the service user want to do about it?
- Does the service user want help to do that?
- What are the applicant's own wants?

Then analysis of 'cause':

- How is the problem maintained: by beliefs, emotions, the social system or attempted solutions?
- What are service user's beliefs about the situation and about the want? Are the beliefs accurate? Consistent?
- If the 'cause' is an attempted solution, is it seeking utopian goals, trying too hard or seeking attitudinal change?

Stage 3. Problem classification

- How can the problem(s) be classified? (What type of problem/s?)
- Which, and how many, of the eight types are involved? How serious is each one? How frequent?

- Is there any interconnectedness between problems?
- What meaning does the problem have for those concerned?

Stage 4. Agreeing a goal or goals

- Is the want/goal specific?
- Is the goal achievable?
- What constraints make change difficult?
- What needs to change, for the goal to be reached?
- How long will it take to reach the goal?

Stage 5. Agreeing a task or tasks

- What tasks will be required to make the necessary change?
- Will the service user be able to carry them out?
- What task/s will the social worker or others carry out?

Stage 6. Task implementation

- What help or rehearsal will be needed to prepare for task implementation?
- What other resources will be needed?
- When will the work be reviewed?

Stage 7. Task review

If tasks are not done:

1. Has the service user a clear enough understanding of the task and its relevance?
2. Has the service user any adverse beliefs, such as thinking that the task has little value or that doing it will be frightening? Has s/he the necessary self-confidence to perform the tasks?
3. Does the service user have the necessary skill to perform the task completely and consistently? If not, how can this be acquired?
4. Does the service user have the necessary concrete resources to carry out the task? These may be money, accommodation or the support of friends.
5. Are there reinforcements necessary to encourage the service user in the persistent carrying out of the tasks? If so, from whom could they come?
6. Are the social worker's attitudes affecting the service user's performance? Does the service user's forgetfulness or anxiety annoy the social worker, or do his/her behaviours or attitudes make the social worker feel contemptuous in any way?

On first reading, these questions may seem to be too obvious and simplistic but that is really their strength. It is all too easy to make assumptions and end up putting words into the mouths of service users; it is good practice to take nothing for granted and to ask all the 'fundamental' questions necessary. Even where the nature of the problem is clear and specific, we still need to learn from service users how best to help them proceed in small steps towards their goals. Encouragement over small achievements and seeing them as a cause for optimism are vital elements in the 'coaching' process. Small successes improve motivation to progress further.

CASE STUDY: THEORY INTO PRACTICE

The K family: a social services department received a complaint from neighbours that they could hear shouting, and what seemed like a child being hit coming from the K family's house.

The visiting social worker explained who she was and the purpose of the visit, making use of good engagement skills to gain access to the home despite some early hostility and fearfulness on the part of the Ks. The couple had been together for three years and there were two children, Sarah aged 12 and Jason aged 3. Sarah was Mrs K's child from an earlier relationship, and Mrs K had lived alone with Sarah for several years. She had a low-paid, part-time job and struggled to pay her way, accumulating £4500 in debts. Mr K had not been aware of the debts until about 18 months previously when a court letter arrived. He had felt very angry and had started to drink more than usual, often on his own. He also had back trouble and had been unemployed for the past 6 months, which was getting him down. Mrs K also said she felt a bit depressed and that everything seemed to be falling apart. They agreed that there had been loud arguments; he was angry over the debts and she would respond that his drinking and attitude were making things worse. Over the past 18 months, they seemed to talk only when they rowed; he had hit her once (a 'slap on the face') and he had lost his patience with Sarah. They both said he had not hit Sarah but he had frightened her and made her cry. At one point, he had briefly left the family, returning for Jason's sake.

■ Sum up the wants of each person and identify which are acknowledged.

Given these data, the worker was able to establish that Mrs K wanted to be less depressed and more able to deal with the debts (her two main acknowledged wants), and she felt that Mr K should help her more in the home instead of just shouting about things. Mr K wanted his wife to be honest over the debts and to be more firm in dealing with Sarah (two 'attributed' problems), but he did acknowledge that he needed to watch his temper in order to avoid hitting anyone in the family. Both Mr and Mrs K, however, expressed feelings of hopelessness about the future in that debt, unemployment and health problems were seriously frustrating and heightening the risk

Problem type(s)	Nil	Low	Some	A lot	Serious
Interpersonal: Aggressive arguments				X	
Social relations: Few friends					X
Formal organizations: Courts		X			
Roles: Budgeting				X	
Decisions:	X				
Emotional distress: Feeling depressed			X		
Resources: Debts. No job			X		
Others: Drinking Backache		X		X	

Figure 7.3 Completed problem sheet

of abuse and family break-up. This led to a vague acknowledgement that they needed some help or guidance of some sort. At this stage of the assessment, they could be said to have a mixture of attributed and acknowledged problems, some vague goals and many constraints. The social worker next showed them a 'problem scale' and, talking them through it, asked them to enter their problems and use ticks to show how serious they considered the issues to be. With some encouragement and advice, they produced the sheet shown in Figure 7.3.

This exercise helped to set out the situation in a non-blaming way so that, for example, Mr K was able to accept that drinking was at least a minor problem. The completion of the scale led to some discussion on the *interconnectedness* of the problems. Did the fighting make the depression worse? Did this affect their ability to tackle the debts better? Did the drinking make the rows and the debts worse, or were they causing it? Where would the most effective starting-point be? At this point, they were not ready yet to face up to the problems of their relationship, their inability to talk things out or their lack of social life. They were, however, more clear that something needed to be done, and they were willing to have the worker see them again to plan some action together.

Before leaving, the worker left two copies of the want sheet with them and suggested the *task* of completing their sheets separately and privately, then sharing them for discussion one evening when the children were in bed. A second visit was arranged for a week later.

As she departed, the worker began to consider what obstacles might be blocking this couple from satisfactory functioning:

THINKING POINT

- Pause here and consider what obstacles might be maintaining the problems of Mr and Mrs K.

Obstacles to problem-solving

1. *Beliefs.* As she had listened to their accounts, she had a sense that they believed they were each being blamed by the other, that they were caught for ever in growing debt and that they had lost any real hope of financial coping or of happiness. Mr K seemed to think that his back was permanently damaged, but he had not continued with medical checkups. The social worker could gently discuss and question these beliefs with the family.

2. *Emotions.* The belief in the loss of prospects could explain the depression. Mrs K was also isolated in that there was little communication with Mr K, so she might have been feeling unloved and alone. This depression and sense of isolation could be addressed by examining the underlying beliefs.

3. *The social system.* Reduced welfare benefits and a shortage of employment were affecting the family, as was the lack of nursery school places in the area. It may be possible to act as advocate concerning these issues.

4. *Attempted solutions.* How had they gone about the debt issue? Was Mr K's drinking an attempted solution? There was no evidence of utopian thinking in the session. It would be useful to check what efforts, if any, Mr K had made to respond to his wife's depression. Attempts like 'Cheer up!' tend to make the other person feel worse. These questions could be explored at the next meeting and tasks could be negotiated to help counter any such attempted solutions.

In the next session, the social worker planned to use these questions to obtain a more in-depth assessment of their situation and review the task with them. By the end of the second meeting, the couple were clearly saying they wanted help in improving their relationship in terms of talking with each other and their children. Using incremental steps, Mr K decided he would visit his doctor about his back and both parents would attend for debt counselling. Additionally, they agreed to spend 15 minutes talking, at least two nights a week, without the television on and when the children were in bed. This constitutes three simple tasks that would be monitored over four more sessions with the social worker, who by now was well placed to write a report on this family and the likely prospects of their being able to care safely for their children. The review element of the task-centred approach would provide further assessment should the tasks not be done or should they fail to bring about the service users' desired changes.

Critical comment

Reid (1978) suggests that this approach is suitable for any specific, acknowledged psychosocial problem that is capable, with some help, of resolution by the service user's own action. It can serve 'as a basic approach for the majority of clients served by social workers' (p. 98). Used in full, as the sole method, its range is narrower than if it is used along with other approaches. For example, as well as engaging in tasks, victims of trauma and people in grief may need to talk at length to an understanding listener who can facilitate their self-expression. Given some creativity in developing appropriate tasks, this approach is suitable, therefore, for most potential service users who are capable of rational discussion, perhaps with the exception of those with existential problems, seeking for meaning and identity. These need time for a lengthy, 'searching and free-ranging self examination' (ibid. p. 99).

Various texts criticizing the relevance of Eurocentric approaches to social work with black service users and their families (see for example Logan *et al.*, 1990; Devore and Schlesinger, 1991) find task-centred approaches less problematic than those in the maps described earlier. Logan *et al.* (1990) maintain that this is because the task-centred approach acknowledges the person – environment interaction and the place or impact of the social system on the personal. It also respects the beliefs, values and perceptions of the service users and listens to their definitions of their problems and their concerns. In this approach, 'the problem' is always 'the problem as defined by the service user'.

This approach also encourages service users to select the problem they want to work on and engages them in task selection and review. Logan *et al.* (1990) found that minority ethnic groups preferred this level of personal responsibility, as well as the action orientation of the task-centred approach. They add, however, that white workers need to concentrate on keeping a 'strength focus', assuming the existence of community and cultural strengths and seeking to locate them. The task review is clearly vital for checking cultural appropriateness and whether different world views are being overlooked. Issues such as language differences also need to be addressed. Staying with specifics reassures members of some minority ethnic groups who may feel threatened when a lack of specificity by social workers suggests that they are attempting to take over the person's whole life. Last, it clearly helps to develop service users' confidence in social workers if the latter show themselves willing to carry out their share of tasks, especially if they show themselves to be assertive brokers of services, actively helping to remove environmental barriers, locating information and conferring with other agencies and with those the service user considers relevant, such as community leaders and also helping with resources. And, just as they review the efforts of the service user, social workers ought to review their own performance of tasks, what they have and have not done, and the reasons why. This accountability is assisted by the clear data display developed in the assessment process. In this way, the approach can be seen to be truly collaborative, empowering and taking into account the social dimension.

Mick is a 50-year-old kitchen fitter employed by his local council. He has been off work with depression since being disciplined for racially abusing a colleague. His GP considers him fit for work but Mick stormed out of the consulting room when he was refused a sick note and verbally abused surgery staff. He later attempted to hang himself but is now recovering well in hospital. At initial interview he tells you that he doesn't want to go back to either his home or his job as he only gets harassment at both places; he lives with his elderly mother in a terraced house in an area where most residents are recent immigrants and he is 'bothered' by gangs of youths. At work, he is on the receiving end of taunts about being a single man, with the implication that he's gay.

- What tasks might you expect Mick to undertake, and which would be your responsibility?

It will be clear that, because this approach prefers to assess *during* intervention rather than before it, time and care must still be spent in carrying out a useful assessment. However because tasks will have been tried out, much more realistic practical information will be available. In a period of three weeks or so, a considerable number of trials/experimental tasks can be completed, provided these are started at the end of the first meeting without waiting to plan the perfect action. In this way, service users have an opportunity to demonstrate their capacities as well as their needs and, together with the worker, gain a useful understanding of what is maintaining the problematic situation and what might be a helpful way of dealing with it. It is also our experience that this collaborative style, with its focus on actions rather than feelings, sets the scene for the mutual bridging of difference gaps in an unthreatening way. The tasks are set to attack the problem and they, and not the person as such, are the focus.

In our view, there are few disadvantages to this approach if it is used rigorously although its capacity for empowerment perhaps needs to be more explicit. In the case example of the K family, the children are not directly empowered or involved; children should be heard and their views taken into account. Some social workers, believing the approach to be value-free and intrinsically non-oppressive, take this as read and make no further efforts to address issues of empowerment and anti-oppressive practice. The coaching role of the worker could be open to abuse, perhaps encouraging an overworked social worker to be overly directive. Like all other approaches, it needs to be accompanied by the values of anti-oppressive practice set out in Chapter 2. Additionally, the emphasis on simple tasks may give rise to concrete solutions that can obscure the advocacy role mentioned earlier.

Although, in theory, the approach should be ideal for group and community work, there are few examples of this happening. It may be that, like the approaches already discussed, it lends itself most easily to individual and family problems.

Outcomes

After years of research, Reid and Epstein (1972) published several results showing a high degree of progress within limited time scales; for example, in a study of social work with children in their last year at school, 80 per cent of the children reported that their overall situation had changed for the better, with 20 per cent reporting no change. However, when independent assessors studied the files, they reported evidence of improvement in only 21 per cent of cases, although in the opinion of other people involved with the children ('collaterals'), there was improvement in 60 per cent of the cases. Reid and Epstein provide examples of work with families, where 72 per cent reported improvement in the main problem and 56 per cent said the problem was either better or no longer present; 45 per cent felt a lot better.

Similar results were obtained in Britain by Goldberg *et al.* (1985) in a study of the method's use in various settings. Of the clients who completed the series of sessions, most reported that they were pleased with the approach and that their problems had reduced. Sadly, owing perhaps to the brevity of their training, workers decided that because there was no agreement about the target problem at the problem clarification stage, the approach was unsuitable for a third to a half of cases and there was no improvement for those out of touch with reality and those who lived life as a series of 'cliff-hanging' crises. They did not report what other approach was more useful for these service users. Gorey *et al.* (1998) suggest that where the target for change involved a social dimension (such as some element of the environment or of a social structure) the task-centred approach did better than the cognitive-behavioural approach.

SUMMARY

- Task-centred work involves a six-stage process, in which problems are viewed as temporary breakdowns in coping with unmet wants.

- It sees the 'causes' of problems as those *obstacles* that prevent resolution, that is in the four obstacles that maintain problems, namely beliefs, emotions, attempted solutions and the social system.

- It offers a unique problem classification and problem clarification process.

- Goals are reached by taking action, by performing tasks, and coaching in task selection and task preparation is central to the helping process.

- Time limits and task reviews aid motivation and promote optimism and empowerment.

- A sound assessment is best made after task analysis and task experimentation. The more time there is for this, the better.

FURTHER LEARNING ACTIVITIES

- Discuss the various ways in which the task-centred approach differs from cognitive-behavioural approaches.

- Using the case of Dean (see p. 127), what difference would this make to how you might approach the assessment?

FURTHER READING

Reid, W. J. (1978) *The Task-Centred System*. New York: Columbia University Press.
Doel, M. and Marsh, P. (1992) *Task-Centred Social Work*. Aldershot: Ashgate.
Marsh, P. and Doel, M. (2005) *The Task Centred Book (Social Work Skills)*. Abingdon: Routledge.
Payne, M. (2005) *Modern Social Work Theory*. Basingstoke: Palgrave Macmillan, chapter 5.

NATIONAL OCCUPATIONAL STANDARDS

For students working with the British National Occupation Standards for Social Work (see Appendix):

- This chapter relates to *practice elements* 5.2–3; 9.1–3; 11.1–4; 17.1–4.

- With which of the *knowledge* requirements does this chapter help you?

CHAPTER 8

A Navigator's Map: Solution-Focused Approaches

What this chapter is about

This chapter presents the first of two theoretical maps which belong to the 'third wave' of social work theory. Unlike the approaches outlined in the previous three chapters, it eschews pathology and problems. A solution-focused approach has some features in common with a task-centred approach in that it is largely a cognitive approach and frequently leads to tasks to be carried out by the service user. However, the focus is quite different. While task-centred approaches focus on understanding *problems* and seeking ways of removing or at least alleviating them, solution-focused work focuses on understanding *solutions*, maintaining that it is not necessary to understand a problem in order to understand its solution. Any link between the problem and the solution may be nominal. This approach begins at the end (the solution) and works back from there, rather like a navigator plotting a sea journey, pinpointing the destination first and then drawing a line back to the present position.

MAIN POINTS

➤ Wider theoretical issues: social constructionism, postmodernism, philosophical assumptions.

➤ Implications of solution-focused practice for assessments.

➤ Practice techniques: miracle and scaled questions, goal setting, tasks, feedback.

➤ Meeting agency risk assessment requirements and service user needs: a safety approach.

➤ Influence of safety approaches on assessments.

➤ Critical comments on some possible drawbacks of this approach if not used thoughtfully.

➤ Outcomes of evaluations of this approach in working with a wide range of people.

Wider theoretical issues

This approach originates mainly from work developed at the Milwaukee Centre for Brief Therapy by Steve de Shazer and his colleagues. In a succession of publications, de Shazer (1985, 1988, 1991, 1994) set out the solution-focused approach, which can be described as postmodern and constructionist. The central characteristics of social constructionism have been identified by Burr (2003) as a critical stance towards taken-for-granted, 'scientific' knowledge on the grounds that our understanding of certain social facts changes over time and depends on the cultural context in which we see them. These understandings are sustained by social processes, particularly the 'naming' of problems; and knowledge and social action go together, for example, 'naming' a problem will result in resources being made available to 'treat' it. Postmodernism is a collection of critiques of ways of thinking and can be viewed, says Myers (2007b), as the broader academic movement in which social-constructionist ideas have flourished. Although de Shazer claims that solution-focused practice is atheoretical, it is based on social constructionism in that it uses the 'local knowledge' of service users (which is theoretically limitless) rather than depending on 'professional knowledge'. Thus it embraces one half of the evidence-based practice development, namely effectiveness, remaining cautious about the evidence-based practice which makes generalizations about the nature of people. It is deeply sceptical about the ability of the 'grand' modernist theories and explanations to deliver truth, holding to a plurality of truths, including those contained in the 'local' theories of service users. Therefore it avoids any form of diagnostic labelling and sees professional categorization of people as disempowering. For example, the Finnish psychiatrists, Furman and Ahola (1992), reframe 'depression' as 'latent joy' and 'borderline personality disorder' as 'a search for a new direction in life'.

De Shazer's philosophy is based largely on the psychotherapeutic ideas of Milton Erickson (1959) and on the theories of language and meaning of Derrida (1973) and Wittgenstein (1980). This philosophy is set out more fully in Parton and O'Byrne (2000) and Milner and O'Byrne (2002). At its simplest, its practitioners hold an unwavering belief in the capacity of service users to discover their own, workable solutions to their problems. Examining in great detail 'what worked', de Shazer's team perfected a set of economical techniques that form the foundation of the approach. Many of the techniques will be familiar to social workers adopting different approaches, but solution-focused workers use them to explore service users' futures, not to understand past events.

Those using the solution-focused approach take a *not knowing* stance towards people's problems, preferring to remain *curious* about people's stories and views, about their strengths and potential, about occasions when the problem was less, and about how that happened – curious about the seeds of solution. Rather than seeking to understand (based on some grand theory), they merely seek more *helpful* 'misunderstandings'. There is a preoccupation with *difference*, with what was different when things were better and what needs to be different for them to be better again. They utilize each problem-free aspect of the person and engage in *problem-free talk*, engaging the person, rather than the problem. Indeed, they see the problem as outside the person: the person is not the problem, the *problem* is the problem. The social worker joins the person *against* the problem and thereby gets a different story. Therefore, this approach seeks not to be pathology-based and thus its assessments are not based on identifying deficits. This is particularly so in the assessment of dangerousness, solution-focused workers finding it more useful and easy to assess safety, which is measurable, rather than risk, which resists quantification; in other words, it is easier to assess the presence or start of something, such as safety, than it is to assess the absence or cessation of something, for example, risk.

This solution-focused approach seeks to find the seeds of solution in a service user's current repertoire, seeking those occasions or *exceptions*, however small or rare, when the problem is less acute in order to identify when and how that person is doing or thinking something different that alleviates the problem. This involves listening carefully to, and then *utilizing*, what the person brings to the encounter, focusing on problem-free moments, constructing an envisaged future when the problem is no longer there, and getting a very detailed description from the service user of what will be different then and whether any of that is already beginning to happen.

CASE STUDY: THEORY INTO PRACTICE

Thelma has recently left her husband after years of physical and emotional abuse but is facing a number of legal battles over her divorce, contact with her daughter, and compensation for her husband selling her house and furniture behind her back. She is also struggling with the fact that he is pleading with her to take him back (she still has some feelings for him) and the financial pressures of living in a rented house she can't afford. She tells you that she can see no future for herself now that she is getting older and feels like giving up.

■ What initial questions would you ask Thelma?

When asked how she keeps going even though she feels like giving up, Thelma says that she still takes care of her appearance, walks the dog each day, and helps relatives. Although there is nothing joyful in her life, she can remember times when she was joyful. She keeps going because she has hope and reminds herself of this by having red roses in the house.

Assumptions

Myers (2007a) provides the following list of key assumptions as an aid to practice.

Assumptions about problems

- The problem is the problem; the service user is not the problem.
- Problems do not necessarily indicate a personal deficit.
- Problems happen in interactions between people rather than inside them.
- Problems are not always present; exceptions occur.
- Complicated problems do not always require a complicated solution.

Assumptions about the past

- Events just happen: exploring the past leads to blame whereas the goal is to develop responsibility for the future.
- Exploring a problem-free future avoids having to dwell on or understand the past.
- A diagnosis does not have to determine the future.

Assumptions about change

- Change always happens; nothing stays the same.
- What may appear to be small changes can be hugely significant.
- Change can be constructed through talk.

Assumptions about talking

- Hearing what the service user has to say is important.
- Take a *not-knowing* stance that reduces premature and imposed worker judgement.
- Stay on the surface of conversations rather than looking beneath; any search for meaning is likely to be the worker's interpretation.
- People experience and make sense of their world in different ways; their reality may not be yours.

Assumptions about solutions

- Identify what is going right rather than what is going wrong.
- Service users have the solutions to the problems; assist them in finding these.
- Solutions generated by the service user are more likely to be meaningful, achievable and successful.
- Imposing *what works* for others does not always work for the individual; seek what works for them.
- Increasing service user choices will enable behaviour change.
- Goals need to be meaningful for the service user in order to be successful, but they also need to be legal and moral.

Implications of solution-focused approaches for assessments

Look again at the questions Thelma was asked. Having listened to the problem and the feeling of 'having no future', rather than lingering unduly with how bad things are for her, the social worker asks about what is not so bad – what seed of solution might be present. Notice how it brings a very different person with different possibilities for the future.

In partnership, both the service user and the social worker build a picture of a possible future without the problem or with the problem lessened. Talk (language) is seen as powerful enough to construct life; talk of life with the problem constructs a problem-laden life; talk of life without the problem constructs a problem-free life. Talking in detail of what will be happening, what people will be saying, what effect this will have on relationships, and so on, provides the *experience* of a glimpse of that life; that life then becomes a possibility and the person experiences a sense of personal agency in setting out to construct it. The new story can even include a changed or different self, especially an accountable self. Ferguson (2003, 2004) refers to this as creative reflexivity in which service users have new opportunities to shape their lives. Assessments that fix people's identities, conflating the person and the problem, are avoided as new possibilities become visible. From this assessment process, messages and tasks emerge for the service user to consider between sessions.

This approach thus has a view of assessment different from most others. Rather than assuming that information about a problem will help to find its solution, the assumption is that we can understand a solution without necessarily knowing a great deal about the problem. Searching for an understanding of a problem usually leads to a laundry list of deficits or negatives, whereas this approach says that what is needed is a list of positive strengths and *exceptions* to the problem. Lists of deficits often risk overwhelming both the service user and the social worker, engendering hopelessness and a tendency on the part of the social worker to use such expressions as 'unmotivated', 'resistant' or 'not ready to change'. In solution-focused assessments, 'resistance' is regarded as an inability on the part of the worker to recognize the service user's 'unique way of cooperating' and an indication that more careful listening needs to happen. For example, Iveson (1990) says that when people repeatedly shout about their complaints, or complain in other ways that we find difficult to hear, they are invariably people who are not being heard. To hear them we must accept their language as rational and meaningful, even when it appears irrational, unreasonable or perverse. The solution-focused approach 'can be summed up as helping an unrecognized difference become a difference that makes a difference' (de Shazer, 1988). This happened with Thelma.

Repeated complaints are especially likely to happen in child protection assessments when neither parents nor social workers feel they are not listened to:

> Parents stuck in protracted disputes tend to repeatedly tell the same story in the same particular way. This is unproductive and unsatisfying as it makes the parents feel a sense of disputation and powerless. It is important to listen to the parents' story in a way that does not feed the frustration of the denial dispute. (Turnell and Essex, 2006, p. 55)

As Durrant (1993) puts it, psychological assessment tends to assume that qualities are measurable entities, that there are 'normative' criteria for determining healthy functioning and that we need to identify deficit and fault before planning intervention. He contrasts this with the solution-focused approach, which assumes that the meaning of behaviour and emotion is relative and constructed, that psychological and emotional characteristics are partly a product of the observer's assessment and interpretation, that intervention need not be directly related to the problem, and that social workers should build on strengths rather than attempt to repair deficits. This approach, therefore, develops an apparently 'atheoretical, non-normative, client determined view' (Berg and Miller, 1992, p. 5) of difficulties in which change is regarded as constant and inevitable. As a result, it makes sense to find what bits of positive change are happening and to use them to develop a solution. If social workers do not look carefully for what the service user is doing when the problem is not happening, or is not perceived to be a problem, these exceptions will go unnoticed. The most striking example of this is the 'pre- session change' question. Because de Shazer's team believe that change is constant, that no problem, mood or behaviour happens all the time or to the same degree, new service users are asked what has changed since the appointment was arranged. The team found that a considerable proportion of people reported some change. By then asking 'How did you do that?', they quickly got a solution-focused assessment under way. The exceptions can be very small indeed but still very valuable.

CASE EXAMPLE

Helen's aftercare worker put a lot of effort into preparing her for independent living after many years in a children's home but found, two years on, that Helen was depressed, tearful, unable to leave her flat unaccompanied, spending most of the day watching television or telephoning her worker and relatives with long tales of her misery, developing an eating disorder, and on poor terms with her natural father and brother, and making heavy demands on the worker's time. Intensive psychodynamic-based work on helping Helen to come to terms with the effects of her abusive past on her current functioning and behaviourally based work on her fears of going out alone failed to effect any improvement.

Taking a solution-focused approach, the worker discovered that Helen was free from sad and intrusive thoughts when she watched television programmes about the archaeology of Roman Britain. Helen became animated when discussing her one interest and talked about her preferred future as an archaeologist. Rather than dismissing this as utopian thinking, the social worker built on this exception. Helen began to read books about Roman history and then had to get on better terms with her father and brother as she wanted a lift to visit local museums to further her interest. She bought a book on Roman cookery during one such visit and tried out some of the recipes at home, thus developing a solution to her eating problems. Her 'depression' lifted considerably and three months later she had applied for, and been accepted on, a distance-learning module of a university degree in Roman archaeology; applied for a grant to pay for her studies; approached a charity for assistance with buying a computer; and paid off her debts so that she could change her telephone system to enable her to access the internet for her studies. In order to complete her module, she will have to attend a residential study weekend at a Roman site so she will soon have to find her solution to her inability to leave the flat alone. Her aftercare worker is feeling better too as the work has become much more interesting for her.

Practice techniques

The main techniques are simple questions, the 'miracle question', scaled questions, coping questions and future questions, all aimed at eliciting and defining goals and progress.

The 'miracle question' is helpful in developing goals with people who are not sure what their goals are or who find it difficult to believe in a better future:

Suppose tonight, while you are asleep, a miracle happened and the problems you have today are gone in a flash, but because you were asleep you don't know this has happened. What would be the first difference you would notice in the morning?

This is followed by gentle prompts about new behaviours, new attitudes and new relationships, followed by 'Is any little bit of this happening already, sometimes?' So the miracle question helps to get a picture of the future without the problem and the follow-up searches out small exceptions to the problem. When these are found, the key question then is 'How did you do that?' This is not only a compliment but it presupposes personal agency and builds up possibilities of repeating what they are able to do at least once. With some small exceptions, a minimum of motivation and a little imagination, when we use constructive questions the possibilities are boundless and the potential service user can get ready for change without analysing the problem – the subject can 'describe what they want without having to concern themselves with the problem and without traditional assumptions that the solution has to be connected with understanding or eliminating the problem' (de Shazer, 1994, p. 273).

Although the miracle question is the key element of solution-focused practice in the US, many UK practitioners find it too formulaic – although the answers never are. Some British solution-focused workers (see, for example www.brieftherapy.org.uk) have found that asking a service user what their best hopes are, works as well as the miracle question for goal development. Macdonald (2007, p. 14) provides the following list of key questions for goal-setting:

- What will it be like when the problem is solved?
- What will you be doing instead?
- When that happens, what difference will it make?
- How will others know that things are better?

- Who will notice first? And then who?
- What else will be different?
- What else?
- What else?

Scaled questions are used in a particular way in this approach. These questions can be directed at service users' estimations of the severity of their difficulty, at their level of confidence about reaching their goal or at their willingness to work hard to make progress. A scaled question is usually put like this:

> Suppose we had a scale of 0 to 10, with 0 being 'the pits' and 10 being 'there is no problem', where would you put yourself on that scale?'

This scale is set up 'in such a way that all numbers are on the solution side' (de Shazer, 1994, p. 104), although it is impossible to be sure about what any number really means, even for the service user. They and we know that 5 is better than 4 and less good than 6, so answers provide a way of grading progress – or its lack – for both social worker and service user. But, more importantly, scaled questions and their answers help to make concrete what is not concrete, making it easy to describe what is hard to describe.

Numbers get their meaning from the scale to which they belong; they are content-free in so far as only the subject has any idea what they mean. But when we ask 'How will life be different when you move from 5 to 6?' and 'What will important people in your life notice that is different?', these future-oriented questions help the service user to begin constructing progressive change. Scaled questions also make it much easier for a service user to talk about behaviour which either embarrasses them or reminds them of failure and censure.

> ### CASE EXAMPLE
>
> Fourteen-year-old Jade had been told at every school exclusion meeting that her aggressive behaviour was unacceptable, to which she reacted in a sullen manner, but she could describe her efforts to control her temper through scaling: 'I've only got to four or five (she had hoped to get to six during the summer holidays) and I'm worried it'll go down to one or two when I start back at school. But it's better than it was. I was minus five at middle school!'

In discussing a problem such as depression, scaled questions help us to get away from the idea that one is either depressed or not, as if depression had an 'on – off' switch. Suppose a worker asked, 'So if 0 is how depressed you were when you asked for help and 10 is when you will be unaware of any depressing feelings, where are you now?', any reply above 0 would indicate that the depression is less bothersome now and that things are already moving towards the goal (de Shazer, 1994).

Kral (1989) produced an assessment device, the 'solution identification scale' (S-Id), to aid this process (see Parton and O'Byrne, 2000). Referrers are asked to score 39 different strengths as not at all, just a little, pretty much and very much, examples of strengths being such details as 'Sleeps OK,' 'Is happy,' 'Is considerate,' 'Tells the truth' and 'Shows honesty.' While this helps to focus attention on strengths, and allows weaknesses to be acknowledged, it also ensures that progress is not ignored, thus providing a better chance that the location of steps towards solutions can be found. It has the added advantage that it can be completed by potential service users as well as referrers, giving tangible evidence of a partnership approach. Kral also suggests four basic questions at the initial assessment stage:

---

1. To estimate self-concept, he asks 'Think about the best person you could be and give that person 100 points. Now tell me how many points you would give yourself these days.' Most people without serious problems give themselves between 70 and 85. If a service user says, for example, 60, this would influence the second question.

2. 'On a scale of 1 to 10, how much are you satisfied with your score of 60?' Most people are not satisfied with their score but a high satisfaction with a low score could mean that the person is doing as well as they can in very difficult circumstances.

3. 'When you move from 60 to 70, what will be different that will tell you that things have changed?' or 'Have you been at 70 before and if so what was happening then?' or 'What is the highest you have ever been and what was going on then?' Although these variations of the same question ask nothing about the problem, they open the door to finding exceptions, in which will lie the seeds of solutions. They also clarify for the service user what change is within his/her control.

4. 'What are the chances, on a scale of 1 to 10, that you could do that again?' This question hints that the person should make such a change, thus helping to estimate commitment and pave the way for a task assignment.

Clearly, these questions have nothing to do with why the problem is happening. They are about goals, where people are positioned in their situations and what the service user is doing that is different when there is less of a problem or no problem. They are about 'putting difference to work' (de Shazer, 1991): the questions explore what is different when the problem is not happening.

A distinction can be made between problems and unhappy situations. 'Problems' relate to patterns of behaviour, attitudes, beliefs and moods; 'unhappy situations' relate to losses (for example, loss of work, of a person, or a resource) and to environmental events (for example, the weather). While there are solutions to problems, many unhappy situations have to be coped with. In their case, *coping questions* are important, such as 'How do you manage to get by?' 'Are there times when you can cope better?' 'What helps?'

Tasks

Based on solution-focused assumptions, a set of tasks is used. These are developed with the service user, who is invited to have a go or experiment with them and keep a track of any difference made. The invitation is a permissive one in that service users can change the task or do something else that occurs to them that might be more useful. Unlike cognitive-behavioural approaches there is no expectation that the task will be done or have a specific effect. They are merely ways of enabling the service user to note changes that are beneficial (for fuller details see Milner and O'Byrne, 2002).

Where a situation is vague, a standard first session task can be given, asking service users to list all those things happening in their life that they want to continue happening. By listing what does *not* need to change, this exercise helps the clarification of appropriate goals. Sometimes people are so overwhelmed by their problems that they say they want to change everything, and here it is useful to ask them to 'take a step in a direction that will be good for them'. This helps them progress towards taking responsibility for their futures and, thus away from victimhood.

When a service user is unable to recall an exception, a *pretend* task is suggested, for example pretending to be not depressed one half of the week and noticing what is different or what other people see is different. This helps to develop and identify possible exceptions that make a difference to the problem.

Where exceptions are spontaneous or the result of other people's efforts – that is, not deliberate on the service user's part or seen as outside their control – service users can be asked to *predict* when spontaneous exceptions are going to happen. For example, a service user who steals compulsively could be asked to predict days when the urge to steal will or will not come. It has been found that service users can improve their ability to predict this correctly with practice and, of course, when they can get a high proportion of predictions correct, the question is 'Are the exceptions really spontaneous, or do you have some control?'

Where there are clear exceptions, the person is simply asked to do more of them.

Feedback

Solution-focused practice recognizes the importance of constructing helpful feedback for people at the end of sessions in order to build solutions. De Jong and Berg (2003, p. 128) identify three main aims of feedback:

- To assist in the development of clear goals.
- To focus people on the exceptions that are related to the goals.
- To encourage people to notice what they and others may be doing to make the exceptions happen.

Verbal feedback is given at the end of each session; however, we find it useful to follow this up with written feedback so that the service user has a record of progress – or lack of it – on which to reflect. Written feedback is also important in terms of transparency and accountability. Service users are concerned about what is written down about them. Solution-focused work lends itself to being entirely open with the service user as there are no hidden agendas behind the questioning of the worker; they are eliciting information from the person and seeking their meanings rather than analysing it from a professional perspective. In this sense, it is relatively easy to explain to people how you work, emphasizing that they are the person who knows themselves the best; that everyone has the capacity to change and the strengths to achieve this, and that your role is to work with them to further their progress towards their goals. This contrasts with some other approaches where the worker is looking for hidden meanings and it can be difficult to explain the theory behind such interventions.

To assist people identify their progress and how they did it, the written feedback is formatted in four sections: problem description, goals, exceptions and progress (what has been done), solutions (how it was done), and tasks/next steps. The example below shows how feedback is constructed in this way and employs the service user's own words. Feedback notes are not only for service users; they constitute an accurate agency record of each session. Some social workers find the use of the service user's words unprofessional but to re-author these words would be against the basic assumptions of the approach: honouring the service user's knowledge, accuracy and transparency.

CASE EXAMPLE

Session notes
Name: Denzil   **Date**: 3 January

Problem: Denzil is excluded from school at the moment because of his behaviour and attitude. He was re-admitted last week but didn't make enough effort. Now he is ready to change. He would like to be able to understand why he's running away and behaving in an odd manner so that he can choose a different option and get out of the state of mind that makes him want to run away or take something.

When he's got out of this state of mind, he will able to control himself more, not let his emotions take over, and think about things. His friends won't notice much different about him when this happens but others will. His teachers will notice that he is talking to them politely, getting on with his work and not talking to others in class. His mum will notice that he does things at either the first or second time of asking and he will be happier because then she'll want to sit down with him and talk about what he's been doing all day. His friends in school will notice that he's not talking to them, not messing about in class and not being sent out or in detention so much. He will be ignoring them when they talk to him in class.

When all this happens, he will be staying in school, getting on with his work, and getting good grades in his SATs so that he can be a lawyer or a psychiatrist when he's grown up.

Progress

1. Denzil can be quiet in class and get on with his work. He did this in art when he was drawing masks (this work is brilliant)

2. He can do being polite to teachers.

3. He can be responsible, like when he looks after his mum's best friend's sons and when he's form rep.

4. Denzil can take criticism without getting annoyed.

5. Sometimes Denzil can control his state of mind and avoid trouble, like the time he found a fiver on the floor and thought 'Wow, I can do a lot with that', but he turned round and walked away from temptation.

6. Denzil can think quickly and control situations that are moving fast and need control and care – like his free running.

Solutions

1. Denzil was quiet in class and got on with drawing the masks because he controlled his excited state of mind. He set himself a goal and got there by talking and laughing – but not too much – with a friend who can talk and work at the same time. He also concentrated a lot; he drew the word 'mask' four times to get it just right.

2. It's easy for Denzil to be polite to teachers because he is a polite person – only sometimes he forgets to be polite to teachers he doesn't like or respect.

3. He does responsibility mostly when he's interested and is controlling his state of mind. It's easy when he's not getting all excited and looking for a buzz.

4. Denzil can take criticism because he listens to people and takes what they are saying on board.

5. He controlled his state of mind when he saw the fiver by thinking that it would cause stress for his sister and get him into trouble. He controlled the excitement and felt good after he had walked away. He knew how to do this because he has worked out that it is no use taking advice on how to control his state of mind at stage two (when he's in the middle of it). It's more helpful to control it at stage one (when it's about to start). Then he can walk away or resolve the issue before it gets to stage two.

6. Denzil can do free running without getting hurt by planning three or four steps ahead and then using his energy and just going for it.

Tasks

1. Denzil will go to school with his mum and tell them most of his plan for handling his state of mind, getting on with his work, and his determination to do this (this is at eight and a half out of ten). His plan is use his skills in free running; he will plan three or four steps ahead and then just do it so that he can walk away from the excitement factor which he knows means he is at stage one of the state of mind that gets him into trouble.

2. He won't tell anyone about his plans for handling Miss B. She always shouts, never has a good word, and has a nasty attitude. He will be extra polite to her and this will probably really annoy her because she thinks that Denzil is an easy target for her bad temper.

3. Doing his plan for school will take a lot of energy so he will go more gradually at changing his attitude and behaviour at home. On Wednesdays (his hardest day) he will come home from school and do his jobs around the house. If he's late from school, he will do some jobs when he arrives and the others later. He will surprise his mum and sister by doing the hoovering, tidying, kitchen, whatever. They won't know what day he's going to be doing these things.

Subsequent sessions

These follow the same format as first sessions; see the flow diagram developed by Wilgosh *et al.* (1993). This diagram shows how progress, or the lack of it, is assessed in this approach and how changes, or the lack of them, are responded to. Where something is better, this is explored in detail, using the EARS process:

- Eliciting from the service user what exactly the changes are.
- Amplifying these changes by asking the service user what difference the changes made, who noticed the changes, what they saw that was different, and so on.
- Reinforcing the change by complimenting the service user.
- Starting again, discussing any further changes that are reported by the service user and how s/he can 'do more of the same'.

See Figure 8.1.

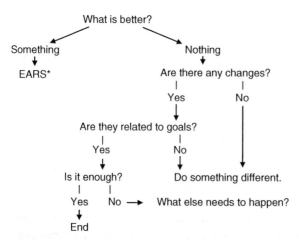

Figure 8.1 Flow diagram of the exploration of responses in solution-focused work (EARS: Elicit, Amplify, Reinforce and Start again)

Meeting agency requirements and service user needs

There are many situations where service user and social worker goals differ, especially where there is obvious vulnerability. For example, Hawkes *et al.* (2003) give examples of how people who have been diagnosed with mental illnesses, particularly psychosis, are routinely dismissed as not having the capacity to make rational decisions or choices, therefore becoming subjected to interventions that reduce opportunities for collaborative work. They give the example of someone hearing voices who has a goal of becoming the next England football manager, which may on the face of it seem part of a complex of irrational belief systems. Hawkes makes the point that this diagnosis is irrelevant to a great extent, as the steps needed to become the England manager require concrete actions about going to football training, taking his medication to assist him to worry less, and making his bed to get on better with his mother, all actions that are helpful for him generally and over which he can have some control.

Equally, practitioners may worry that a person's goal may be life-threatening; for example, someone with an eating difficulty may have a goal to lose even more weight, or a severely depressed person may be contemplating suicide. We discuss these particular problems in more detail in Chapter 11, but here we outline solution-focused practice principles which enable practitioners to work in partnership with families where one member's violent behaviour and goals potentially threatens the safety of more vulnerable family members.

A solution-focused safety approach

This approach accepts that risk assessment defies accurate quantification. Telling a person what they ought not to do consists of nothing more than the absence of something, and we can rarely be sure that an unwanted behaviour has ceased. Neither does it help a person who is violent, to work out how they will be when they are non-violent. Instead, a solution-focused safety approach emphasizes identifying existing indicators of safety, which are measurable; develops these indicators; and expands them so that a safe care plan can be put in place. The service user is helped to do this, but is held accountable for their behaviour in the future. Six safety practice principles developed by Turnell and Edwards (1999) are outlined below.

Understanding the position of each family member

Basically, this means accepting people who are violent as people worth doing business with. Jenkins (1996) comments that we treat those who are violent to others with considerable disrespect at the same time as we expect them to learn how to show respect to others. Practitioners working with people who are violent often operate from a position of self-righteousness, therefore the first step in building a partnership approach is to quell one's own 'inner tyrant' and seek to identify and understand the values, beliefs and meanings of the violent person as well as the victims'. This does not involve colluding with an offender's mitigating account of the violence; rather it means listening respectfully to accounts of perceived unfairness, encouraging them to explore the meaning of their behaviour to them and the underpinning beliefs. Cavanagh and Lewis (1996) found that this helps offenders to move beyond superficial responses. Respectfulness also involves not reframing people's concerns as poor motivation, denial, victim blaming or resistance to change. A central feature of solution-focused practice is seeking the person's unique way of cooperating. Listening carefully to their accounts of their lives avoids a sullen stand-off often initiated by confrontation.

Practitioners often have firm hypotheses about violence and its causes which make a person who has already been humiliated by the circumstances of arrest only too aware that the damage they have done is disproportionate to the satisfaction or tension release the violence provided in the first place and, worried about the consequences, feel even worse about themselves. For example, Scourfield (2003) discusses how social workers treat sex offenders within a rigid template, one that assumes recidivism and untreatability, but this is reading one's own hypothesis into another person's life story, one that ignores the complexity of violent behaviour: Kearney describes this as 'therapy's insufficient awareness of its own narrative process as it sought to unravel and negotiate an extremely sophisticated and unconscious web of history and story' (2002, p. 41). At the Barnardo's Junction (Rotherham) project for young people whose behaviour is sexually concerning or harmful, the young person is asked how they would like to be helped, what effect the problem has had on them, how things have changed for them since the problem came to light and so on, acknowledging them as people who have concerns about their own, as well as other people's, safety (Myers, 2005). It is much easier for a person to begin accepting responsibility for changing their behaviour in the future when they have been listened to and permitted to explore their own beliefs and meanings.

Ensuring that all family members are heard is crucial to this approach and, particularly where the family is remaining together, it is helpful to hear how others view the unwanted behaviour. This can allow for clarification for the violent person about the impact of their behaviour and begin the process of developing a measurable safety plan located with the people most involved in the day-to-day monitoring of change. Partners and children are encouraged to voice their understanding of the situation and to consider solutions and think about what is needed to support a change in behaviour.

Finding exceptions to the violence

The occasions when the person was frustrated and angry but was not violent are examined in great detail – when, where and how – so that these abilities can be used in other situations – 'Can you do this again?' Asking a person to tell you about a time when they could have been violent, but were not, helps a person who talks about being overwhelmed by violent feelings which 'just explode' to recognize that they do have some control over their behaviour. This control may not be directly linked to the violent context which led to the referral, and it may be a very small exception, but it can be used in solution-building (for a fully worked case example see Milner, 2008a).

Where exceptions exist and the person can recognize how they did them, they are developed by setting homework tasks that involve 'doing more of them'. Sometimes, exceptions are discounted as chance events ('I don't know, it just happened') or the result of other people's efforts ('If she doesn't wind me up, I don't get mad'), and then a prediction task is given. When a person gets a high proportion of their predictions correct about the days when they are going to be non-violent, they are asked if the exceptions are really spontaneous or do they have some control over their behaviour. This control is again analysed in great detail, so that they can increase their chances of 'doing it again'. Exceptions are the first signs of safety, although it is not always easy to confirm that they are present. While it is simple to check with other family members that physical violence has decreased, this confirmation is harder to come by when the victims are not known, or when a person is reporting exceptions to sexual urges. Here, a tangential approach is needed, checking for allied behaviours which are measurable – such as increased respectfulness to others, responsibility taking over a wide range of situations, truthfulness and so on. Where there is a total lack of exceptions, the person can be given a pretend homework task: pretending not to be angry or frustrated one half of the week and noticing what is different or what other people see is different. This helps to identify possible exceptions. *Where there are few indicators of safety, a higher level of dangerousness is apparent.*

Discovering strengths and resources that can be used in the problem situation

A focus on deficits discourages people; violent offenders are rarely told what they are doing well, so begin to believe that there is nothing good about themselves – especially when it is written down in psychopathological terms. This does not aid engagement in the therapeutic process as the person will resist hearing bad things about themselves or become depressed. Looking at existing strengths validates the totality of people's experiences, places current problems in context (few people are completely evil), and makes contact with professionals less threatening. More importantly, it helps the person develop a more competent self – it is easier to do more of something that is working than to stop doing something that is problematic.

It is not always easy to elicit strengths and resources. Solution-focused practitioners find that when they ask service users to detail the good things about themselves, they often reply that there aren't any (see, for example, Milner and Jessop, 2003). Where this happens, a series of prompts are needed, such as 'What would your mother say makes her proud of you?', 'Can you tell me about a time you were being caring?' or 'What is it about you that means you have been able to keep the same friends?' With young people a set of 'strengths' cards (http://www.stlukes.org.au) can be used to identify not only what strengths the child already has but also what strengths they would like to develop. Strengths in any area of life can be used, as all strengths and resources are transferable skills.

Focusing on the goals of all involved people to ensure the safety of those most vulnerable

The setting of goals is vital to the process of assessment as this enables clarity about the nature of the problem and what can be done about it. In solution-focused practice, goals must be measurable, achievable and ethical. It can be difficult for an offender to develop a realistic goal because other professionals may have predetermined goals. For example, Scourfield (2003) noted that social workers tended to expect women to separate from an abusing husband in the interests of the children's emotional wellbeing. As most women and children prefer for the violence to stop rather than the family to be split (Lipchik and Kubicki, 1996; Milner, 2004a), there are often conflicting goals which hinder the assessment process. Similarly children whose behaviour is sexually harmful pose particular problems for parents and foster-carers who have a duty of care and love to both the offender and the other children in the family (Milner, 2009).

Achievable, ethical goals are set through negotiation with all parties with an emphasis on the measurable safety of vulnerable people; for example, rather than setting a blanket goal of no violence, a more detailed one is developed around what *will* be happening differently after the violence has stopped. For example, what will the offender be doing differently that would make workers confident enough to close the case? A 'victim' is asked what he or she will notice differently about the offender when they feel safe; the offender is asked what they need to be doing differently to ensure the safety of others *and* their own safety from accusations. This latter is especially important in situations where sexual abuse is strongly suspected but denied. Essex (Essex *et al.*, 1996; Turnell and Essex, 2006) makes it the responsibility of the suspected offender to devise a safety plan that will ensure the dual safety demands. Thus, the emphasis is always on developing a goal that meets everyone's needs and is measurable – the signs of safety that are measurable.

The solution-focused practitioner is not surprised if the offender finds it difficult to describe a clear goal in the early stages, not least because they would not have been likely to resort to violence had they already possessed a well-developed repertoire of solutions. Lee *et al.* (2003) spend time helping people to develop goals as this offers choices and aids change. They suggest the following questions to clarify goal setting for men who are violent (p. 57):

- What would we see if you were going for your goal right here today?
- What might your wife notice that would be different when you are going for this goal?
- How might she respond to you going for this goal?
- How do you think it will be helpful to you?
- If this goal is helpful, how will you know?
- What do you think you might notice that you are doing differently?
- When will you do this?
- Can you do this now?

Goal-setting of this kind shifts practitioner responsibility for monitoring dangerousness and assessing risk on to the service user. For example, a sex offender may well undertake a variety of courses in prison (victim empathy, alcohol control and so on) and the probation officer may have put in place a number of monitoring devices in the community but, unless the offender can say what s/he will be doing differently when s/he is released from prison that will ensure the safety of others, and how this will be measured, then there are no indicators of safety. The goal of getting out of prison by being a model prisoner is not an ethical, measurable goal that involves the person in doing something differently to ensure the safety of others.

Scaling safety and progress

Professional risk estimation is often based on the *absence* of risk/danger, which makes quantification problematic, as it is difficult to say that because something is not happening it will not happen again. This drive to eliminate risk can lead to practice that does not address the local circumstances of the people involved, imposing professional answers that are not achievable and reducing the potential for safe partnership. Solution-focused practice avoids these dilemmas. Quite simply, the person who has been violent is asked how safe s/he rates other family members on a scale of 1 to 10 and their ratings are compared. Then they are asked what they need to do differently for everyone to feel safe. Other family members are given the opportunity to talk about their safety without the potentially violent person being present and provided with ways of communicating any unsafe feelings; for example by means of the provision of stamped, addressed 'help' postcards to alert a trusted professional about any concerns. With children a *helping hand* can be devised. The child is asked to draw round their hand and write the names of people they trust on each digit so that they know who they can talk with about anything that is worrying them (for more details see Myers and Milner, 2007). All parties – family and professionals – are asked for evidence of any changes. In cases where safety is impossible to imagine then more direct preventative action will have to be taken, but this process aids clarity of decision-making for the family.

Using scales makes it possible for people to acknowledge when they are not making sufficient progress without making them feel like complete failures. The range of points on a scale means that they are rarely condemned and recognizes their aspirations to 'do better'. The scales can be constructed in such a way as to make it easier for families to discuss what they need to be doing differently even when the subject is emotionally charged. For example, in instances of child abuse, a mother can be asked to rate her mothering ability on a scale of 1 to 10, with 1 being Rosemary West and 10 being Mother Teresa (the role models differ depending on current dominant images). When the scale is so wide, the person can readily locate themselves at some point. Where this point is doesn't matter at all as long as what needs to be done differently to move up the scale is identified. For example, 'You rate your parenting at 5 but I rate it at 2. What do you think you will be doing differently when we can agree?' In complex situations where an offender is separated from partner and children and the courts are involved, questions can be asked such as: 'When you are asking the judge for contact with your children, what will you say that will convince him/her that your child is safe with you?' Again, this places the responsibility for developing a safety plan, and putting it into effect, on the person whose violence led to safety concerns in the first place.

Assessing willingness, confidence and capacity to change

Although it is important for offenders to take responsibility for their behaviour in the future, Turnell and Edwards (1999) make the point that practitioners have a responsibility for setting the scene so that motivation can be improved. Adversarial relationships with professionals reduce the possibility of this, causing unnecessary frustration and increasing feelings of powerlessness at the same time as the offender is expected to exercise self-control. Willingness to change can be increased by assessing whether the person needs help with motivation or ability to change. This is done by creating separate scales for each of the behaviours: for example, 'If 1 means you can't be bothered and 10 means you will do anything it takes, where are you on this scale?' And 'If 1 means you have no confidence in your ability to change and 10 means you have complete confidence, where are you on this scale?' The lower of the two scores becomes the focus of the work; that is, 'What will you be doing differently when you are one point higher?' It is also important to ask, 'If 1 means you haven't a clue about what to do differently and 10 means you know exactly what to do to change, where are you on this scale?' People may be well motivated to change their behaviour, but lack the knowledge or confidence to make the necessary changes so solution-focused practitioners assume nothing, asking questions to which they genuinely don't know the answer and are keen to discover so that they can remain flexible and creative to opportunities for change.

Implications of a solution-focused safety approach for assessment

As the emphasis is on assessing whether there are sufficient, measurable indicators of safety, the social worker has to be very clear exactly what behaviours need to be demonstrated and evidenced for the family to be allowed to remain together or the child/ren to be rehabilitated. This is not easy when the social worker has concentrated on identifying risk factors, as these are often vague. Thus the social worker has to have a clear idea about what constitutes wellbeing and safety as well as risk. As noted above, this is especially difficult to determine in cases of sexual abuse and/or when child abuse is strongly suspected but denied. The assessment of young people with sexually problematic behaviour is detailed more fully in Myers and Milner (2007) and adult 'deniers' in Turnell and Essex (2006), but the way in which concerns are clarified and requirements spelled out is illustrated in the following example of an initial safety plan for a man who is separated from his partner but there are concerns that his previous violence and substance misuse may impact on his ability to provide a safe environment for his children.

Initial safety plan for Dale, Bradley (7 years) and Kaiden (4 years).

Concerns

1. Dale has a history of hitting people when frustrated and/or under the influence of drink/drugs.
2. Bradley and Kaiden have witnessed dad and mum fighting. On one occasion, Bradley remembers seeing mum lying in a pool of blood.
3. Dale doesn't recognize that Bradley's disruptive behaviour at school may reflect Dale's behaviour at home.
4. Both children have shown fear of Dale at times.
5. He isn't always honest with social services, so they doubt his assurances that his relationship with Sharon is truly over.
6. He can become frustrated when meeting with social services and they tend to visit him in twos for their own safety and so that things do not blow up in front of the children.
7. He has been disrespectful to the female social worker.
8. He has been drunk when collecting the children from school.

Goals

1. Dale wants the children to live with him and Social Care out of his life.
2. The children want their parents to live together without arguing and fighting. Alternatively, they want some form of contact with their mum.
3. Social services want Dale to be able to work in partnership with them so that they feel confident about his care of the children. When he is doing this he will:
   - be sober when with the children;
   - extend his parenting skills so that he can find ways of handling any difficulties the children present in a way that ensures they are not fearful;
   - control his temper so that he is not angry in front of the children;
   - encourage the children to speak openly about any worries they have;
   - talk quietly, calmly and respectfully with social services;
   - accept that he may make mistakes and be able to own up to these and learn from them;
   - be honest and open with social services, recognizing that openness about difficulties will not necessarily mean that the children will be removed. Rather, they are difficulties to be resolved, and
   - be respectful to women.

Social services will be confident to close the case when:

1. Dale's practical care of the children continues to be of a high standard.

2. He understands the children's emotional needs, can control his anger and be a good role model for the children.

3. He demonstrates over time that his separation from Sharon is complete so that contact between mum and the children can take place without the need for social services' supervision. (Alternatively, should the parents wish to live together again, they can accept that the children will need to be removed while they undertake work on developing more peaceful ways of being together.).

4. Dale is respectful of women and this is reflected in how Bradley treats women teachers at school.

Current indicators of safety

1. Dale's practical parenting skills are good.

2. When he is calm, the children are able to go to him for comfort and affection and Dale is appropriately responsive towards them.

3. Bradley's behaviour at school has shown some improvement.

Time scale

Dale will have up to 4 months to work with his counsellor to demonstrate that he can meet these goals, progress to be reviewed 6-weekly.

Critical comment

Although we argue that the solution-focused approach is intrinsically anti-oppressive because of its central emphasis on empowerment, respectful uncertainty and minimum intervention, feminists have argued that the emphasis on competence and strengths tends to overlook gender and power differences (Dermer *et al.*, 1998). Gender differences are discussed by several solution-focused writers/practitioners (see for example Letham 1994; Berg and Reuss, 1998; Dolan, 1998; Milner, 2001); the main implication is that tracking the service user's language does run the risk of ignoring the reality that much language is constructed by men and may not always allow for a full understanding of women's experience.

There have also been criticisms that there is a danger of being solution-*forced* rather than solution-focused (O'Connell, 2001). Similarly, Darmody *et al.* (2002, p. 18) warn that 'Many novice therapists, in their desire to be solution focused, may rush straight ahead to goals and solution building without having first listened to or connected with their clients.' To seek solutions relentlessly when someone is expressing grief or pain at events that have severely impacted on their emotional wellbeing is not helpful in developing a cooperative relationship, but nonetheless the validation can be expressed in such a way as to sow the seeds of exceptions, agency and change.

Because the approach involves a complete change of emphasis from those traditionally used by social workers there is a danger that the technique might be too hastily applied or used inappropriately or uncritically, neglecting the philosophical basis. It is essential for social workers hoping to employ the approach, to get into the habit of reframing situations and listening carefully to service users. Although the approach creates a good flow to the work, it still requires careful analysis. Using it well is not as easy as it sounds. The notion of understanding a solution without understanding the problem could be misread for finding a solution before knowing anything about a problem. If this latter reading were taken out of context, it could result in muddled work in which people are not sure what they are doing or why they are doing it. Properly understood, however, solution-focused theory is not saying this. The problem is not ignored, but it is not necessarily deconstructed in the traditional way. However, courts and agencies, long accustomed to traditional assessments based on theories of pathology, will take some time to get used to this way of thinking.

Outcomes

Solution-focused approaches have been evaluated more extensively than problem-based approaches – there being over forty outcome studies that demonstrate the effectiveness of this approach. The European Brief Therapy Association publishes a full list on the internet (www.ebta.nu/news.htlm). These studies show that the effects are not only as good as or better than any other known method, but they are longer lasting. An interesting aspect of these studies is that they show no difference according to service user group, ethnicity, age or gender. The approach has been shown to work equally well with anorexia, violence, drug abuse and mental health problems, regardless of learning ability. In one of de Shazer's studies (1991), when clients were followed up again 18 months after completion, their reported success rate was up from 80.4 per cent to 84 per cent after an average of 4.6 sessions. In another study, the success rate at 6 months was 80 per cent, at 12 months 81.5 per cent; at 18 months 86 per cent. It seems that when people realize that they have personal agency and can change their lives, they go on making things better. These studies were based on service users' evaluations of whether they had reached their goal.

SUMMARY

Iveson (2002) sums up this approach as follows:

■ Solution-focused work is an exploration not of present problems or past causes, but of current resources and future hopes. Assessment therefore focuses on:

  – What is the service user hoping to achieve?

  – What will be the details of the desired life after the problem?

  – What is s/he already doing that might contribute to this?

■ Here the worker moves from eliciting exceptions to discuss what the person is already doing that is helpful.

   – What will be different when they take one small step in that direction?

■ The process is shown schematically in Figure 8.2.

Figure 8.2 Schematic summary of solution-focused work (adapted from Iveson, 2002)

Jackson and McKergow (2002, p. 7) provide a useful summary of the differences between a problem-focused and a solution-focused approach (Table 8.1).

Table 8.1 Differences between problem-focused and solution-focused approaches

Problem focus	Solution focus
The past	The future
What's wrong	What's working
Blame	Progress
Control	Influence
The expert knows best	Collaboration
Deficits	Resources
Complications	Simplicity
Definitions	Actions

O'Connell (1998, p. 21) provides an excellent outline of solution-focused theory and practice in counselling, providing a helpful comparison of the sort of questions and conversations that arise from the above differences (Table 8.2).

Table 8.2 Typical questions asked in problem-focused and solution-focused counselling

Problem-focused questions	Solution-focused questions
How can I help you?	How will you know when therapy has been successful?
Could you tell me about the problem?	What would you like to change?
Is the problem a symptom of something deeper?	Have we clarified the central issue on which you want to concentrate?
Can you tell me more about the problem?	Can we discover exceptions to the problem?
How are we to understand the problem in the light of the past?	What will the future look like without the problem?
How many sessions will be needed?	Have we achieved enough to end?

FURTHER LEARNING ACTIVITIES

- Think of a conversation you had with someone that had a positive outcome for the other person.
- How did you both agree about the nature of the problem?
- How clear were you with them about your perception of the problem?
- How did you both agree about what should be done?
- In retrospect, could you have helped the person come to a solution more quickly? If so, how?

FURTHER READING

Milner, J. (2001) *Women and Social Work. Narrative Approaches*. Basingstoke: Palgrave Macmillan.
Parton, N. and O'Byrne. (2000) *Constructive Social Work*. Basingstoke: Palgrave Macmillan.
Myers, J. (2007) *Theory into Practice: Solution Focused Approaches*. Lyme Regis; Russell House.

NATIONAL OCCUPATIONAL STANDARDS

For students working with the British National Occupational Standards for Social Work (see Appendix):

- This chapter relates to the following *practice* elements 1.1, 5.1, 11.1–4, 18.1–3.
- With which of the *knowledge* requirements does this chapter help you?

CHAPTER 9

A Forecast Map: Narrative Approaches

What this chapter is about

This chapter presents the second of the theoretical maps belonging to the 'third wave' of social work practice; like the previous chapter it is more interested in service users' futures than pasts, in potential rather than pathology. As the term narrative implies, the approach provides options for the telling and retelling of service users' stories of their lives (developing alternative stories), but the term has been developed further than the storytelling involved in psychodynamic or cognitive-behavioural approaches. Narrative approaches share the solution-focused notion that there are no fixed truths but, additionally, emphasize that some 'truths' have more weight than others. Hence the intention of narrative assessments to take into consideration the 'climate' of social work, addressing power issues explicitly through the deconstruction of dominant cultural stories which have the capacity to marginalise and oppress service users. Building on the service user's own metaphors, it develops a 'forecast' that adds in all those 'sunny spells' that often are edited out when problem stories are told or written, without ignoring the 'highs' and 'lows' of oppression by powerful narratives.

MAIN POINTS

➤ Wider theoretical perspectives: narrative theory.

➤ Implications for assessment.

➤ Practice techniques: externalizing the problem, externalizing the internalised narrative, thickening the counter-plot, evaluating the interview, and narrative feedback.

➤ Meeting agency requirements and service user needs.

➤ Critical comments on the conceptual nature of this approach and comparisons with the solution-focused approach.

➤ Outcomes of this approach as compared with Cognitive-behavioural approaches, and on the benefits of the emphasis on externalizing oppressions.

Wider theoretical perspectives

A narrative approach challenges people's beliefs that a problem speaks their identity; instead of a totaling effect which conflates the person with the problem, such an approach seeks to separate the person and the problem, and develop a sense of incongruity between the two that opens up new possibilities for responsibility-taking and accountability. Traditional psychotherapeutic concepts are reconstructed in narrative approaches: interpretation is how service users can make meaning of their lives rather than be entered into stories by others; and resistance is the way in which they can resist the influence of the problem on their lives.

Narrative theory

The approach was developed mainly in Australasia by White (1993, 1995, 1996; White and Epston, 1990; Epston, 1998). It is more political, cultural and social than other approaches, being based on the sociology of the post-modernist Foucault (1972, 1973, 1980, 1988) and the sociolinguist Halliday (1978) concerning the oppressive effects of dominant narratives on people's understanding of the validity of their ways of living. White (1995) argues that there isn't a single story of life which is free of ambiguity and contradiction and that can handle all the contingencies of life. These ambiguities, contradictions and contingencies stretch our meaning-making resources; especially when there are dominant cultural stories about particular sorts of behaviour. These stories tend to concentrate on identifying the behaviours seen as desirable by the most powerful groups of people, thus people whose behaviour does not conform to this become storied as deficient in some way. White refers to this as being entered into a story, a story which people come to believe about themselves:

> [T]hese stories or narratives form the matrix of concepts and beliefs by which we understand our lives, and the world in which our lives take place; and there is a continuing interaction between the stories we tell ourselves about our lives, the ways we live our lives, and the future stories we then tell. (Payne, Mn. 2006, p. 20)

Whereas solution-focused assessments search for exceptions to problems and, therefore, concentrate on problem-free talk, in narrative assessments the problem is first deconstructed. This takes the form of searching for *unique outcomes* or *sparkling moments* (Bird, 2000) – times when the service user actively resisted the influence of the problem, a contradiction to the dominant story, or plot in Epston's terms (1998, p.11). Deconstructing the problem is done by reflecting with service users how they came to be recruited into a *problem-saturated story*. This includes discussing that story in a way that separates the problem from the person, developing a sense of alienation between the person and the problem. This *externalizing* conversation is helped by giving the problem a name of its own and by asking questions that establish the influence of the problem on the person, and their influence on it. This can be seen as discussing the *person's relationship with the problem*.

CASE EXAMPLE

Following the discovery that 6-year-old Liam had been sexually abused by his father and a number of male relatives, he is fostered with Sylvia and Dave. He has settled well in his foster home but is exhibiting sexualized behaviour at school: touching girls and boys, exposing his private parts, and going into the girls' toilet. He also messes about in lessons. He was reluctant to discuss his behaviour until it was talked about as the *touching problem* (Myers et al., 2003). He says that the *touching problem* happens mostly at school; he doesn't do it as much at home. He can desist at home because Sylvia says 'Don't do that' in a nice way and he doesn't think about it much because he is always busy. Liam can listen to Sylvia most of the time (although he sometimes ignores her), and this works. Sylvia has also talked with his teachers and since his move up a form with a new teacher, he has been provided with more structure at school too.

Using Liam's abilities, it is suggested that because he can listen to Sylvia, maybe he can do more listening to his teacher and get on with his work.

Also Liam's ignoring could be put to use – he can ignore the *touching problem* when it tells him to do things. Liam knows how to do ignoring – he puts his fingers in his ears.

White (1996) states very clearly that while the alternative narrative offered may be seen as part of radical constructionism he does not accept that 'anything goes' simply by giving it a new name. Because narrative is constitutive of people's lives, shaping and structuring them, we must be accountable to those we seek to assess or help. Not all stories are equally good in their effects. And not only do service users enter themselves into stories but so do social workers; consider, for example, stories about women as powerless victims of domestic violence (Augusta-Scott, 2007), and men who sexually abuse as inherently recidivist (Scourfield, 2003). Payne, Mn. (2006) discusses the implications for social workers of deconstructing their own stories. While he acknowledges that racism and patriarchy are cultural beliefs rejected by most social workers, he reminds us of the need for constant vigilance against the more subtle manifestations of these stories; for example, the way sexism may be demonstrated through verbal tone and the dominance of conversations. This is particularly problematic for male social workers as they live in a culture in which such attitudes are embedded; for example, a man attending our domestic violence programme told us that his male probation officer cut across his telling of his marital difficulties by challenging his use of the term 'bird' to describe his partner: 'Listen to you! "Bird"!'. No doubt the probation officer believed that he was challenging the service user's sexism but, at the same time, he was demonstrating his own capacity for oppression. Jenkins (1996) refers to this as the danger of acting from a position of self-righteousness and moral superiority. In narrative assessments, therefore, critical self-monitoring and regular checking out with other people is essential (as we discussed more fully in Chapter 3).

There is a fine line between responsible assessment and intervention and therapeutic abuse, says Jenkins:

> I work hard at establishing a context for a client to own his own 'discoveries' and do not see myself as the architect of his new thinking and behaviour. Yet, all the same time, I am acting strategically and intervening towards this end. Is this really self-enhancement? (1996, p. 129)

He advises being mindful at all times of the risk of insensitively pursuing our own agendas at the expense of service user experience, and this is particularly complicated where social workers are impelled by agency-led assessment requirements. Payne, Mn. (2006) also addresses the ethics of externalization, concluding that the process is transparent as the service user can hear exactly what the worker is saying. Nevertheless, in deconstructing and reconstructing stories, social workers need to be aware that the choice of questions asked is influential on the way the assessment is focused, and that differences in values, beliefs and meanings between the service user and the social worker require explicit attention (Milner, 2001).

Implications for assessments

The service user, having been invited to explore the effects of the problem – for example, 'It causes arguments,' or 'It means I might lose my kids," – is then asked if that is something they want in their life or not (an evaluation of the problem or their relationship with it). If they do not want it, they are asked to justify that evaluation by explaining, for example, reasons for not wanting it, and what that says about them as people. In this way they make a decision to start reclaiming their life from the influence of the problem and this clearly makes for a promising assessment. Then questions are asked to elicit unique outcomes, and aid goal-setting, such as:

- How did the problem seduce you into thinking that way, or going along with it?
- What influences led to your enslavement by the problem?
- What prevented you from resisting it? What were the restraints?
- Does it really suit you to be dominated by it?
- What effect or influence does the problem have on your life, or on those close to you, on your relationships, on your self-image?
- What effect do you have on the life of the problem?
- Given a choice between life with the problem and life free of the problem, which do you choose?
- (When the problem has been named), tell me about the times you made Anxiety wait. How long has Conflict been making your life miserable? Tell me about a time you didn't fall for the story Anorexia has been telling you?

- (When there are unique outcomes), what are the implications for the sort of person you are when you refuse to cooperate with the problem's invitations?
- What does it say about your ability to undermine the problem?

Note that these last two questions are reflecting on the qualities of the person rather than on their actions. White refers to this as adding to the *landscape of consciousness/identity*, enriching a possible alternative story through a *language of action*. The language is the language of resistance and liberation and it is used to understand how the service user submitted to the problem's ways and how these ways are not liberating, or not ideally suited to the service user's preferred way of living. This involves looking back at the past to some extent, before going on to becoming future- and solution-focused, but it is not a blaming look at the past or a search for deficits. It is empowering in that it develops a sense of the service user being intrinsically okay, as *not being* the problem, but as being oppressed by it and sometimes giving in to it. Thus the explanation that is developed is not one that seeks the cause of the problem in the person but one that seeks to understand how this, basically okay, person became ensnared by the problem's invitations.

Substance misuse is an obvious example here. Narrative approaches query the addict story, with its accompanying 'Just Say No' story. Instead, they seek to acknowledge the substance misuser's social knowledge, hard-won wisdom and harm-reduction strategies (see for example Sanders, 2007). As Couzens (1999) points out, how to talk about substances needs thoughtfulness:

> There's often this concept that everything about drugs and alcohol is negative. It's pretty hard to have an interesting conversation if everything is negative! I mean obviously drugs and alcohol are negative for the body, but there are some positive things to talk about too especially in relation to the stands people have made in relation to alcohol and other drugs, and about how people can care for one another. (Couzens, 1999, p. 26)

Narrative questions for substance misusers would include:

- Is [the substance] for you or against you?
- How did [the substance] con you into thinking this way, going along with the story?
- What influence does [the substance] have on your life, on those close to you, on your relationships, self image?
- Given a choice of life with [the substance] or a life free of it, which would you choose?
- Does it suit you to be dominated by [the substance]?
- Tell me about the times you made [the substance] wait.
- What are the implications for the sort of person you are when you refuse to cooperate with [the substance's] invitations?
- What does it say about your ability to undermine [the substance]?

- In the times you have felt in control of [the substance], what are the things that helped you have that control?
- Tell me about a time when [the substance] didn't stop you being in touch with your hopes and dreams?

Frequently, part of that enslavement is caused by societal attitudes, such as attitudes that suggest that the consumption of alcohol is socially necessary or that women should be the main carers in families. More accurately, people are *restrained* in these ways from resisting the problem or from taking responsibility in various ways. A narrative style, storying the separate lives of the person and the problem, encourages a sense of ownership of one's life; a sense that the service user and social worker can co-author a future story, breaking away from the performance of the past unhelpful story and thus experiencing the capacity to create change. New narratives yield a new vocabulary and construct a new meaning, new possibilities and new self-agency. White (1996) has found that more service users than expected are able to re-author their lives and we cannot assess their capabilities to do so until we afford them the opportunities created by narrative promptings.

Practice techniques

Narrative approaches to assessment are fluid and wide-ranging. The service users' alternative stories are developed via the techniques of *externalizing the problem, externalizing internalized narratives* which support dominant stories or plots about the problem, *thickening the counterplot* to strengthen the alternative story, *evaluating the interview*, and the provision of *narrative feedback*. As all these techniques reveal and increase unique outcomes, they are not necessarily used sequentially.

Externalising

Central to externalizing is remembering how people have come to believe that they are the problem; so separating the two via externalizing conversations is an effective way of identifying unique outcomes (White and Epston, 1990, p. 95). These unique outcomes include not only when the service user actively resisted the influence of the problem but also ways in which they subverted it, endured it, or delayed its effects. In order to encourage a service user to have a different relationship with both the problem and the narrative that supports it, early on in the assessment, the problem is spoken of as an external enemy oppressing the person. This aids the non-pathologizing of the service user; it is the problem that is the problem. Externalizing conversations help the service user to stand back from the problem and recover a sense of self-agency as they separate themselves from their own subjugation and begin to resist the influences that recruited them or that invited the problem into their lives.

To aid separation of person and problem it helps to give the problem a name as soon as possible, using the service user's own narrative metaphors. Often the service user can suggest a richly descriptive name for the problem; for example, we have experienced 'temper' named as Total Upset, Fiery Red Bomb, Black Cloud, and Raging Bull. Equally common is a more anonymous naming, such as 'It'. In naming the problem, service users then find it easier to describe the influence of the problem on their lives.

> ### CASE EXAMPLE
>
> Zaffir was so crippled with anxiety following an unprovoked assault on the street that he was unable to go to school. The assessing social worker's initial name for the problem was thus 'anxious non-school attendance' or 'school phobia'. Zaffir talked at length about his anxieties about the possibility of a further assault but, once he had named these anxieties as *Sad Fear*, he was able to recognize the influence of *Sad Fear* on all aspects of his life. It was making him tearful, stopping him eating or keeping himself smart, and ruining his hopes of getting an education. He did not want to keep *Sad Fear* in his life and the one unique outcome he could identify was when he had 'talked back' to a voice in his head that told him to be 'more scared'. Through this externalizing conversation he was able to extend his unique outcomes by telling the voice to go away if it couldn't come up with something new to say or swear at it in Punjabi. Thus there was no need to assess possible depths of anxiety or relabel him as suffering from post-traumatic stress disorder.

Externalizing conversations are particularly useful in the assessment of service users who hear voices. Instead of assessing for the possible presence of auditory hallucinations or delusions, the social worker interrogates 'voices' as unhelpful beliefs which can be resisted or subverted. For example, Jacob (2001, p. 70) provides a set of cartoons depicting 'Monster Bashing Methods' for thoughts and beliefs underpinning eating difficulties. White (1995) suggests that it is helpful to question the purposes and motives of the 'voices':

- Are these voices for you having an opinion or are they against you?
- These voices throw you into confusion. Whose interests are best served by this confusion?
- What is it like for the voices to have to listen to your thoughts for a change?
- (And later), what is it like for them to know that you are developing a disrespect and mistrust of them?'

For a more comprehensive questionnaire on 'voices' see Romme and Escher (2000).

Thus a narrative approach is very different from traditional approaches to the assessment of mental health states; not only are the 'voices' questioned but so also are the effects of psychiatric labelling. Mikey da Valda of the Hearing Voices Group in Manchester (2003) talks about the way in which a label offers a new identity, one which can be soul-destroying because friends and family treat a person differently; and which can be dangerous as it becomes an excuse for not having any control over one's life or actions:

> I am particularly interested in how issues of class influence mental health. I believe that working class people are especially at risk in the interactions with mental health professionals. If you approach a psychiatric service without a given amount of knowledge and education you are incredibly vulnerable. In my experience, working class people are a little more likely to accept their label and live it, act it out and become the schizophrenic they are told they are.
>
> If you consider the plight of the sub-working class voice hearers, the risk is more extreme. Those within prisons for instance, who ask for the help of a psychiatrist, are almost always drug users and with histories of trauma. They seem almost guaranteed to acquire a psychiatric label before too long. Initially I thought this was true for me. But about a year ago, I went back to a local prison to facilitate a group for people who are designated as having psychiatric problems and hearing voices. Out of a dozen lads, there were a dozen paranoid schizophrenic labels ... They had been discovering that their minds were now habituated to hallucination. They now have vivid dreams and experiences that are akin to drug use but without taking any substances. While they have been told this meant that they are now paranoid schizophrenics, actually this is not the only explanation. These bizarre experiences can be fantasies, they do not have to be connected to delusions or what is known as schizophrenia. Nobody explains to working class lads in general, even outside of the jails, the different things that can happen in our minds. (da Valda, 2003)

Externalizing conversations thus aid the development of alternative stories and encourage the service user to take action against the problem. They emphasize context, deconstruct the objectification of people, and challenge dominant stories through which 'disorders' and 'pathologies' are constructed; what Epston refers to as 'spy-chiatric gaze' (1998, p. 127). Externalizing conversations invite people to take up a position towards the problem and consider whether they want to continue living with it. In the case of violent or other oppressive behaviour on the part of a service user, accountability is not minimized; instead the beliefs and attitudes supporting the violence are externalized, *externalizing the internalised story*, enabling other ways of responding to situations to be discovered. Here the work of Jenkins (1990, 1996) is particularly useful. He suggests that much male violence is supported by dominant stories about 'being a man' in which the need to 'be someone' is exaggerated and extreme. He invites men to take responsibility for their behaviour by asking questions which externalize this internalised story, the 'blueprint' of their marriage. The man is invited to externalize patriarchal restraints and consider their influence in his life and the extent to which he has slavishly and blindly followed a set of oppressive and unhelpful beliefs:

- If a man takes this recipe on board, what sort of marriage is he going to be building?
- Is he going to want his wife to be her own person with her own ideas or his person with his ideas?

- Is she likely to respect him more if he tries to get her to be his person or if he allows her to be her own person?
- If she was just doing what she is told, would she be more likely to give out of love and desire or out of duty? (Jenkins, 1990, p. 82).

CASE EXAMPLE

Stephen explained his hitting of his wife as a result of his frustration with her unfair treatment of their 3-year-old child. An argument would start between the adults when he came home tired from work and his wife would vent her frustration on the child. Stephen was extremely critical of her mothering, about which he had a clear set of beliefs – a dominant story about nurturing motherhood under all circumstances. When asked about his blueprint for being a husband and father, he said that it varied, depending on what he had seen on television. Sometimes he saw himself as a 'lad' and sometimes as a caring parent. As stories about how to do being a father are not well developed in our society, he had only internalized the mothering half of his family story, supported by a dominant cultural story that said it was okay for men to tell women what to do.

For more narrative questions in response to 'excuses' for violent behaviour see Augusta-Scott (2007).

It matters little what sort of blueprint people develop for living in their marriages as long as this story works equally well for both partners. Narrative questioning does not aim to push a particular story or suggest that a person is thinking distortedly; it aims only to assist a person to tell a different, more useful story. Externalizing the internalized story also differs from the insight-giving of psychodynamic approaches in that ways of interacting with others are not revealed as maladaptive attachment patterns. This is only another (psychological) story; one that has become embedded in contemporary stories about commitment and 'being there' for friends. We find that many young women have internalized this story and then struggle with friendships which do not meet their expectations. They tell us that they think there is something wrong with themselves but, rather than assess them for deficiencies in intimacy, we ask them questions about their story of friendship:

- What is the most important thing you get from your friends? Support when you are troubled? Having a laugh? Someone to go out with?
- Can all your friends do all these things?
- Can a person expect the same level of commitment from all their friends?
- Which friends are you closest to?
- What is the difference between your supportive and unsupportive friends?
- Are some of your friends emotionally supportive and others social friends?
- Perhaps there are different sorts of friends – silver, gold and platinum?

Similarly with women service users particularly, and many social workers, we question stories about the all-nurturing nature of mothering ('failure to protect', 'putting her needs before those of the children'):

- Who comes first in your family? Second? Third? (And so on.)
- Does it feel comfortable always to be at the bottom?
- How can you put yourself a little higher without being selfish?
- What support do you have?
- Are your expectations of your mothering reasonable? Attainable?
- How much responsibility can a mother take for her family's behaviour?

Another totaling and restricting story we frequently interrogate is the story of 'low self-esteem'; one which is popular with both social workers and service users.

> ### CASE EXAMPLE
>
> Despite Suzie being affected at birth with mild cerebral palsy, and then being rejected by her family after she disclosed her sexual abuse by a close relative, she managed to live independently as long as she had intensive support. Every time she appeared to be coping well and that support was reduced, she reverted to cutting her arms. A reassessment then focused on externalizing the internalized story which told her she could not function without intensive support. She had entered herself into several contradictory stories: her story of sexual abuse told her that she was worthless; her story of support provided her with feelings of self-esteem but that she needed to work through her experiences of sexual abuse; and her disability story told her that she was a worthless cripple. Cutting herself was her form of resistance to feelings of worthlessness. So the disability story was interrogated, questions focusing on 'where she belonged' – using her words. This enabled her to develop an alternative story of her life, one in which she could mix with other adults who had the capacity to make her feel good about herself.

It may be worth mentioning here that in child protection work this approach turns Finkelhor's theory upside down (Trepper and Barrett, 1986). For Finkelhor, abuse happens when a perpetrator breaks through the 'blocks' of internal inhibitors, external inhibitors and child resistance. Therefore, it is suggested that work needs to *strengthen* these blocks in order to prevent further abuse. The perpetrator has some deficit that makes an abuse of power possible and that makes stronger blocks necessary (deficits may be such as to limit responsibility). In the narrative approach, however, the perpetrator is presumed to have started life 'okay' but his/her capacity for caring became *inhibited* by various factors that *restrained* caring and *invited* inappropriate self-indulgence. The person is not 'damaged' and is held fully responsible for accepting the invitation. Therefore, the worker's task is to *weaken* these invitations and restraints, to undermine them and to expose their lies, excuses, methods and thus their influence, so that caring is no longer inhibited and signs of safety can be built up.

Thickening the counter-plot

Although 'thin' descriptions of life (that edit out unique outcomes in the old plot) often arise from a person having been subject to 'expert' diagnoses and commentaries, and 'thick' descriptions are elicited by examining the service user's actuality and complexity of life (for a fuller discussion see Payne, Mn., 2006, pp. 30–1), a problem-saturated story has mass and considerable evidence to support its momentum:

> Problematic stories have an advantage. They've been around for a while. Their plot is thick [thick with deficits; thin on strengths]. Like a snowball, they have packed together certain incidents and episodes in the family's life, finally freezing them into a solid mass. The once innocent snowball becomes a force with which every-one has to reckon. These problem-saturated stories can become very pervasive. The trouble is that their effects are negative and discouraging. (Freeman *et al.*, 1997, pp. 94–5, our parenthesis)

Thus the alternative story, the counterplot, needs strengthening. Juxtaposing the plot and counterplot thins the plot and thickens the counterplot, and this is done in assessment by specific questioning:

- What kind of alternative story would be required if the service user/family/ social worker were to tell another version at odds with the problem's story?
- How might the service user/family/social worker look and act in an alternative story different from the way the problem's story told them to look and act?
- How might the anomalies, irregularities and strangenesses that lie outside the predictive reach of the problem's story be considered meaningful events in the life of the service user and powerful antidotes to the problem?

An additional way to thicken the counterplot when there is no-one in the service user's life to tell the new story to, is to use narrative metaphors which emerge in externalising conversations. These can be more complex than the simple 'naming' of the problem; for example, Pete had no particular name for his problem with temper and frustration, although he knew that these were worse when he had been drinking heavily. Paradoxically, his unique outcomes occurred when he was responsible for controlling temper and frustration fuelled by drink in others: when he worked as a nightclub bouncer and as a barman he could 'see things from the other side' and be different. 'Turning to the other side' emerged as a metaphor which strengthened his counterplot, enabling him to incorporate this more fully into his life; for example, he literally turned over in bed when he wanted to switch from sad thoughts, about all the losses he had incurred as a result of his temper outbursts, to a 'happy side' when he wanted to explore the possibilities for his future life.

Also aiding thickening of the counterplot is asking the service user's permission to broadcast the news. This could take the form of developing *communities of concern*, but the main intention is to thicken the emerging alternative story by asking the service user what advice they would give to people with problems similar to their own. Thus they have to explain how they overcame the problem, and how they spotted its sneaky ways of setting up the service user for slipback.

CASE STUDY: THEORY INTO PRACTICE

Although Geoff feels that he is not likely to harm a child after having counselling for his childhood experiences of physical abuse, successfully completing an anger management course, and stopping using cocaine, he told his social worker that his previous counsellor had told him that it would take a long time for him to come to terms with the pain of his previous experiences of physical abuse. He is being assessed for his dangerousness towards his partner (he has hit her several times) and his child (as a teenager he sexually abused his sister). This psychological story is not only unhelpful in that it provides him with an excuse for his behaviour: it also maintains him as a victim of circumstances, thus limiting his ability and willingness to take responsibility for his behaviour.

- What questions could you ask him that would externalize this internalized story and thicken the counter-plot?

Evaluating the interview

Evaluation is carried out at various points in the interview to check that the assessment is collaborative and that partnership is developing. Evaluative questions would include:

- How is this conversation going for you?
- Should we keep talking about this or …?
- Is this interesting to you? Is this what we should be spending time on?
- What would we be talking about if I was being more helpful?

And, at the end of the interview:

- How helpful has this interview been for you?
- What would I have been doing if I had been more helpful?

Narrative feedback differs from the more usual formal social work assessments where the social worker gives the service user a copy of the completed assessment report. These reports can distance the social worker from the service user when the former becomes the expert author of the latter's life. White and Epston (1990) argue that such an author has a 'library of terms and descriptions that have been invented by and considered the property of this particular domain of knowledge' (p. 188). This 'expert' knowledge, combined with the invisibility of the author, creates the impression of the possession of an objective and detached point of view that does not actually exist; one that bolsters a view of the social worker as benevolent expert, with the moral assumptions implicit in their specialized narrative hidden by their construction of the subject. Permitting the service user to read such an assessment report does not allow them the scope to do more than disagree with factual errors; the meaning-making (interpretation) being the social worker's.

Narrative approaches challenge this view of recording by providing the service user with regular written feedback which uses their own words and explanations: what Epston (1998) considers to be the work of a conscientious scribe, 'who faithfully notes down the proceedings for posterity and makes available a client's history, capturing on paper the particular thoughts and understandings with which they make sense of their lives' (p. 96). This provides a check on the social worker's accuracy of perceptions, reduces power imbalances between the worker and service user, and encourages co-authorship. Epston writes long letters which include the metaphors people use to tell their stories and any unique outcomes, commenting on these as a means of expanding the externalizing conversation (see also Speedy, 2004; Smith, 2005). Letters need to be adapted to the reading and concentration levels of service users; for example, children with learning needs may need a pictorial record of any unique outcomes, while a card briefly summarizing recent events is more appropriate for elderly people with memory difficulties (for a fuller discussion see Milner, 2001). Letters are also unsuitable for most agency records, particularly where the assessment is risk-focused. We find that the format of written feedback described in the previous chapter is appropriate for both solution-focused and narrative approaches. In the illustration below, the social worker was assessing a lone parent family where there were concerns about maternal drinking; her 15-year-old son, Dan, had touched his sister, Krystal sexually and was truanting from school; Krystal (9 years) had not only been subjected to sexually concerning behaviour by Dan but was also reportedly going 'into bushes with lads', getting into fights with peers, being rude and disobedient at home, accidentally starting a small fire in her bedroom with a candle, and riding her bike in the middle of the road. The feedback notes were posted to Krystal after a session which aimed to assess her self-protective awareness. The font used is Comic San MS as this is more child-friendly than formal fonts, and smiley faces and star stickers were added where appropriate.

CASE EXAMPLE

Session notes

Name: Krystal   **Date:** 17 May

Problem: Krystal isn't always well behaved so she thought Judith had come to talk to her about being naughty! Judith had come to talk to Krystal about keeping safe because she is worried about the things that have happened to her recently – like the touching Dan did, lads at school telling her she's sexy, getting racial abuse from local kids, and stuff like that.

What Krystal has done right

1. Krystal has been in so much bother lately that she has forgotten the good things about herself – but she did remember some of them.

2. She knows how to keep herself safe from Dan's touching.

3. Krystal knows how to be safe with hot water.

4. She knows how to handle knives and scissors safely – even if she sometimes forgets to do this.

5. She knows her road safety for crossing the road but forgets it when she's on her bike.

6. Krystal can do respect a bit. She nearly got a line in the 'bingo game' we played for that.

How Krystal did it

1. The good things that Krystal remembers about herself are that she is pretty, she can dance (and mum thinks she might make a good singer too). She presents herself nicely (mum says she always looks good for school). She is helpful (she made Judith a nice cup of coffee). She can stand up for herself when she gets racial abuse. She likes horses and she has a good memory.

2. When Dan touched her, she told a teacher at school. She knows all about good touches and bad touches and when people can touch each other on private parts. She can say no to Dan now. She has a Helping Hand with the names of people she can tell if she's upset. On her Helping Hand are: her teacher, mum, grandad (she has his number in her mobile), her friend, Poppy's mum next door, and dad (his number is in mum's phone book).

3. When Krystal is making coffee with hot water, she lifts the kettle by the handle with both hands.

4. Krystal knows that she should pass knives and scissors by the handle.

5. For road safety, Krystal stands on the kerb and looks left and right. She looks and listens as she crosses the road.

Homework

1. For remembering more good things about herself, Krystal will put a Post-it on the fridge every time she notices a good thing about herself.

2. For safety, Krystal will practice doing more safe things and then she can go in for her safety certificate (see below for details). She already has two safety stars.

3. Krystal will practice doing respect and then she might win the next bingo game. She might start with being a good sport, or she might start with listening and turn taking in talking. Or she might start somewhere else.

The use of certificates is frequently used in narrative approaches to validate and honour people's acts of resistance to problems (see for example Payne, Mn., 2006, chapter 6).

KRYSTAL'S SAFETY CERTIFICATE

Krystal will do all these things:

- she will handle knives and scissors safely
- she will not play with matches, lighters, cigs or candles
- she will ride her bike safely
- she will remember where she has put her mobile phone
- she will keep safe from boys at school
- she will tell mum where she's going
- she will ring mum if she goes somewhere mum doesn't know
- she will remember that her private parts are private
- she will be dressed when she is downstairs
- she will lock the bathroom door

When Krystal can do all these things, she will get her safety certificate.

Meeting agency requirements and service user needs

A central dilemma for social workers for many years has been how to manage the tensions between care and control; between individual and social needs, risks and safety. Narrative approaches to assessment manage this perhaps more fully than any of the other approaches, enabling the assessing social worker to incorporate her understanding of oppression most fully. The approach clarifies partnership without neglecting responsibility-taking and, by highlighting service users' local knowledge, has the capacity to produce individual assessments which have real meaning for service users.

For example, where there are concerns that young women's risk-taking behaviours put them at risk of sexually transmitted diseases, unwanted pregnancy, substance misuse and prostitution, it is useful to focus an assessment on questions that elicit and encourage safety rather than talking about consequences and dangers. Thus questions would include:

- When you are [running away from home, getting drunk with your mates and so on] how will I know you will be all right?
- What can you do, and what can I do, to help me understand that you will be all right?
- What are the things that make you know you are going to be all right?
- Could you share them with me? I might feel a whole lot safer about it if I knew these things.

For more safety questions see Milner (2003, 2004a).

Additionally the approach has a wide range of applications. The type of problem does not limit its use – it being effective with service users of limited intellectual capacity, including elderly people who are muddled in their thinking, people with learning needs, and those who might be storied by others as having major mental illnesses. Like solution-focused approaches, it can be used with individuals, families and groups. These groups include support groups for people with 'anorexia' or 'schizophrenia', community groups of aboriginal people tackling problems of diabetes that are partly the result of poverty, and groups of AIDs workers in villages in Malawi. In larger group work, externalizing conversations have been shown to lead to an exposition of the problem that empowers the taking of community and political action (see various reports in the *Dulwich Centre Newsletter*, Adelaide, South Australia).

Critical comment

Strand (1997a, 1997b) suggests that externalizing the problem and its internalised narrative in an attempt to unmask the relationship between self and hidden political realities requires advanced conceptual understanding, whereas a solution-focused approach demands only a rethink of the definition of one concept – the problem – without concern for its effects on self-definition. This, he thinks, makes narrative approaches unsuitable for people of limited intellectual ability. We have not found this to be the case. Indeed, the similarities between narrative and solution-focused approaches in terms of their theoretical base, particularly the relevance of social constructionism, means that the approaches can be combined in assessments. There are also similarities in practice techniques, despite the terms used; for example, there is little difference in practice between the narrative technique of *haunting from the future* (Epston *et al.*, 2006) and Dolan's (1998) solution-focused technique of *consulting a wiser, older self.*

O'Hanlon (see for example O'Hanlon and Beadle, 1994) has combined the American and Australasian approaches in a creative fashion which stresses the importance of language. In his view language can easily make difficulties sound, and become, fixed. His aim is to reconnect people's sense of possibility and hope when things seem unchangeable. He is concerned about the danger of 'iatrogenic injury' whereby problems are caused or worsened by an assessment or attempted intervention; stressing the importance of avoiding negative assessments 'that discourage, invalidate, show disrespect or close down possibilities for change' (O'Hanlon and Beadle, 1994, p. 10). He maintains that, since service users are experts in their own lives, we need to check our work with them as we might with another professional. Included in this approach is Milton Erickson's principle of *utilization*, considering carefully how a social worker can identify and use fully the strengths, exceptions, or unique outcomes that the service user brings to the assessment. Like White, O'Hanlon holds service users accountable for behaviour that impacts on others but this is about accepting responsibility for future behaviour, not blaming, looking for bad intention or suggesting that service users are bad people. People are presumed to be resourceful enough to deal with changing, the social work task being to connect them with their – often unrecognized – resources and join with them in locating these and any other resources they may need, be they external, personal, inter-personal or spiritual – in a word, possibilities. Milner (2001) offers a combined approach which specifically addresses gender differences in both assessment and intervention in social work in the UK. Jacob (2001) demonstrates how the approaches can be combined in work with people with eating difficulties (see also Jasper, 2007).

The main disadvantage for social workers trained and experienced in other approaches is the very real difficulty of deconstructing their own stories; for example, they would need to question cautious notions about 'setting up the service user to fail' because narrative approaches are based on a premise that the service user is 'set up to succeed'. Thus they have to be prepared not only to make their 'stories' explicit but also to abandon cherished theories about the nature of people. Some social workers also find it more difficult to start an assessment using this approach, in view of its fluid nature. Also the emphasis on using the service users' own language does run the risk of colluding with male metaphors of control, the notion of resistance readily lending itself to 'fighting talk'. Thus, linguistic oppression must always be guarded against.

Outcomes

Research into narrative approaches is in its infancy, yet Gorey *et al.* (1998) found that where there is a 'mutual client–worker strategizing' to change an external target 'the prevalence of moderate to large interventive effects may be fivefold greater' compared with cognitive-behavioural approaches. They found that when the problem is defined as transcending the individual, 'that is the problem does not reside "under the person's skin"' the work is 'very effec-tive' (p. 274). They add that practice based on oppression theories has possible greater effectiveness compared with traditional problem-solving approaches, for example in work with survivors of abuse. We are also aware of the work of Fisher *et al.* (1998) in studying the externalization of problems in work with compul-sive adolescents. They made the problem 'the enemy' and found that 11 of 15 participants who provided follow-up data showed significant improvement following a 7-week programme. There are also numerous qualitative research articles on narrative approaches listed on www.dulwichcentre.au

SUMMARY

- The narrative approach believes people are multi-storied and endeavours to make the service user the privileged author of their life.
- It encourages multiple perspectives and acts to deconstruct stories of 'expert' knowledge.
- Deconstructing problems in a liberating narrative is helpful and promotes the separation of the person from the problem.

- It encourages a perception that change is always possible.
- It encourages many possible futures through the co-construction of alternative stories.
- Written language as feedback helps people to reflect on how to break free from difficulties.

FURTHER LEARNING ACTIVITIES

1. In a seminar group, ask one person to volunteer to act as a service user who lives with parents and hears voices which are made worse by cannabis. Father says 'stupid, ignore them'; mother criticizes father for saying this.
   - The group then asks the service user for feedback.
   - The service user can elaborate the role as they wish.
2. Chose a service user who has a formal psychiatric diagnosis where you are making an assessment.
   - What are the benefits to the service user of this label?
   - Are there any possible drawbacks to the label which limit the service user's possibilities for self-agency?
   - How might you discuss with this service user what the label means to them?

For more details see Macdonald, A. J. (2005) '"Voices": An exercise in developing solution-focused conversations with the mentally ill', in Nelson, T. S. (ed.) *Education and Training in Solution-Focused Brief Therapy*. New York: Howarth Press.

FURTHER READING

Payne, Mn. (2006) *Narrative Therapy*, 2nd edn. London: Sage.
Brown, C. and Augusta-Scott, T. (eds) (2007) *Narrative Therapy: Making Meaning, Making Lives*. London: Sage.

NATIONAL OCCUPATIONAL STANDARDS

For students working with the British National Occupation Standards for Social Work (see Appendix):

- This chapter relates to *practice* elements 5.1–2; 9.1–3; 11.1–4; 17.1–4.
- With which of the *knowledge* requirements does this chapter help you?

CHAPTER 10

Assessment in Children's Services

What this chapter is about

This chapter outlines briefly the statutory context for the assessment of children and the values and principles underpinning it. It describes the theoretical and research evidence on the aetiology and maintenance of child abuse commonly used by social workers in making assessments, illustrating the lopsided nature of this research. The problems accruing from attempts to eliminate risk are discussed. Then the evidence of good practice in the assessment of need is presented and outcomes for children are discussed. The chapter concludes with suggestions as to the ways in which the wishes and needs of children can be assessed and good working relationships with parents can be promoted. The learning exercises in this, and the following chapter, are intended to complement student placement and work experiences.

MAIN POINTS

> ➤ The statutory framework.
>
> ➤ Types of assessments and processes.
>
> ➤ Values and Principles.
>
> ➤ Theoretical and research evidence in the aetiology and maintenance of child abuse.
>
> ➤ Assessing risk, problems with the research evidence.
>
> ➤ Assessment of need.
>
> ➤ Assessing the wishes and needs of children.
>
> ➤ Critical comments on the lack of attention to people's competence/strengths and on the difficulties of group decision-making.
>
> ➤ Difficulties in intra- and inter-agency decision-making.

Introduction

Assessment in children's work takes different forms, depending mostly on whether it is a case of unmet need, of protection from harm, or of adoption. In

182

all these categories, the work is driven by law and government guidance, which in turn is driven by failures in the system that have led to tragic deaths. Reports investigating the unfortunate tragedies made several recommendations that are now enshrined in the law and in a tide of government frameworks, checklists, forms and definitions of terms. Children's services and local authorities have added policies and principles and have produced protocols and procedures of their own. The result is that it is difficult to discuss the subject adequately in one chapter, and trainee social workers need to spend time familiarizing themselves with local practice and documentation.

Much of this chapter is about the legal context, processes, assessment forms and so forth, so we remind the reader that the ideas in the 'maps' chapters, Chapters 5 to 9, about ways of helping people to be self-determining, take responsibility for their actions and words, take child safety seriously, mobilize their own resources (internal and external), be creative and engage with professionals, are to be drawn on if assessment is not to be separated from intervention. The response of a person to such help is a key element in any assessment.

The reader may also wish to refer back to the section on the legal context in Chapter 1.

The statutory framework

The essential bedrock of the law in this area is the Children Act 1989, in which Section 17 deals with children in need and Section 47 with deals with children at risk of significant harm. Following its passing, further tragedies, often blamed on the failure of agencies to share information that had it been known more widely could have prevented the deaths, led to further official guidance and eventually this led to the Protection of Children Act 1999 which was followed closely by the *Framework for the Assessment of Children in Need and their Families* (2000). Scotland has the Children (Scotland) Act 1995. The Assessment Framework was issued to address increasing government concerns about poor assessment practice in children's social care and to promote a more broadly based approach to assessment of need and the provision of services, the idea being that better assessment leads to better services (for a fuller discussion see Ward and Rose, 2002; Cleaver and Walker, 2004; McAuley *et al.*, 2006).

This framework required that information should be organized according to three 'dimensions' (sometimes known as 'domains'). These are: the child's developmental needs, parenting capacity and environmental factors. Each dimension included a list of aspects (or sub-dimensions) to be considered and an assessment recording form was devised setting out questions or prompts relating to each aspect, for example, health, emotional development, relationships, self-care, safety of the child; the parent or carer's ability to provide basic care, emotional warmth, stimulation, guidance and boundaries; and for the environment, family history, housing, employment, income and community resources. Notes were made of any help offered and of the responses to that help, and social workers were asked to engage in analysis, judgement and decision-making as they summed up the information.

Meanwhile the Climbié tragedy occurred and the report was published in 2003, which again stressed interagency work and a new accountability structures. This led to the *Every Child Matters* government documents for England and Wales, with an agenda on children's rights to be healthy, safe, able to enjoy and achieve, make a positive contribution and gain economic wellbeing. The Children Act 2004 followed, enshrining these outcomes in law. The Scottish Parliament published *Getting It Right for Every Child* in 2004. Section 10 of the 2004 Act required local authorities to make arrangements to promote interagency cooperation with a view to improving children's wellbeing, which includes protection from significant harm and neglect. Section 11 required services to ensure that their work safeguarded and promoted the welfare of children in need. 'In need' is defined as 'likely to suffer significant impairment of health or development without services'. Section 12 required that data bases be set up nationally. Section 11 also set up Local Safeguarding Children Boards (LSCBs) which produce their own principles and guidance, much of it rehashing earlier guidance but stressing interagency work still further, as well as cooperation with parents and other carers and especially emphasizing the need to be child-focused and to take into account what children have to say.

At the same time the *Common Assessment Framework* for children and young persons (CAF) was devised and published in 2005, to be used nationwide by the end of 2008. (In Scotland the document is known as the *Integrated Assessment Framework*, and in Wales as the *Unified Assessment Framework*.) This explicitly states that the principles of the assessment should include:

- Collaborating – working *with* the family to find solutions – they will often know better than the worker
- A focus on the child's and family's *strengths* [original emphasis] as well as needs and these strengths should be recorded. (DfES, 2006, para. 4.8)

The *Common Assessment Framework* improves the earlier framework (DoH, 2000) by revising the dimensions and their headings, making it available for all agencies dealing with children, and capable of being shared more easily so that service users would not be asked for the same data again and again. This framework however was not considered sufficient for cases where there was reason to suspect significant harm or severe neglect; for such cases, a s. 47 investigation is needed and the headings of the 2000 framework form part of that. The 2000 framework had spoken of some families needing specific services to assist them in achieving a child's outcomes in terms of health and development, for example if they required help with particular stress factors. However there is a sense that the pressures of assessment writing and court cases dominate social workers' lives and that supporting families in need has taken second place. While it is good that help for parents is now emphasized more than ever, it is not clear how it will be provided, as much of modern practice is about referring out to the private sector and voluntary agencies. Thus assessments may be accurate but, without time scales and ways of determining whether the required changes have taken place, families still risk being offered inadequate or inappropriate support which will inevitably lead to re-referral, and yet another assessment (Thoburn *et al.*, 2000).

CASE STUDY: THEORY INTO PRACTICE

Peter (12 years), Laura (9 years) and Michael (7 years) live with their mother, Sharon, and have contact with their father, Doug, for full weekends every other week, alternating with Saturday visits. Following Doug's complaints about the effects of Sharon's drinking on the children's wellbeing and her counterclaims that his concerns are malicious attempts to control her as he did through a violent marriage, Social care have investigated twice in two years. On both occasions the case was quickly closed. Recently the two younger children confirmed Sharon's drinking; their wishes are to continue living with mum and seeing dad at weekends but for the drinking to stop. Peter is supportive of his mum, saying she only gets 'happy drunk sometimes'. Sharon has difficulty disciplining Peter, who roams the district and comes in late. Although pleasant and polite with adults, he also tends to dominate his brother and sister. A s. 36 investigation is underway. The investigating social worker does not consider there to be sufficient grounds to institute a s. 47 investigation and is recommending that the children remain with Sharon but that they are referred to a voluntary agency which supports the children of parents with drink problems.

■ To what extent do you consider the children's needs and wishes to have been met?

By 2007 the government project *Every Parent Matters* had published further documents, looking at interagency support and help for families as well as how *all* children could have assured outcomes. An overall plan for children's services became clearer, and the relationship between the 2000 Framework and the new Common Assessment Framework (CAF) was spelt out, and a continuum of needs and services, at four levels (A–D) was introduced (See Figure 10.1.)

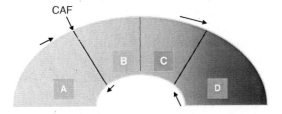

Figure 10.1 Windscreen diagram (adapted from Common Assessment Framework for Children and Young Persons – A Manager's Guide, 2006. London: DfES)

The continuum of needs and services

A 'Children with no additional needs.' This is the level of service for the majority of children. The majority have good enough parents and need only the general services, a local doctor, a dentist, a school, and so on. There is no lead professional.

B 'Children with additional needs, when *a single professional* is involved.' Targeted support. At this level a CAF may be started (see note below). This work could be in any agency such as a school with a mentor service, or health visitor services. Ideally an intervention plan should be started and reviewed at set periods.

C 'Children with additional needs, with *integrated targeted support and a lead professional.*' A CAF would certainly be done here, if not already started, as well as an intervention plan, and planned reviews. B and C services would cover much of the work with any child 'in need', but not investigations where a child was considered to be at risk of significant harm.

D 'Children with "complex needs" (especially safety), with integrated support and detailed enquiries by *a statutory or specialist service.*' In this area the 2000 Framework is used and s. 17 or s. 47 enquiries are done by child protection teams. The work may conclude with a CAF assessment if the work is referred back to level C.

PLACEMENT THINKING POINT

1. Chose a family you are aware of and identify the needs and risk factors.

2. Locate the children on the continuum.

What needs to be done to move them back towards A?

The Common Assessment Framework covers the topics of the 2000 Framework, minus the risk investigation/ s. 47 enquiry work. Levels B, C and D involve services *sharing information* with each other in various ways. Cases may move back or forward on the continuum as they are reassessed; indeed managers monitor whether cases are 'drifting' at an inappropriate level. Many referrals come in at level D and about half are moved back to a lower level because the needs are not very 'complex' or there is no serious risk to the child. Various services may have differing threshold criteria for the four levels.

(Note: The CAF *is to be used* when it will help a child meet one of the five outcomes in *Every Child Matters* (see below) and there are concerns about a child's progress, or needs are not clear, or support of more than one agency is needed. The CAF is *not used* when a child's progress is good, needs are identified and being met, and needs are clear and can be met by the family/assessing agency.)

Types of assessments and processes in child protection

(Table 10.1 lists and explains briefly some of the terms and initials used in this section.)

Table 10.1 Some of the terms and initials used in child protection

S.17	Section 17 of the Children Act 1989 referring to children in need.
S.47	Section 47 of the Children Act 1989, referring to children at risk.
CAF	The Common Assessment Framework.
CP	Child protection.
Failure to thrive	The rate of growth is significantly below normal due to inadequate nutrition. It usually applies to the first three years.
Framework (2000)	The Framework for the Assessment of Children in Need and Their Families (2000).
Harm	'Significant harm' which is any physical, sexual or emotional abuse, neglect or injury, or impairment suffered from seeing or hearing the ill-treatment of another, that is sufficiently serious to adversely affect progress or the enjoyment of life. There are no absolute criteria – it can result from a single event or an accumulation of events.
In need	Unlikely to attain a reasonable standard of health or development without the provision of services.
Suspect	'To have reasonable cause to suspect.' Having a sensible reason for thinking that a child MAY be at risk of being damaged or not protected by an adult who should be ensuring safety and wellbeing. This criterion is lower than 'beyond reasonable doubt' (as in criminal cases) or 'the balance of probability' (as in civil proceedings) or having a reasonable belief that that something is true.
Core assessment	Full assessment using the Framework (2000) or the CAF.

Referrals

A case starts when a referral is received expressing concern about the safety or welfare of a child:

- More detail may be sought from the referrer.
- Is the information direct or third-hand?
- Is there maltreatment?
- Who else knows?
- What is the name and location of child?
- Any family details?

Records are checked. If these show an existing *core assessment*, this is updated. Other agencies may be contacted, including the police. The referral is acknowledged within one day and the contents discussed with a manager. Based on an assessment of the information (the nature of the concern, how it arose, what the needs seem to be, whether risk of harm is suggested and if urgent action could be needed) a decision is made to start an *initial assessment* or take no action, or perhaps to refer on, unless urgent action is needed. (We explain the process for this later, below.) The decision is sent to the referrer and recorded.

Initial assessment

This is to be completed within seven working days. The work may involve:

- Consulting again with the referrer.
- Consulting other agencies who know the child or the family.
- Checking records.
- Interviewing the parents and the child.
- Ascertaining the child's wishes.
- Visiting the home.
- Taking some family history and listening to the various accounts and explanations given.

It involves assessing the seriousness of the concern, its duration and repetition, the vulnerability of the child, the family context and interactions as well as any risk factors such as mental illness, misuse of drugs or domestic violence. The Common Assessment Framework criteria for interagency sharing apply. If there is no reason to suspect risk of harm or need for support then feedback is sent to the referrer. If there is reason to suspect risk of harm then a 'strategic discussion/meeting' is held (see below). If there is no concern about harm but there is unmet need, there is a team discussion about what help/support is required. More assessment may be needed for this and services may be put in and reviewed.

The strategic discussion/meeting

This is to decide whether to take immediate protective action, or to have a s. 47 enquiry (child at risk of harm), and/or a police investigation, or declare the child 'in need' and start a core assessment under s. 17 and offer services to the family.

S. 47 enquiry

If an s. 47 enquiry is agreed, a 'core assessment' under s. 47 is started at the same time, if not already started. Meanwhile a discussion with managers is needed to consider/assess:

- Can the child can be protected at home?
- Can this be agreed with parents?
- Should the alleged abuser be asked to leave the home?
- If not, can the child be placed with relatives with parental agreement?
- If so, is this arrangement sufficient?
- Should legal action be taken?

The enquiry focuses on the information most important in relation to the risk of harm and, if it finds that concerns about risk of harm are substantiated and the child is continuing to be at risk, a *Child Protection Conference* has to be convened within fifteen days of the last strategy meeting.

Core assessment

This is a full assessment following the dimensions and headings of the Framework (2000) or the Common Assessment Framework. It may include a s. 47 enquiry. It may include judgements about responses to help that has been offered, and decide that either:

- further help is appropriate, or
- there is no risk of harm but there are unmet needs, and a plan would then be agreed, with planned reviews, or
- the concerns are substantiated and, while significant harm may not be a concern, a 'child protection conference' is justified to ensure ongoing welfare, or
- there is continuing risk of harm and a child protection conference is needed, if such a conference has not already been arranged.

The initial child protection conference

This has to meet within 15 working days of the last strategy discussion. The conference receives a report from the social worker, the core assessment or as much information as can be found, and makes one of two decisions:

- Concerns about harm are not substantiated but the child is in need of a plan for ensuring future welfare. It may decide how matters are recorded in the completion of the core assessment.
- There is risk of harm and the child will be subject of a child protection plan (formerly known as 'placed on the Child Protection Register') and a key worker named who will arrange a 'core group meeting' within 10 working days, and lead the core assessment completion (by 35 working days). The child is now known as 'a child subject to a child protection plan'.

The core group

This group, made up of the main interagency staff involved in the case including the key worker, puts into action the recommendations of the CP Conference. The key worker draws up a plan for, or implements, any interventions that are needed, and holds the first child protection review conference within 3 months, and further reviews every 6 months, with a revised plan if necessary. If the plan is not working and there are still some serious concerns, the key social worker raises this with the social work team, and the manager may discuss the case with the legal department if court action is a possible option.

Urgent action

Where protective action is thought to be necessary at any point to ensure the immediate safety of a child, this is termed taking 'urgent action'. To do this an immediate 'strategy discussion' is held, involving the local authority, the police and any other agency dealing with the matter. With legal advice they decide that either:

- urgent action is needed and parents are informed. A s. 47 enquiry is also started if the process has not already reached that point.
- urgent action is thought to be not needed but the child or family may or may not be in need of further time or services to ensure future welfare.

Section 8 enquiries relate to orders for residence, contact, prohibited steps and special issues.

Section 36 enquiries relate to making education supervision orders.

Useful flowcharts for all of the above processes are provided in the West Yorkshire Consortium procedures manual (part 4). This is available on www.wakefield.gov.uk/LSCB/chapters/contents.htm

The Children and Family Court Advisory and Support Service (CAFCASS) has its own flowcharts and processes for protecting children for whom the courts are making decisions.

Values and principles

LSCBs often include statements of principles for this work. Typically they require that social workers:

- Practice in a child-centred way, listening to and taking into account the child's voice where possible.
- Keep the child's welfare as the primary goal and protect it promptly.
- Allow enough time for people to absorb the professionals' concerns and the processes involved.
- Offer confidentiality, but with the limitation that information will be passed on if this is necessary for the child's safety.
- Be open and honest about concerns and responsibilities.
- Use appropriate language in engaging with people.
- Identify difficulties but also build on strengths and potential to resolve problems.
- Work in partnership with parents and carers and children.
- Enable maximum participation by all the family.
- Listen and endeavour to understand people's concerns.
- Respect the dignity of all people and their need for privacy.
- Ensure people know their rights and responsibilities concerning participation and cooperation.
- Keep an open mind, and an attitude of uncertainty.
- Acknowledge errors and misunderstandings as well as possible bias.
- Base the assessment on sound evidence – what is seen and what people say.
- Keep recordings up to date.

Theoretical and research evidence on the aetiology and maintenance of child abuse

Social workers are asked to make judgements about what is good enough for meeting children's safety and wellbeing. This involves assessing parents' capacity to parent and also to evaluate a child's development, using the sub-headings of the three 'dimensions' in the 2000 framework. The framework encouraged the use of various scales and checklists, for example the work of Cox and Bentovim (2000), Caldwell and Bradley (1984) and Bentovim and Bingley Miller (2001) for the gathering of information and for thinking about what is good enough parenting and good enough care. Hepworth *et al.* (2002) developed a list of factors to be considered, information about these being obtained through verbal report, observation and worker self-awareness. The factors they listed are: manifestations of the problem, severity, strengths and obstacles, interactions, unmet need and wants, developmental stages, the meanings people ascribe to events, behaviour (frequency and duration), substance abuse, emotional reactions to the problem, coping efforts, skills needed, cultural, societal and class factors and the external resources needed, cognitive/perceptual functioning (reality testing, values, judgement, misconceptions), emotional control, family boundaries, power structure, decision-making processes, expression of feeling, goals, communication, roles, strengths, and problem-solving. But these are only headings, prompts or a checklist – they do not tell us what is good enough.

Jones (2000) comments that it is not possible to ascribe a numerical value to aspects of parenting, and that parenting capacity can only be understood in the context in which it operates. We can, however, draw on what it would be reasonable to expect of parental care to a similar child in a similar situation. There is extensive literature about parenting capacity; see, for example, Jones (2000) and Cleaver *et al.* (1999).

When considering whether parents who have maltreated a child have made progress in their parenting, Silvester *et al.* (1995) have indicated signs that suggest a poor outcome:

- Not fully acknowledging responsibility for the child's state.
- The child is blamed.
- The child's needs are not recognized and parents' needs are put first.
- Frequently showing lack of concern about problems such as alcoholism or mental illness.
- Relationships within the family or between family and professionals remain at breaking point.

Jones (1998) reported on research findings that indicated the features associated with good outcomes:

- The children did not have residual disability, developmental delay or special educational needs.
- The children had been subjected to less severe abuse or neglect.

- The children had the benefit of corrective relationships with peers or a supportive adult.
- The children had developed appropriate attributions about the treatment they had received.
- There was cooperation with the helping agencies and professionals.
- There was engagement in therapeutic work
- The psychological component of the abuse was amenable to change.

Silvester *et al.* (1995) found that the family's capacity to change remained uncertain where:

- It was not clear the parents were taking responsibility for the abuse.
- It was unclear whether the parents put their own needs first.
- Parent–child attachments were ambivalent or anxious.
- Family patterns were inflexible.
- Relationships with professionals were ambivalent.

Such families should, however, be given help and the best chance to make the necessary changes, so long as the child does not have to wait too long, depending on their particular age and development. Following the Adoption and Children Act 2002, parallel planning for both rehabilitation and adoption was encouraged to prevent delay and drift for looked-after children (Wigfall *et al.*, 2006).

The ability to set *clear and firm limits* for a child is stressed in the literature, as children need the security of firm boundaries as well as *warmth and encouragement*. This is becoming a difficult area to assess as children gain increasing freedom in many families where parents cannot or do not wish to say 'No' and children can be said to be burdened with more choices and power than is appropriate. The Winnicot (1964) term 'good enough parenting' suggests that if parents do the following, especially in the first five years of a child's life, while they may not be super parents (if such is possible or desirable), they are good enough:

- They attend to the basics – physical care, nutrition and protection.
- They attend to emotional needs by unconditionally and consistently showing love, care and commitment.
- They set reasonable limits.
- They facilitate overall development with:
  - A high level of warmth and constructive criticism and a low level of negative criticism.
  - A high level of time spent with the child and child focused activities.
  - A high level of communication.
  - Good parental cooperation, showing unity and enjoyment of each other and the children.

Assessing risk: problems with the research evidence

Child protection work is strongly underpinned by discourses (theories, research evidence, policies and protocols) of risk assessment and management which have led to risk assessment tools being relied on, often uncritically, to assist in what is actually a complicated and uncertain area of work. Stanley (2005, 2006, 2007) argues that risk assessment has developed to manage incidents rather than to address families' needs. He identifies three risk periods:

- A growing anxiety towards children in the 1970s where risk was used to identify those children at risk and those not at risk (see, for example, Parton *et al.*, 1997; Parton 1998).
- This was followed by a period where risk assessment tools and risk management policies were developed to define degrees of risk (see, for example, Kemshall, 2002; Myers, 2007a).
- More recently, a period of legitimacy has emerged, where discourses of risk are drawn on to legitimise assessment decisions. Bessant (2004) refers to this as a 'science of risk'. Here risk is seen as something that can be located and resolved; thus evidence and certainty are privileged and ambiguity and uncertainty are expected to be managed through risk assessment procedures: 'if the tool predicts violence and this occurs, then the organization is defended; if the tool has been followed and an unexpected outcome occurs, then it is at fault and requires further development' (Milner and Myers, 2007, pp. 28–9). Webb (2006) suggests that social workers use these risk discourses to make 'risk claims' to argue for or against a particular decision (p. 154).

The difficulty with such certainty is that both actuarial and clinical assessments of risk have only modest predictive accuracy. For example, the AIM model for children who have sexually harmful behaviour consists of a series of factors or characteristics – based on research evidence and clinical consensus – that are categorized as either concerns or strengths. These factors are allocated a high, medium or low numerical value. These are plotted on a grid to indicate the level of risk of the person being harmful in the future. The grid has two axes: high-concern – low-concern, and high-strength – low-strength; thus a young person with high concerns and low strengths would be considered as needing intensive interventions. While appearing 'scientific', there are a number of problems with the model. There is no agreed definition of what constitutes sexually harmful behaviour; a key study informing the model (Skuse *et al.*, 1998) consisted of only eleven boys. This study was designed to explore recidivism, and three factors are prioritized as warranting a high concern categorization regardless of other considerations (for a fuller discussion see Myers, 2007a). Not least of the problems with this model is what interventions are indicated when the assessment reveals high concerns and high strengths.

A major problem with risk assessment tools is that the research evidence is skewed towards the aetiology and maintenance of abuse, with little known about what constitutes safety. Thus practitioners tend to focus their assessments on a search for what the research indicates is risky behaviour at the expense of other domains in the assessment framework, particularly the impact of family and environmental factors (Jack and Gill, 2003; Cleaver and Walker, 2004). Risk assessment defies accurate quantification so social workers can never be sure that risky behaviours have ceased, although they are preoccupied with risk elimination. This, say Turnell and Essex (2006), leads them to adopt a one-position response, such as insisting that a mother leaves her husband or a teenage daughter is not allowed to live at home. As families rarely agree with this one-position response, such assessments are not likely to lead to constructive planning and interventions. We have noted that social workers have a tendency to institute yet another assessment in these situations, involving families in protracted, and often intrusive, questioning about their past behaviours. Where the children are young, there is often a hidden one-position response – bolstered by the need not to delay permanency. Parallel planning often disguises intent to adopt – the ultimate risk elimination strategy. This is frustrating and distressing for parents who believe that rehabilitation is a genuine option.

Second, much of the research is flawed. For example, a persistent recommendation from the research into good outcomes mentioned above is that parents fully acknowledging responsibility for the abuse is a key factor. This is not actually the case; for example, there is no evidence that denial of responsibility has any effect on recidivism in cases of sexual abuse (Hanson and Bussiere, 1998; Hanson, 2004; Christodoulides *et al.*, 2005; Cooper 2005; Craig *et al.*, 2005; Henning *et al.*, 2005). Neither does denial influence recidivism in cases of physical abuse; as Turnell and Essex (2006) point out:

> There are very few benefits to be accrued by an alleged perpetrator in admitting abusing a child. A person who takes responsibility for seriously abusing a child may garner a clearer conscience but they may also very likely face criminal charges, job loss, exclusion from family and community, as well as other major negative repercussions. This highlights the inappropriateness and injustice of framing denial solely as an individual psychological distortion of an evident truth, when there are so many strong and interactional pressures that make denial a compelling response. (p. 29)

It is entirely possible that the research finding about accepting responsibility being associated with good outcomes, may be an artefact of the way in which social workers frame outcomes in the first place; Stanley (2005) found that social workers were more likely to leave children at home when their parents acknowledged the concerns and 'came on board'. However, there is a great deal of difference between social workers and families sharing the same perspective: what Platt (2007) refers to as congruence, and cooperation, the extent to which a social worker perceives family members to be working with social services in a constructive and compliant manner. Cleaver and Freeman (1995) found that parents rarely shared the same perspectives as social workers at the beginning of a case; indeed, family members tended not to share the same perspectives between themselves. Where there were good outcomes, the families' and professionals' perspectives came together gradually – not as the result of families accepting the social workers' account, but by extreme sensitivity, tolerance and awareness at the point of confrontation by the assessing social worker (p. 89).

> ### CASE EXAMPLE
>
> Eight-year-old Jonathon was placed with foster parents when he was 2 years old. It is strongly suspected that his mother physically abused him but she has consistently denied this. She has been permitted monthly 2-hourly contact with Jonathon and has not missed a contact in 6 years. Jonathon is happy in his foster placement but has recently expressed a wish to see his mother more regularly. She has asked for more contact several times and is now applying for his care order to be revoked.
>
> The social worker is opposing this on the grounds that mum has never admitted harming Jonathon and that this means that he cannot be safe with her, or that she can 'move on' until she admits responsibility for the earlier abuse.

Third, social workers do not always use the research evidence well. As we have discussed in Chapter 1, there are several organizational reasons for this, but it does result in the formation of working hypotheses about families, that are based on the selective use of research findings (for a fuller discussion see Scourfield, 2003). These are dangerous when they gain the status of a mantra; for example, the research into the deleterious effects of domestic violence on children has become a reason to remove children, whatever the circumstances of the violence (Milner, 2004a). Other commonly held working assumptions include: the 'fact' of male abuse of power in all domestic violence (this ignores female-on-male and female-on-female violence); the inherent recidivism of sex offenders (see above); that previous behaviour is the best indicator of future behaviour; and the primacy accorded to secure attachments (see Chapter 1). These are all powerful working hypotheses that influence assessments. Other well-identified risk indicators, such as the effects on children of parental mental illness and substance misuse (Cleaver, 2002; Falkov, 2002; Smith, 2004) figure less prominently in child protection discourses.

Check your assumptions

> ### CASE STUDY: THEORY INTO PRACTICE
>
> Following concerns about her mother's substance misuse and her neglect of her daughter, 4-year-old Casey has been with foster parents for eight weeks. During this time, her mother has maintained regular contact with Casey. You are concerned that Casey does not wait too long for a decision to be made about her permanent placement.
>
> ■ What working hypotheses about family reunification inform your preliminary planning?

■ Read:
Biehal (2007) 'Reuniting children with their families: reconsidering the evidence on timing, contact, and outcomes', *British Journal of Social Work*, 37: 807–23.

■ Does the evidence support your hypotheses?

Fourth, the need to make an 'at risk' or 'not at risk' claim leads social workers to depend heavily on 'expert' assessments. Stanley (2007) notes that these are used to legitimize social workers' preferred decisions, despite the fact that they mask important ideas about the way risk is constructed differently by psychologists and social workers. The former are even more likely than social workers to depend upon a barrage of risk assessment tests, despite their poor predictive power. These reports are immensely powerful documents in that they determine blameworthiness and creditworthiness, and remain durable across time and space (Taylor and White, 2000). They may well have been prepared after only one session of fixed questions with the parents (the exchange model does not figure highly in these sorts of assessments), yet these psychological assessments will override any social factors which may well be relevant; for instance, a report may indicate medium risk yet ignore evidence of high need. They also encourage certainty where certainty is unknown. For instance, one man complained after a psychologist told him that his was 'the typical profile we would expect of a sex offender'. The man complained that he had merely answered a set of predetermined questions about stress responses, drinking and so on, to which the possible responses were 'very much, sometimes, not at all' and that he had replied 'sometimes' to all the questions. Such a question format is not only highly 'unscientific' but it is also dangerous in that person who is deciding on the questions is framing the subject as a sex offender on predetermined but spurious criteria – as the meta-analyses demonstrate, due to the heterogeneous nature of this group of offenders, there is no current consistent profile of the sex offender (Craig *et al.*, 2005).

Assessment of need

The tendency of social workers to overemphasize the psychological dimensions has distorted assessments, particularly, as we noted above, the neglect of environmental factors on the lives of children. However, there is evidence that the Common Assessment Framework is encouraging more parental participation. Cleaver and Walker (2004) found that three-quarters of parents in their study felt involved in the assessment: social workers had explained why the assessment was being carried out, how it would be done, and what it would entail. They felt less satisfied with the care plan, however, except where they had a shared perspective with the social worker about the difficulties and had been involved in the choice and development of the plan. Millar and Corby's study (2007) confirms that the Framework's format has improved communication in the ways parents are involved. Particularly relevant to feeling involved in the assessment was being given copies of the assessment decision and plan:

> Parents liked to know what was being said about them, and valued the chance to make comments that were recorded and openly discussed. We suggest that the format of the framework helped to produce this transparency of approach, *encouraging explicitness about social workers' concerns and a dialogue about them.* (Millar and Corby, 2007, our emphasis)

However, the improved communication between parents and social workers was mainly found in families where there was less extreme conflict over perspectives – those with disabled children or complex caring problems. It seems that the framework has more effect in improving communication in assessments of need than risk (see also Tunstill and Aldgate, 2000).

Boddy *et al.* (2006) identified the elements of successful assessments of families in need where children had either complex disabilities or complex needs. These assessments were genuinely collaborative and the active participation of parents in the process shifted the emphasis from 'services' to 'solutions' by:

- Using accessible language.
- Explaining the assessment process and discussing this with parents before asking any checklist questions.
- Conducting the assessment in either the home or a familiar community building.
- Sharing information with parents.

Other elements included having confidence in the lead professional, and developing 'joined-up working' from bottom-up initiatives rather than depending on strategic-level decisions.

As Brandon *et al.* (2007) found, where parents are not part of the assessment and not in agreement with the resulting plan, they will be reluctant to accept the help offered. This is an expensive waste of time and resources, which leads only to reassessment. While all assessments should be fluid and on-going to meet changing circumstances, they are rarely successful without the full participation of parents. As families in need tend to have lower priority than families at risk, it is important for social workers to consider how to assess unmet need in their communities as well as individual families. It is not uncommon for specific groups of potential service user needs to be researched and assessed in a participatory way by voluntary agencies (the Barnardo's project (Rotherham), on assessing the needs of asylum-seekers' children, is a good example of this), but we suspect that in areas of high deprivation whole communities of children's needs are unmet. Dealing with the more acute incidents that arise under child protection assessments is not only insufficient for families but frustrating for social workers. A test of a good assessment is the outcomes that follow it, and these have been made explicit by government in the *Every Child Matters* document.

Every Child Matters (DoH 2005a) – the Outcomes Framework:

- Be healthy – physically, mentally, emotionally, sexually, in lifestyle and the avoidance of illegal drugs.
- Be safe – from maltreatment, neglect, violence, sexual exploitation, bullying, discrimination, crime, anti-social behaviour, and be cared for and have security and stability.
- Enjoy and achieve – be ready for school, attend it and enjoy it, achieve educational standards and social development, and be able to enjoy recreation.
- Make a positive contribution – engage in decision-making, support the community and the environment, be law-abiding, develop positive relationships, not bully or discriminate, be confident, deal with changes and challenges, be enterprising.
- Achieve economic wellbeing – engage in further education, employment and training, live in decent homes, have access to transport and material goods, live in a household free from low income.

In Scotland the outcomes are slightly different: safe, nurtured, healthy, achieving, active, respected and responsible. (*Getting it Right for Every Child*, 2004)

Assessing the wishes of children

Whether the situation is one of possible risk or of unmet need, or both, the focus of assessment is the child. As part of making a positive contribution, children are expected to be able to engage in the decision-making process, but the Cleaver and Walker study (2004) found very little evidence of informing or *consulting* children and young people during the assessment process. They suggest that this may be because social workers are so involved with case management that they have little experience and/or confidence in direct work with children (p. 265). Taylor (2004) suggests that there are other factors at play here. She identifies the reinforcement of social work's reliance on psychological knowledge as a means of understanding behaviours and relationships and identifying causes for concern, particularly the use of child development theory. Viewing children as preparing for adulthood, rather than viewing them as people in their own right, living their lives and accomplishing things in the here and now, means that their capacities for understanding and reasoning are underestimated, and they are not deemed competent to make decisions. Ferguson (2004) noted also that social workers are often at a loss regarding how to communicate the enormity of a child protection investigation to children. Children are aware that something major is happening in their lives when they see their parents distressed, the police coming to their home, or a sibling taken to hospital or foster care. Without an explanation, they often make up their own; for example, Turnell and Essex (2006) tell of a 5-year-old boy who witnessed his stepfather being arrested for alleged sexual abuse. Later, he saw a television news story about an IRA bombing and came to the misguided conclusion that that was why his stepfather had been arrested.

CAFCASS social workers possibly have the most experience in this area of work, not only in child protection assessments but also because of the growing number of s. 8 reports prepared for the courts when parents are contesting issues of contact, residence and/or parental responsibility. There are difficulties here, most notably the very real issues for a child of not offending the residential parent and how to assess whether or not a parent is attempting to promote a partial view (for a fuller discussion see Mantle *et al.*, 2007; Hobbs, 2002). There is also the issue of possible disagreement between the children about contact; for example, in the case of Peter mentioned above, he did not want contact with his father as he found it more difficult to get his own way under the stricter discipline in this home. This meant that his mother's initial solution to the concerns – only drinking when all three children were with their father – was impossible to operationalize. To what extent should children's wishes be accepted as paramount, and to what extent do they have free choice when this impinges on the rights of other siblings to have their wishes and needs met?

CAFCASS workers have a wealth of materials for assessing the wishes and needs of children which could be made more widely available to social workers. As Cleaver and Walker (2004) found, social services' workers have little confidence in direct work with children. Partly, this may be due to their preoccupation with case management but there is also evidence that they rely heavily on interviews with parents and the parents' willingness to cooperate to make judgements (Holland, 2000). This means that it is the quality of the worker–parent relationship that forms the basis for decision-making, not the quality of the parent–child relationship (Taylor, 2004). Rarely are there in depth observations of this relationship, except where contact is supervised. This supervision is not usually undertaken by the social worker and we have evidence from our work that these observations tend to focus on deficits rather than competencies. What seems to happen is that the assessing social worker makes a token attempt to assess the children's wishes separately from the parents. Thus, the child is either seen in school or taken out for a burger or to the local park, while the parent or parents wait anxiously for their return. This is not entirely satisfactory for a number of reasons:

- If the child has not been given an explanation for earlier events that led to Social Care involvement in the family, they will be puzzled as to why they are being taken out by a relative stranger and may not understand why they are being asked about their wishes. This leaves the social worker with having to 'interpret' any chance comment made by the child.

- Where the child knows only too well the seriousness of the situation, they may hesitate to talk freely as they may worry how the social worker will use any information given. They do have to return to the home and may well face questions from parents about what they said.

- Many children do not like being interviewed at school as this leaves them with the need to invent a story for their classmates.

> **CASE EXAMPLE**
>
> The investigating social worker in the case of Peter, Laura and Michael (above) interviewed Michael at school. This interview consisted of direct questions about his mother's drinking and the preparation of an eco map. She was left in a quandary after this interview as, on the one hand, Michael confirmed that mum's drinking worried him but, on the other hand, his eco map left out dad's new partner. The worker was worried that contact with dad was impacting on his welfare as much as mum's drinking.
>
> Michael's mum later complained to us that she did not want her children interviewed at school as it 'showed them up'. Michael confirmed this: 'It was right embarrassing. The teacher sat in with us and I didn't want her to know all that stuff.' When asked about his eco map, he added: 'I did it right quick, just to get it over with so I could get back in class.'

Smart *et al.* (2001) show that children are capable of a sophisticated understanding of issues and dilemmas and able to construct ways of dealing with them, so it is more productive to provide children with an honest explanation of events and issues, however young they are. Turnell and Essex (2006) use words and pictures as a way of explaining *the concerns* to children, along with the parents. This process covers the following areas:

- Who is worried about the children.
- What they are worried about.
- What happened then.
- Private parts (in cases of alleged sexual abuse).
- What we (family and professionals) are doing about the worries.

> **CASE EXAMPLE**
>
> **Assessing Jonathon's wishes and needs**
>
> Jonathon's foster carer was very worried about Jonathon being talked to about his previous abuse and she also complained that he wasn't very good at writing and was 'fed up' with the 'wishes' questionnaires his social worker had asked him to fill in, so an introductory session consisted simply of explaining our role and asking him to make a list of the things he's good at for the next visit. The second session with Jonathon took place with his carer present. After discussing his list of good things about himself, one of which turned out to be 'good at drawing', Jonathon was then asked what he understands about court and he surprised us by giving a sophisticated answer: 'It's where judges make decisions about bad people.' He had seen this on *Coronation Street*. We explained that family courts are rather different, and what they do to protect children, and asked him to draw a picture of a court.

His drawing was remarkably accurate; he even drew an accurate representation of the insignia on the judge's bench. We explained who sat where in court and he drew stick figures representing the judge, solicitors, social workers and his mother and family. We then asked him what happened at school when someone has been naughty and a teacher says 'Who did that?'; we agreed that all the children say 'It wasn't me.' We then explained that's what everyone said when the judge asked who gave Jonathon the bruises, and the judge then said that, to keep Jonathon safe, he would send him to live with his foster carer. Jonathon understood this and asked if he could keep the picture in his life story book.

We then fast-forwarded his life six years and talked about him now having two mums, and how he would like this to be. Jonathon was very clear that he would like to see his mum every other week, sometimes at her house, sometimes at his foster carer's house. He wanted his foster carer to be present at these contacts.

Both mum and the foster carer could readily accept Jonathon's wishes, mum because it gave her more time with him to build up their relationship, and the foster carer because it removed her fears that Jonathon would be suddenly removed from her care.

Interviewing children separately from their parents *to ascertain their views* on family life (not *to make a decision*) is sometimes necessary, but we find it most useful to ask all family members for their views on the concerns, what needs to be different when everyone feels safe, and what their best hopes are as a family. Even families where there are serious child protection concerns still have high hopes and aspirations for a better and more satisfactory family life; and, often, elucidation of these also brings out the Common Assessment Framework third-dimension factors that are preventing the family from living a better life. We do this by means of listing the concerns and asking everyone for details of the good things about living in this family (a 'thin' answer from a child to this question frequently encourages a parent to change their behaviour so that they can get a better response next time the question is asked). Then we ask everyone the miracle question (for more details see Chapter 8). We give everyone a piece of paper and a pencil and ask them to write down the answer to the question we are about to ask (pre-school children are invited to draw their answer; very young children are given a sheet of paper, stickers and crayons to make a picture which they can then present to an adult; and older children without speech are linked with another family member who the family has identified as the person best able to represent them). We keep this lighthearted by reminding them that no-one must see their answer and to put their arm round the paper as they do at school to prevent copying. Then we ask: 'Suppose, while you are asleep tonight, a wonderful thing happens and everything that is worrying Social Care has disappeared. When you wake up, what is the first thing that you would notice that would tell you that things are better?' It is helpful for the social worker to do this too as it helps him/her to identify precisely what evidence of safety would look like and present this to the family.

Reminding everyone to keep their answers hidden, we then ask them in turn to guess what another person has written. This is not done randomly; we ask the non-abusing parent to guess what the youngest child has said as this is relatively non-threatening and gives that person the opportunity to demonstrate his/her understanding of the child's needs and wishes. Then we ask the most confident child to guess what the (alleged) abuser may have put. Finally, we ask the abuser what they think a child has said (we usually select the most vulnerable child here). Where a family gives superficial answers, such as 'He would have a new bike,' we add the family pet to the exercise and ask everyone what the pet would notice. After this has been talked about, we ask each person what they actually put and discuss differences of perceptions. This exercise has several advantages:

- It gives children the opportunity to express their needs and wishes.
- It enables parents to hear these.
- It encourages discussion about what changes can be made.
- It enables a non-abusing parent to talk about the difficulty of being what one parent described as 'piggy in the middle'.
- It provides a snapshot of family dynamics in action.

The latter observations are important as they reveal family strengths (for example, a parent being unexpectedly caring towards a child) and weaknesses (for example, the children fighting and the parents unable to handle this). It is less threatening to point out weaknesses during the exercise and parents enjoy their competencies being noticed and commented upon. Observing families is easiest when the social worker makes an effort to see them at ordinary family times; we cannot stress strongly enough the value of visiting families outside working hours. Families can be very different in the evening and at weekends.

Dumbrill (2006) and De Boer and Coady (2007) found that families are most likely to make changes that will benefit children when social workers exercise their power softly and judiciously, treat families with kindness, dignity and respect, and are honest and genuine. This is not always easy to do when the assessing social worker is faced with organizational pressures to prioritize maintenance of the records by which the agency will be audited, and we suggest that establishing genuine working partnerships demands enormous moral courage on the part of social workers as well as endless persistence (and sometimes resistance) in responding to organizational pressures.

Critical comment

Although the framework has had the effect of improving information collection and the involvement of parents, especially in the assessment of need, Rose *et al.* (2006) note that practitioners are still encountering difficulties when it comes to analysis, judgement and decisions about when and how to intervene. This is understandable given the theory and research evidence that is promoted in government guidance.

There are two major problems with this guidance. First, the research evidence is lopsided in terms of understanding child abuse and thus encourages practitioners to search mainly for 'risk' factors. This does not facilitate shared perspectives about concerns between parents and professionals, and leaves the worker with a plethora of negative information on which to make decisions about safety. The guidance does include advice to focus on strengths as well as problems, but this is not emphasized enough.

Second, the underpinning theory is largely psychological, leading to other dimensions of the framework being neglected. This is especially the case where there is low risk but high need. Additionally, the emphasis in the guidance about the importance of attachments ignores the fact that such an assessment should logically lead to psychodynamic interventions but these are rarely provided as they are lengthy and expensive. Not only would such interventions mean delay for a child, but there are no adequate resources available for them. As a result, assessments and subsequent interventions are often theoretically inconsistent, as the example below demonstrates.

> ### CASE EXAMPLE
>
> Jacob is a large 13-year-old with mild learning difficulty who has raped his 10-year-old sister, Paige. An AIMs assessment identified him as low-risk but he has been re-referred following acts of disruption, vandalism and violence which have resulted in him being excluded from school.

The social worker's assessment identified several risk factors:

- Jacob has ADHD which is partially controlled by medication. He remains impulsive.
- His parenting is inconsistent: his mother tends to find excuses for his behaviour while his father is critical and demanding.
- Disagreements about handling Jacob's behaviour have put the marital relationship under severe strain.
- Paige is unwilling to talk about the rape and has refused to be interviewed by the police.
- Her parents support her in this as neither of them want it 'dragged up'. They are uncomfortable in talking about sexual matters.
- The family are financially stretched as they have recently bought a large house that is in need of extensive renovation.
- The parents are unable to have a social life as they feel the need to supervise Jacob and Paige at all times.

Not having identified family strengths, and ignoring the community and environmental factors, the social worker instigated interventions based on psychological factors. A referral was made for marital therapy for the parents, and adolescent psychological services for Jacob. Additionally, Paige was offered counselling and a referral was made to a specialised service dealing with young people whose behaviour is sexually harmful. Jacob was provided with a support worker. The social worker saw her role as managing the case, not offering any direct work.

On the surface, this sounds like a reasonable package of care. However, it turned out to be completely inconsistent: the marital therapy was based on systemic family therapy ideas; the adolescent service used cognitive-behavioural therapy, the counselling was person-centred, the work on sexually harmful behaviour was solution-focused, and the support worker used the Good Lives model. Not surprisingly, the family were totally bewildered by the differing demands and therapeutic advice offered. There was no change in Jacob's behaviour.

Difficulties in intra- and inter-agency decision-making

All government guidance prioritises intra- and inter-agency working as a means of sharing information and improving decision-making. However, there are three serious distortions that can occur when we work in groups, especially when making decisions involving risk (for an overview of the psychological factors involved in team work see Nicholson *et al.*, 2006, chapter 7).

Groupthink

One popular explanation of reasons for defective decision-making in groups is the concept of groupthink. This describes decision-making in groups under stress where a group engages in particular types of behaviour. When Janis and Mann (1977) studied several disastrous policy decisions, they found that these behaviours include:

- Shared rationalizations to support the first apparently adequate course of action suggested by an influential group member.
- A lack of disagreement between group members.
- A consequent high level of confidence in the group decision.

This concept of groupthink has already been aired in the child protection literature, and suggestions for improving case conference performance with reference to making corrections to the symptoms of groupthink have been promoted in training packs (Lewis *et al.*, 1991). However, there are two fundamental problems with the application of correctives.

First, the concept of groupthink itself suggests that once a group is subject to its symptoms, it will be too deeply entrenched in its behaviour to see a need for re-evaluation or change.

Second, it may be the case that an individual can exert far more influence on the decisional direction of the group owing to framing effects.

Group polarization

Whyte (1989, 1993) suggests that rather than alter the original framing of the problem, a group would be subject to the effects of group polarization, and this would *accelerate* the tendency to risk or caution of the original framing, group polarization effects demonstrating that people in a group take a more extreme position than they would as individuals (Moscovici and Zavalloni, 1969). This, suggests Whyte, means that rather than act as a countercheck to any unwarranted optimism, if the decision is framed in terms of losses, the group will commit resources to a course of action initially agreed on by the group, even when it is failing. Group members will bolster this decision by self-justification, such as 'The plan needs more time to work,' or 'We need more resources.' The group then has the potential to become so risky that there is always the possibility for a decision fiasco. This group behaviour is not only found in social work assessments of risk. As Leiss and Chociolko (1994, p. 31) comment on industrial risk assessment: 'The significance of an event's probability tends to decrease as conceivable consequences increase, until what is possible becomes more feared than what is probable.'

An analysis of child protection case conference decisions (Kelly, 2000) showed that:

- Most child protection assessments are framed in the domain of losses.
- The *key decision-maker* is the individual social worker who deals with the initial referral and prepares the report for the case conference.
- The case conference does not act as a check against this initial assessment (it does, as Whyte predicted, escalate rather than reduce risky decision-making).
- Although individual social workers perceive other case conference members to be more powerful than themselves, these members actually have little influence on the decision.

This does not imply notions of unwarranted optimism or careless assessment work on the part of social workers *per se*. The social-psychological theory explaining these effects is universal and there is no evidence that other case conference forums are any more effective in realistically assessing risk (Whyte, 1989, 1993). What it does imply is that an individual social worker would make less risky decisions than a group when a losses frame is applied, and that an interagency group can operate more effectively when a gains frame is applied. O'Sullivan (1999) cautions that social situations are complex and uncertain, with sound decisions arising from a process which includes involving service users to the highest feasible level; consultation between *all* the stakeholders; careful framing of the decision situation; and making a systematic choice between options.

Prospect theory

Kahneman and Tversky (1979) offered an explanation of how individuals make decisions that tend towards the direction of risk or caution depending upon whether or not the initial choice is framed in terms of options that involve gains or losses. If the possible options are framed in terms of gains, individuals will be risk-averse; that is, they will opt for a certain, although perhaps smaller, gain as opposed to another larger gain that is uncertain or risky. In other words, they will be less likely to gamble or risk losing the certain gain. However, if the options are framed in terms of losses, individuals will be more risk-seeking and will tend to avoid a certain, although smaller, loss in favour of another, larger loss that is uncertain. They will be more likely to risk the gamble, exposing themselves to a potentially greater risk. Positive framing leads to caution, and negative framing to risk-taking. The various options open to social workers are often all unattractive, desired outcomes usually having a low probability and less desirable outcomes having a high one. All the options can usually be framed either positively or negatively, and this will affect riskiness in decision-making.

Many of the dilemmas in social work involve choices between two unattractive options. For example, a social worker is faced regularly with leaving children in an abusive family or placing them in different foster and children's homes. While family support and specialized fostering services remain underdeveloped, the first option in these examples is highly desirable for the social worker, but, in opting to avoid a certain loss, other possible (uncertain) losses are ignored and risky behaviour sets in (see, for example, Kelly and Milner, 1996b). Cautious behaviour, that is seeking to achieve certain gains, is more likely to lead not only to re-evaluation and contingency plan-making, but also to creative and effective social work. To avoid a shift towards risk-taking, they need to frame options in terms of certain and uncertain gains. Solution-focused and narrative approaches facilitate this more than do other types of intervention as they emphasize safety, which is more easily measured than is risk.

SUMMARY

- The law relating to child protection is complex, the policies are specific and the guidelines are numerous.
- The *Every Child Matters* agenda involves interesting progress in childcare, certainly in the management of it.
- It has at least shared the focus on children at risk with children in need, who should get a better joined-up service in the future.
- The frameworks for assessment are comprehensive checks that ensure nothing should be ignored if they are followed. On their own, however, they do not guarantee effective assessments in terms of ensuring the outcomes.
- Outcomes have been defined better than before, although how they will be achieved via the high level of strategic planning and the commissioning of services is not clear.
- The research basis for assessment of risk is not without its critics.
- The emphasis on partnership with children and their families is a step in the right direction but it needs to be practised with a high level of professionalism. It is not a guarantee of service.
- Intra- and inter-agency work does not necessarily improve decision-making. Cognitive distortions can arise in group decision-making.

FURTHER LEARNING ACTIVITIES

- Select one of your cases where you are frustrated with the parents' lack of cooperation with your assessment and/or your concern about their untruthfulness. Make a note of the possible reasons for this and what you have already done to promote partnership.
- Read: Platt, D. (2007) 'Congruence and co-operation in social workers' assessments of children in need', *Child and Family Social Work*, 12: 326–35.
- Discuss to what extent the CAF restricts or enables your assessment.
- Discuss whether organizational demands limit your preferred way of undertaking this assessment.
- Consulting the Values and Principles listed earlier in this chapter, what could you be doing differently that would encourage these parents to cooperate with your efforts?

FURTHER READING

Wilson, K. and James, A. (2007) *The Child Protection Handbook*, 3rd edn. Edinburgh: Baillière Tindall.

Department for Education and Science (2005) Various publications in the 'Every Child Matters' series of guidelines. Nottingham.

Cleaver, H. and Walker, S., with Meadows, P. (2004) *Assessing Children's Needs and Circumstances. The Impact of the Assessment Framework*. London: Jessica Kingsley.

Hothersall, S. J. (2006) *Social Work with Children, Young people and their Families in Scotland*. Exeter: Learning Matters.

McNeil, F. and Whyte, B. (2007) *Reducing Offending: Social Work with Offenders in Scotland*. Edinburgh: Willan.

NATIONAL OCCUPATIONAL STANDARDS

For students working with the British National Occupation Standards for Social Work (see Appendix):

- This chapter relates to *practice* elements 1.1–3; 2.1–4; 3.1–2; 4.1–4; 5.1–2; 6.1–5; 7.1; 9.1–3; 11.1–4; 12.1–3; 13.1–3; 17. 1–4; 19.1–5.
- With which of the *knowledge* requirements does this chapter help you?

CHAPTER 11

Assessment in Adults' Services

What this chapter is about

In this chapter we will focus on some of the larger categories of service users, particularly older people, people with mental illnesses, and people with disabilities. We will stress, however, that all the groups have many problems in common, for example, health, safety, housing, income support and discrimination. They all can be vulnerable and neglected and, in the not too distant past, the services responsible for them were seen as Cinderella services, which depended on unqualified workers and were underfunded. Many services are now fully staffed with qualified workers and there is a promise from government of a large-scale transformation in adult services, based on entitlement and choice and involving individual personalized budgets. We will look at some current protocols and practices as well as adding critical comment.

As much of this chapter is about the legal context, processes, assessment forms and so on, we remind the reader that the ideas in the 'maps' chapters, Chapters 5 to 9 – about ways of helping people to be more independent, take responsibility for self-care and for behaviours (physical and mental), keep a positive outlook, mobilize their own resources (internal and external), be creative and engage with others – are to be drawn on so that assessment is not separated from intervention. The response of a person to such help is a key element in any assessment.

MAIN POINTS

➤ The statutory framework and the main guidance from government.

➤ Types of assessment: the single assessment process, carer's needs assessment, assessing for eligibility.

➤ Values and principles.

➤ Decision-making and risk.

➤ Assessing vulnerable and/or dangerous adults: older people, mental illness, dual diagnosis, physical impairment, learning difficulties, challenging behaviour and parents with learning difficulties.

> ➤ Preservation of independence, potential and dignity as primary outcomes.
> ➤ Critical comments on assessment tools, protocols and standardized procedures.

The statutory framework

The National Health Service and Community Care Act 1990 introduced a new set of principles and procedures for practice in the care of adults, and paved the way for care management in the UK. It requires local authority social services to ensure that services are available for those in serious need. There followed throughout the 1990s several guidances such as *Caring for People* (1991), *Care Management and Assessment* (1991) and *The Challenge of Partnership* (1995). The *Care Programme Approach* (CPA) for those with serious mental illness was introduced in 1995 and the Health Act 1999 enabled partnerships between primary care trusts, social services, housing and other community services, so that some social services teams now include workers who are trained nurses. The intention was to get services to join together in designing and delivering services around people's needs, rather than worrying about the boundaries of their organizations. 'Assessment of need' and 'care packages' became commonplace terms. Community mental health teams (CMHTs) looked after patients in the community, and user-centred assessments and holistic approaches were encouraged in working towards 'quality of life' for all those needing care. Practitioners were encouraged to look at situations from the services user's perspective rather than the professional's perspective. Debates about risk abounded.

In 2000, we saw the government papers *A Quality Strategy for Social Care* and *Reforming the Mental Health Act*. The 2001 *National Service Framework for Older People* introduced the *Single Assessment Process* (SAP), followed in 2002 by *Valuing People*, which stressed person-centred approaches in supporting people with learning disability, and 'empowerment' as the core principle in deciding interventions. The *Fair Access to Care Services* approach to assessing eligibility for service was introduced in 2003; in 2004 plans for more integrated care were announced as well. These were followed in 2005 by *Integrated Assessment* for those with long-term neurological problems; 2005 also brought the Mental Capacity Act, followed in 2006 by the White Paper *Our Health, Our Care, Our Say*, which proposed a Common Assessment Framework for adults (combining SAP and CPA). That year the 'Dignity in Care' campaign was launched, speaking of the importance of inspiring people to take action. The right to equal citizenship, meaningful activity, choosing for oneself what to do and not to do – 'real choices', as the Commission for Social Care Inspection (CSCI) called it – and the right to be valued were spelt out. 2007 brought a new Mental Health Act addressing public safety and issues of 'treatability'. Supported risk-taking was developed, and a duty was laid on local authorities to discuss individual budgets with people as the first option. The impact of this plethora of legislation and guidance on assessment practice will be discussed throughout this chapter, but the reader is reminded that guidance continues to be developed and of the need to keep up to date with this rapidly changing literature. First we look briefly at the Mental Capacity Act (2005) and the Mental Health Act (2007). In Scotland the legislation is contained in the Adults and Incapacity Act 2000.

The Mental Capacity Act 2005

- This Act states that capacity is to be presumed until proven otherwise. By 'capacity' is meant the ability to comprehend information relating to a decision, to retain that information, to use and weigh it to arrive at a choice and to communicate the decision (even if only by blinking an eye).
- The Act obliges services to take all practical steps to support people in making their own decisions as far as is practicable, in an environment in which the person is comfortable with the aid of an expert in helping him to express his views.
- Capacity is not to be ruled out simply because a person makes an unwise decision – s/he has the right to irrational or eccentric decisions that others might judge to be not in their best interests.
- If capacity is judged to be lacking, services must use the least restrictive option for caring, the option that would least restrict the right to freedom of action.
- A person may lack capacity in regard to one matter but not to another.
- The incapacity may be caused by mental or physical illness, learning disability, dementia, brain damage or a toxic or confused state.
- Any action taken on the person's behalf must be based on their best interest, not simply on age, appearance or assumptions based on condition or behaviour, or assumptions as to whether s/he will have quality of life without treatment. All relevant circumstances are to be considered and none is to be seen as more important than another.
- It cannot be assumed that a person will not recover capacity later on.
- Past and present wishes and feelings are to be considered, and any written statements and religious beliefs.
- The Act does not mean that a doctor has to continue life-sustaining treatment when it is not in the person's best interests.
- The burden of proof of incapacity lies with the assessing health professional, who would work with social workers, as many decisions involve considerations of care provision.

Note: The Mental Capacity Act 2005 is relevant in working with not only those who are mentally ill but also those with dementia and those with learning disability.

The Mental Health Act 2007

This law amends the 1983 Act, the Domestic Violence, Crime and Victims Act 2004 and the Mental Health Act 2005, stating that mental illness can be treated without consent when a person's health or safety, or that of the public, is threatened. The European Court of Human Rights ruled in 2004, however, that detention in a hospital is not lawful unless medical treatment of a person's disorder, considering all the circumstances, is available. Using the principle of necessity to keep a person in hospital is contrary to article 5 of the Human Rights Act. The old 'treatability' test is abolished, and supervised community treatment (SCT) is introduced to ensure people receive the treatment they need and to avoid the 'revolving door' situation.

Types of assessments

The single assessment process

The 'single assessment process' was introduced in the government's *National Service Framework for Older People* (2001c), to help ensure that the health and social services would treat older people as individuals and enable them to make choices about their own care. Services were to be rooted in listening seriously to what people say. The aim was to have services striving to adjust to the person, rather than vice versa. There was an acknowledgement that older people can have as wide a range of problems, views and solutions as anyone else, and that holistic assessments are needed, assessments which, with permission, could be shared between social health services to avoid duplication. The 'Single Assessment Process' was seen as the model on which a 'Common Assessment Framework' could eventually be built to cover interagency assessment. It was seen as more than just stages of assessment, or simply an assessment tool.

The health service has a 'Care Programme Approach' for those with severe mental illness and there are plans to combine it with the 'Single Assessment Process' to form one comprehensive process/approach/framework for continuing healthcare for those who have mental illness and for other adults who need support and care. The term 'single assessment' is used to mean one social care assessment; 'comprehensive assessment' is also used for this, or for a combination of all the approaches. There is talk of movement towards a 'Common Assessment Framework' for adults, as was proposed in the White Paper *Our Health, Our Care, Our Say* (2006c), to be based mainly on the experience of using the single assessment process and the care programme approach. When the common assessment framework for adults appears, it is expected to have documentation and proformas similar to that of the single assessment process. The intention is to promote proportionate assessment according to people's level of need, as well as a person-centred assessment of needs, leading to a personalized care plan and greater transparency around the assessment process and agreed support. It is hoped that it will also avoid treatable health conditions being missed or misunderstood.

At the time of writing there are five main assessments or five assessment documents in SAP:

- Contact assessment.
- Overview assessment.
- Specialist assessment.
- Carer's needs assessment.
- Comprehensive assessment.

Specialist assessment is self-explanatory: for example, assessments provided by psychologists and occupational therapists. A *comprehensive assessment* at present means combining all the assessments available. We now wish to focus on *contact assessments, overview assessments* and *carer's assessments*. Before starting a contact and overview assessment, a referral form is completed to gather basic information, names, ages, addresses, composition of the household and so on, plus some preliminary information about the concerns of the referrer: whether further assessment is needed; the type of case; which professionals are involved; whether there were any previous assessments; and so on. This is the *contact* assessment. The *overview* assessment record checks the basic information with the person, and then obtains detailed information on twelve domains of the person's life. The intention is that the worker should do this in a conversational style rather than routinely going through each question in turn. As the reader will see, this is rather difficult to achieve.

Twelve domains

1. Service user perspectives (9 headings, or subdomains, followed by a decision as to what other domains to address as a result of domain 1.

2. Carer's perspective (9 headings).

3. Health/clinical background (16 headings).

4. Disease prevention (8 headings).

5. Physical wellbeing (13 headings, each with a risk assessment).

6. Activities of daily living – personal care (9 headings, each with a risk assessment).

7. Activities of daily living – household (6 headings with risk assessments).

8. Senses and communication (6 headings with risk assessments).

9. Emotional needs – mental health (12 headings, with risk assessments).

10. Relationships and personal fulfilment (7 headings with risk assessments).

11. Vulnerability and safety (5 headings with risk assessments).

12. Housing, environment and finances (9 headings with risk assessments).

This is the core document of a single assessment process and it looks more like a medical report that neglects to ask a person which parts are healthy.

Domain 1

This begins by asking about past history, strengths and motivation but gives no guidance as to how to do this well. Apart from this first question, strengths are never again mentioned in the process, although there is one question about hopes and fears.

In our view, to deal with domain 1 properly a social worker needs to listen to the person's history, drawing out the successes and achievements, and end this phase by engaging in a conversation to co-construct with the person what would be a meaningful future for them, how they could do meaningful things, perhaps *contribute* to others in some way and not just receive help. How can they be their best selves? Kitwood (1998) comments: 'one of the anomalies in the care of older people, especially in residential settings, is that there is often virtually no knowledge of how they have lived their lives' (p. 326), and he recommends that where people have dementia, the assessor holds conversations with relatives.

Domain 2

This refers to carers' perspectives. Here again there could be prompts about asking how can the carer help the person feel valued? Can they reminisce together? Talk about achievements? Invent possibilities for further contributions to others' lives? Who else could help with such talk?

Domains 3 to 5

These are about health details and disabilities. Some of the detail here is intrusive. We would recommend that where there is a reason to involve a district nurse s/he would be a better person to do these sections. Social workers are not usually able to have meaningful conversations about bowel problems and the like.

Domains 6 and 7

These have a major focus on risk rather than on possibilities or options for change and safety and greater quality of life. The forms leave little room for this, but at least some discussion of these, in positive language, would be more enabling and more likely to engage the person or the carer in considering simple steps to improve safety where it is an issue. The same applies to *domains 10 to 12*; where independence is at risk, a key question must be: what support or action is required to make the situation good enough? This applies especially to items that threaten dignity, independence and choice. In assessments of this kind, it is often difficult to assess areas that people are embarrassed to talk about, such as domestic violence or some form of oppression. Wright (2003) found that many older women in palliative care wanted the chance, however small, to tell in safety what life had been like for them, and needed to be believed and supported (with regard to older people in general, see also Mowlan *et al.*, 2007).

The domains are followed by details of benefits being received. This section is followed by a summary page showing the risk levels for the various sub-domains.

LIKELIHOOD of Harm ↓	SEVERITY of Harm →			
	Negligible	Minor	Severe	Extreme
Unlikely	Low	Low	Moderate	Moderate
Quite likely	Low	Moderate	Substantial	Substantial
Likely	Moderate	Substantial	Critical	Critical
Highly likely	Moderate	Substantial	Critical	Critical

Figure 11.1 Matrix for calculating risk in the single assessment process (SAP)

Risk assessment in SAP

In the introduction to SAP there is a matrix for calculating risk as shown in Figure 11.1.

One could then ask if there are any safety measures or controls in place that would reduce risk as far as possible (and that comply with regulations); if so are they satisfactory? If they are not satisfactory what action would make them so?

Carer's needs assessment

A large and very thorough tool/proform (13 pages, with 130 questions) has been produced for the purpose of assessing the carer's needs. As with SAP, there is a long section for collecting data. This relates to the carer's relationship with the person being cared for, with details of all aspects of the care being given by the carer, problems being encountered, and space for the care manager's comments. There is a section for risk assessment, by which is meant risk to the carer's independence resulting from caring. This has a risk matrix which asks whether the risk is 'critical', 'substantial', 'moderate' or 'low' with regard to four aspects:

- Autonomy (their control over their immediate situation).
- Health and safety (safety from harm within the family or from the person cared for, intentional or unintentional).
- Managing daily routine.
- Involvement (in family life, education, employment, social networks).

Then, there is a checklist asking what services the carer would like, and how these should be arranged if the carer qualifies for them. The intended outcome is that the carer's needs, in relation to health, wellbeing, work, education and leisure are identified, and that they receive the help to which they are entitled.

CASE STUDY: THEORY INTO PRACTICE

William is a 44-year-old man with complex needs. He is cared for by his elderly parents who have always refused respite care services. His father had a stroke recently and his mother is struggling to care for them both.

- How would you give this mother choice and control over her decisions for the future care of her family?
- Suggested reading: Bowey, L. and McGlaughin, A. (2007) 'Older carers of adults with a learning disability confront the future: issues and preferences in planning', *British Journal of Social Work*, 37: 39–54.

Fair Access to Care Services (FACS) – assessing for eligibility

This process was launched by the Department of Health in 2003. Essentially, it is an assessment of eligibility for service in the case of all adults in need. It focuses on four levels of risk to independent living, or rather four categories of help needed to deal with the threat to independence in the immediate and long-term future – critical, substantial, moderate and low. *Fair Access to Care Services* invites the practitioner to focus on health, safety, autonomy and involvement in family and the community (including leisure, hobbies, work, learning and volunteering) but without overlooking risks of accidental harm, self-harm, abuse, neglect, risk to carers and others. Other questions are:

- What are the hazards? Who might be harmed, and how?
- How serious is the risk? What precautions are necessary?
- What support is needed to maximize independence and minimize risk?
- Do others need to be protected as a result of the decision?

Situations are said to be critical when:

- Life is or will be threatened, and/or significant health problems will develop, and/or
- There is little or no choice or control over vital aspects of the environment, and/or
- Serious abuse or neglect has or will occur, and/or
- There is inability to carry out vital personal care or domestic routines, and/or
- Vital involvement in work, education or leisure cannot or will not be sustained, and/or
- Vital social support systems or relationships cannot or will not be sustained, and/or
- Vital family or other social roles cannot or will not be taken.

This level of risk/need will ensure that the person receives services – lower levels may or may not do so, therefore many see this process as a rationing device. Service can also be rationed via the points system in allocating direct payments.

Self-assessment, individual budgets and direct payment

The use of self-assessment and direct payments to increase choice and independence is spreading slowly, despite arguments that it is nothing more than a money-saving device. Figure 11.2 shows an example of how it works.

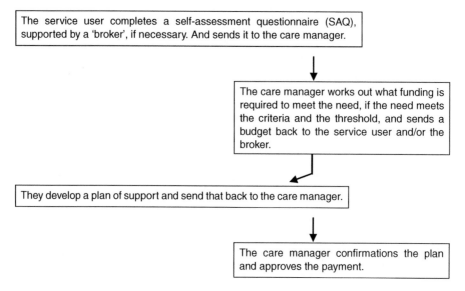

The service user completes a self-assessment questionnaire (SAQ), supported by a 'broker', if necessary. And sends it to the care manager.

The care manager works out what funding is required to meet the need, if the need meets the criteria and the threshold, and sends a budget back to the service user and/or the broker.

They develop a plan of support and send that back to the care manager.

The care manager confirmations the plan and approves the payment.

Figure 11.2 Use of self-assessment and direct payments to increase choice and independence

In this process the broker is the key person. This role may be taken by a relative or other carer or by a professional, and is paid for out of the budget. Some services prefer the broker to be one of their staff, perhaps a social worker. There is some concern that funds may be spent in a wasteful way, leaving social care to pick up the bill when things go wrong, such as a vital need not being provided for, when the money runs out.

The care planning approach

In mental health services assessments and resulting interventions, plans are produced that are not too dissimilar from the 'on-going assessment' in SAP. There is a proposal that they should be combined with the SAP to form a common assessment framework for all adults.

Risk-taking – values and principles

A key area for the assessment of all adults is that of enabling people to make their own decisions while minimizing risk or harm. People using care services or health services want more control over their lives, to be able to make real choices and take control of things just as most people take for granted (Commission for Social Care Inspection, 2006). They say they want a life, not just services. Some interesting steps towards providing this have been made, for example, the use of direct payments to service users and individual budgets (currently being trialled) and there is now a duty (DoH, 2007) on local councils to discuss this with people as a first option. These measures help to place the service user at the centre of the caring process. However, the decisions some people make can seem to be quite risky, placing workers in a dilemma. Avoiding all risk constrains people's choice, yet the worker strives to not make decisions for people. To help with the dilemma, there are some guiding principles:

1. People have a right to live lives to the full, so long as this does not hinder the rights of others.
2. Trying to remove risk altogether can destroy a person's quality of life. Choice, control and dignity are primary values to be respected.
3. Informed choice includes the option to choose 'unwisely'.
4. Decisions made on behalf of those who lack mental capacity must be made in their best interests and be the least-restrictive option.
5. If a choice involves risk of abuse, protective measures need to be put in place.
6. Human rights must underpin the actions of all public authorities.
7. Where there is a duty of care, foreseeable harm and negligence are concerns for the legal system, as is putting people at risk.
8. If a worker is in doubt as to whether going along with a risky decision involves negligence, s/he should consult a manager.

Reports of litigation in the news media have had the result of making managers and workers risk-averse, a state that makes it difficult to honour the above principles, so it is encouraging that policy-makers are now seeking to move from risk-aversion to supported decision-making (in effect, supported risk-taking).

Supported decision-making

How can decision-making be supported? Does supported choice really mean support for the choice you want to make, or for the choice the service user wants to make? Is the main concern of managers to avoid being involved in choice-making, because of the potential risk to the service of blame, should some harm follow? In our view, the process of supported decision-making, carefully carried out in collaboration with a service user, can help to clear up many of the concerns that arise in assessing how best a person's quality of life can be safeguarded and risks managed.

First, we need to check whether service users need to be helped to understand the possible consequences of their decisions and to take responsibility for them and, where necessary, to plan what level of protection would balance reasonable levels of risk. As people exercise more choice, more risks are inevitable.

Risk-taking is a normal part of a free life, yet no worker or service wants to be blamed when things go wrong.

In applying the first principle above, by considering with people the possible consequences of actions and the likelihood of harm, and then setting this against the benefits of a decision for independence and wellbeing, responsibility for decisions can be clarified and, if necessary, a support plan for managing risk can be put in place. However staff in various services, or indeed within the same service, may have differing views on acceptable risk, so a process, involving service users and carers, is needed to resolve disagreements in this area. The service providing the funding will probably have the last say. And of course local authorities have a responsibility not to agree with any plan where they see serious concerns about being accused of placing an individual in danger. However 'having a life' is not possible without some risk and there is acceptance in policy discussion papers (DoH, 2007) that we need to question the culture that says 'minimise all risk', whether it is a threat or not, engaging in helping people to make judgements about reasonable risk, supporting them in balancing the benefit and the risk and in finding possible ways of mitigating serious risk. We need to see vulnerable adults as 'people who want to do things' – people whose best interests are not equated with total safety, people who are often capable of accepting responsibility for their actions. A useful parallel is going to hospital for an operation, being told of the risks involved and the chances of things going wrong, and being allowed by the surgeon to decide whether to go ahead or not. The emphasis is beginning to shift from perceived negative impact to benefits and best interest.

The identification and weighing of risk is an essential part of any assessment in this field and the matrix supplied with the Single Assessment Process (see page 214) will hardly help workers to be less risk-averse. However, the Department of Health has proposed the following supported decision tool to assist when there is conflict between safety and the choices a person may be considering, or wants to make. It consists of a list of topics/questions to be explored in conversation with the person.

Supported decision tool (DoH, 2007)

1. What is important to you in your life?

2. What is working well?

3. What isn't working so well?

4. What could make it better?

5. What things are difficult for you?

6. Describe how they affect you living your life.

7. What would make things better for you?

8. What is stopping you from doing what you want to do?

9. Do you think there are any risks ?

10. Could things be done in a different way, which might reduce the risks?

11. Would you do things differently?

12. Is the risk present wherever you live?

13. What do you need to do?

14. What do staff/services need to change?

15. What could family/carers do?

16. Who is important to you?

17. What do people important to you think?

18. Are there any differences of opinion between you and the people you said are important to you?

19. What would help to resolve this?

20. Who might be able to help?

21. What could we (practitioner) do to support you?

22. Agreed next steps – who will do what ?

23. How would you like your care plan to be changed to meet your outcomes?

24. Record of any disagreements between people involved.

25. Date agreed to review how you are managing.

This tool encourages a conversation that is capable of leading to a more balanced and safer decision, than the use of the risk tick-boxes in the single assessment process. Enabling people to exercise choice and control over their lives is an essential outcome in *Our Health, Our Care, Our Say*, therefore, assessing and managing risk proportionately and realistically is vital. It is also important, however, to ensure that use of the above supported decision tool is accompanied by standard agency arrangements for safeguarding vulnerable people from harm, for preventing unnecessary harm and for not putting people at risk. For social workers engaged in making assessments, treating people in a holistic way means not only promoting independence and clarifying risks that can follow from decisions Independently made, but also considering any health risks and involving health professionals in the process.

While we need to get back to the basic right of people to take an active part in the community, learning new skills, working and developing new confidence (making a contribution) – these things are not possible without some risks. Risk is, ultimately, indefinable as the notion that levels of risk can be categorized as 'negligible, minor, severe and extreme' or 'insignificant, marginal, critical and catastrophic' are not only social constructions of personal perceptions in practice, but also of little use, in that most people fall into the middle range. Professionals making assessments can discuss situations with informed colleagues, preferably including colleagues from other services involved and managers before making judgements about acceptable risk, but good practice focuses on human rights and timely support for decisions that suit people best. In situations of uncertainty, testing the risk is often worth while – for example, when a frail person returns home from hospital and lives alone, having a short trial stay at home can help the social worker to assess the situation better with the person, and answer questions about whether the action is too risky.

Older people

Many, if not most, of the various principles mentioned earlier, apply to work with older people who happen to need social care. Much of the discussion of the *domains* concerning the ongoing assessment of SAP applies. The work is often shared with health professionals and various specialists, but it is the social worker/care manager who usually coordinates the SAP assessments. Here, time is needed for addressing sensitive issues such as safety. Many people fear loss of liberty, loss of home, and so on. They often feel devalued by society and, if their resources are to be mobilized, they need to be valued by workers. They can then be helped to value themselves, and valuing their memories is often central in this. We need to address the following questions:

- How can they value memories of self and others and appreciate their self-worth?
- How can they keep sight of their purpose, rather than become an invalid (or in-valid as a person)?

It takes time to discuss past achievements, contributions to others' lives, work, childrearing, relationships and successes, and then to explore what all that says about the kind of person they are and what they still have to offer. This giving, even if it is only a smile to a tired nurse, is to be valued and is possibly a necessary part of maintaining inner strength in the face of fading physical strength.

People who have faced desperate situations tell us that this is the way to survive well, even when facing the end of life itself. Victor Frankl (1997) survived concentration camps, where people around him were losing the will to live, by finding a purpose amid the madness and hopelessness of his situation. He did this by focusing on some future tasks or unfinished work, or inventing a task like thinking what he could say to others, or how he could benefit his students by sharing his analysis of survival with them after the war. He describes this as 'giving meaning' and 'a purpose' to being alive. He discovered that when he found a *why*, he could manage the most demanding *how*. He found that the most helpful small step was always some giving of himself to another. For him, we are essentially social, and our meaning and dignity are found in our contributions to others, particularly when we find ourselves up against it in some way. Reacting in this way prevents the decline in self-worth that ends in people feeling they are only bundles of flesh waiting in a warehouse to decay.

The outcomes of independence and dignity are not possible if we see our lives as devoid of meaning and purpose. Living alone without purpose can feel like solitary confinement or house arrest, with perfunctory visits from meal deliveries and cleaners. A major need is the mobilization of the person's inner resources as a person with something, no matter how small, to offer others. A little creative constructive talk can develop possibilities during an assessment, making the process therapeutic rather than oppressive or intrusive. Domain 1 in the SAP could usefully be extended with prompts along these lines and a spare page to record the results.

CASE STUDY: THEORY INTO PRACTICE

Ninety-year-old Mrs Willis is reading your assessment and protests about the description of her as 'frail'.

■ What questions could you ask her that would enable her to talk about herself as 'robust'?

Further reading for those working with older people

Hughes, B. (1995) *Older People and Community care: Critical Theory and Practice.* Buckingham: Open University Press.
Phair, L. and Good, V. (1998) *Dementia: A Positive Approach.* London: Whurr.
Ray, M. and Phillips, J. (2002) 'Older people', in Adams, R., Dominelli, L. and Payne, M. (2005) *Critical Practice in Social Work.* Basingstoke: Palgrave Macmillan.

People with mental health problems

Mental illness is a complex problem, and in the eyes of many, a puzzling, mysterious and feared one. It has a rather dark history going back to the early 'madhouses' and huge Victorian asylums which were spread throughout the country up to the latter half of the twentieth century. There have been many models attempting to explain mental illness, mainly that it was a physical brain disorder. The anti-psychiatry movement of Ronald Laing (1961)in the UK and Thomas Szasz (1960) in the USA challenged this, without making much impact on actual practice. Gradually, the *biopsychosocial model* (BPS) was developed. Following the work of Engel (1980), many practitioners in medicine and social work – especially social work – now hold that mental illness is influenced by three factors: physical factors (in particular, disorders in the brain), psychological factors, such as unhelpful beliefs and perceptions, and social factors such as isolation. However, Bentall (2003) challenges all psychiatric diagnoses and argues that we should simply seek to understand and work with the daily experiences and behaviours of psychotic people. In the main, the medical profession resists this view, and it is they who have the principal role in assessing and treating this problem, despite the growth in multidisciplinary teams and the support of government policy for them.

Lester and Glasby (2006) set out five factors that affect the prevalence of mental illness in the population:

1. *Ethnicity and gender* – some ethnic groups are more represented than others in minority communities and women are more represented in some sections of the health system.

2. *Age* – men aged 25 to 34 have the highest suicide rate; suicide accounts for one death in five of young people.
3. *Occupation* – people in certain jobs develop more mental health problems.
4. *Education and work* – poor education, along with unemployment, are the most consistent factors.
5. *Family responsibility* – 28 per cent of lone parents are considered to have mental health problems, and carers are twice as likely to be affected if they give substantial care.

The other popular model is *the recovery model*. This model has moved away from the longstanding deficit models of mental illness that often led to assumptions of incurability. The recovery model proposes the possibility of recovery without necessarily being cured; that is, people being able to get on with leading a satisfying life despite the impairment of the problem, just as a physically impaired person would, provided they had the necessary help, rather than being disabled by society through discrimination or other forms of exclusion. The model also speaks of recovery from stigmatization and from the side-effects of treatments, making sense of their situation and making the most of their talents, not being overly dependant on medication, helping in their own treatment – for example, doing things that help the medication to work better, having more control. In our view, it is tragic that some recent policies do not seem to encourage this approach more.

The 1980s brought considerable changes in the field of mental health. The Team for the Assessment of Psychiatric Services project established in 1985, the work of Engel (1980), the recovery model, the expansion of community mental health teams and community psychiatric nurses all made a difference. Community mental health teams were given the task of assessing and treating those referred to them, as well as supporting GPs. There was confusion, however, over which service users they should focus on. Such confusion seems to be common in this field. The 'care programme approach' was introduced as early as 1991, but it has been increasingly criticized for being driven from a professional rather than a service user perspective, and for being more focused on risk than on developing holistic approaches to promoting recovery on people's own terms.

The twenty-first century brought the addition of specialized teams: 'assertive outreach teams', 'crisis resolution and home treatment teams' and 'early intervention teams'; see the *Mental Health Policy Implementation Guide* (DoH, 2004). Community mental health teams are still seen as the core of the system, liaising with the specialized teams, while caring for those with time-limited problems as well as those with complex problems and long-lasting needs. Assertive outreach teams were to focus on those with persistent severe problems, who had a high use of in-patient facilities, who had problems remaining in contact with services and who had complex needs including homelessness, self-harming and substance abuse. Crisis resolution teams and home treatment teams were intended to aid rapid assessment of people with acute problems and refer them to the most appropriate service, as well as providing home-based 24/7 treatment and supervision for those assessed as suitable for such care, for as long as the crisis continued. Davidson and Campbell (2007) found that assertive out-reach was more successful than community mental health teams in reducing perceived coercion and minimizing the need for coercive strategies, engaging high-risk service users and reducing in-patient bed use. However, a lack of criti-cal understanding by staff can have serious repercussions for the rights of people with high levels of need being supported in the community.

Interdisciplinary partnerships were proposed as the way of the future in the 1999 Health Act, which placed a statutory duty of partnership on local authority social services and the NHS. Pooled budgets, lead commissioning and inte-grated provision were introduced. Section 45 of the Health and Social Care Act 2001 introduced 'care trusts' (NHS bodies), but their setting up was vol-untary and they mainly targeted mental illness and learning disability. Social service staff had concerns about their status in this field, dominated as it is by medical staff and psychologists. As a result, these trusts have not been the smooth fix that was expected. Some of the 'flexibilities' seem to have been imposed without any evidence of their effectiveness, and it was felt that much more thought was needed about how to encourage effective partnerships and joined-up solutions.

Social exclusion is a major mental health issue. Although it is difficult to assess which is cause and which is effect in term of its aetiology, it is clear that it is something to be addressed in any project for supporting those with mental illness. People who behave oddly in public are easily judged as mad and they are quickly avoided. Lester and Glasby (2006) suggest that there are five ele-ments in social exclusion: stereotyping, stigmatizing, discrimination, prejudice and general negative attitudes, especially in the media where violence is asso-ciated with mental illness. With regard to violence by mentally ill people, they list numerous studies that show that only a small percentage (about 5 per cent) of crime is committed by those who are mentally ill and such people are more likely to suffer violence than commit it. Whatever crimes they do commit are committed for the same reasons as other offenders – poverty, substance abuse and relationship problems. Attacks on strangers are extremely rare. As regards predicting their actions, this is very difficult indeed, if not impossible. Blumen-thol and Lavender (2000) provide more detail on risk assessment and they offer a predictive tool, although many see prediction as more an art than a science.

Meanwhile, the drive towards user involvement in social care decision-making continues and the NHS National Centre for Involvement has been set up. Isolated tragic events can, however, have a disproportionate effect on pol-icy, as in the recent decision to make compulsory orders a non-negotiable issue. Peck *et al.* (2002) propose a framework for thinking about user involvement, but though there are a growing number of service user groups, there is still a lack of information, communication and consultation (Webb *et al.*, 2000). Lester and Glasby say that financial costs, time costs, concerns over representa-tiveness, resistance to service users as experts in their own problems and power imbalance are among the barriers to progress. On the other hand, a Social Care Institute ofr Excellence report in 2003 maintained that every effort was being made to include service users on boards.

Mrs Young

Age: 86 Diagnosis: Dementia

Professionals involved: GP(doctor), DN (district nurse), CPN (community psychiatric nurse) consultant psychiatrist, SW (social worker),

Main problems: Weight loss, falls risk, no electricity, no heating, confusion.

Mrs Young lives alone in a rural area of England. She used to enjoy going out, but
now refuses to leave the house. She presents differently every time a different
professional visits. Her mood can fluctuate depending on time of day and there
are mixed reports from different professionals. She has no children or other family
available.

The initial referral was from her GP to DN requesting blood tests due to weight
loss, and falls risk assessment. The blood tests are normal, there is no physical
reason for weight loss and no obvious physical health problems. Her weight loss
was attributed to Mrs Y not eating the meals provided as she gives all her food to
the cats. The SW is asking for more medical/general nursing input. The GP reviewed
her case at home, and insisted that her problems are psychiatric and referred her
back to the CPN. The DN agreed to monitor her weight in the interim, and increase
the care package so a carer visits at meal time to sit with Mrs Y during meals to
ensure dietary intake is adequate. As Mrs Young is unable to prepare meals/drinks
her carers provide all food and fluids.

Her weight increased slightly with the new care package and supplement drinks and
her BMI is now stable. She still has a high falls risk, but has refused a Careline alarm
(not unusual in elderly with or without dementia).

The SW is very anxious about potential weight loss in future, requesting a food and
fluid chart from the DN and a definite action plan should further weight loss occur.
The SW feels that Mrs Young needs to be in residential care, or even a psychiatric
ward for assessment owing to weight loss, but Mrs Young refuses.

She was assessed again at home by the CPN, GP, SW and psychiatrist but didn't
meet criteria for section under the Mental Health Act so a decision was made
to observe and monitor her weight. Mrs Young was also not paying bills, and her
house was in need of repair as it could be dangerous in winter. The SW started
procedures to take control of finances.

MDT meeting on psychiatric ward

Present: DN, CPN, consultant psychiatrist, SW, ward manager.

SW: Asking for residential care – many anecdotes about 'bad days', for example of
not coping, hygiene not good, refuses bath and so forth from carers. Some days dire.

CPN: Less concerned, acknowledged that mood does fluctuate depending on who
visits and what time of day it is. Generally feels there is some deterioration but
nothing acute.

DN: Was concerned about weight loss but now stable thanks to increased care
package. Still high falls risk, especially in the garden which is so overgrown.

Psychiatrist: 'Statistically people are more at risk of falls in residential/nursing
homes.'

DN: 'At least she would have someone to pick her up; if she fell in the garden, no-one would find her.' Did acknowledge that once control of finances is in place a gardener could be paid.

Psychiatrist: 'I think we're being rather paternalistic when advocating residential care. This woman doesn't want to go, doesn't need psychiatric ward admission, her weight is stable, there are issues re finance but these are in hand, she comes in the grey area between mental health section and "not having capacity". I think she hasn't got capacity as she feeds all food to cats and so on, but don't we risk being very paternalistic? Legally where do we stand insisting on residential care? I think we can't. What is wrong with a person staying in the place they want to be with risks that are being in part managed? We can't eliminate all risk. She wants to stay at home. What's better – stay where you want to be with risk and possibly die earlier, or be taken somewhere you don't want to be, causing stress/anxiety, but you have very happy care workers?'

The plan that emerged

Try to persuade Mrs P to go to residential care for two weeks while repairs are done on the house. She is likely to refuse – if so, continue with current care package. CPN to monitor weight and mental state. Review in 6 weeks. Likely to end up in residential care, but not to push this now. If she refuses home improvements, she will die of cold in winter – she was in an acute psychiatric ward all last winter.

Consider

How helpful is the matrix outlined on page 214 in helping you assess the risks to Mrs Young?

- Look at the principles set out in the Mental Capacity Act 2005. Have these been considered here?
- What conversation could the professionals have had with her that would identify any strengths she has?
- Decide which professional view you agree with, and why?
- *Suggested reading*

    Quinn, C. (1996) *The Care Must Be There.* www.fordementia.org.uk.

Assessing the needs and risks of adults with mental health problems is, we suggest, more effective where the worker talks openly with the service user about risks, acknowledging the impact of this on the service user and eliciting their solutions. For example, Henden (2008) provides a graded set of questions for people who pose a suicide risk:

Sample questions to elicit suicidal thoughts

- At this point, how much more do you feel you can cope with?
- How far is this getting you down right now?

- How often, recently, have you felt you are getting to the end of your tether?
- I expect sometimes you feel you have had your lot?
- At the moment, how far do you feel able to go on?
- How close do you feel, right now, to ending your life?
- If you decided to go ahead with the last resort option, what method would you use? How prepared are you should you decide? (Paradoxically, having made preparations is indicative of both very high risk and low risk, as some people are comforted by being prepared and therefore do not feel the need to go ahead with the last resort option.)

Sample questions once suicidal intent has been established

- Tell me about a time in the last week when you felt least suicidal?
- Before you were feeling as you do at the moment, what did you do in the day that interested you?
- What has stopped you taking your life up to this point?
- On a scale of 1 to 10, how suicidal do you feel right now?
- On a scale of 1 to 10, how suicidal were you before you decided to seek help?
- What would you be doing/thinking/feeling to be another half point higher?
- What have you done in the last week that has made a difference to the terrible situation you are in?
- On a scale of 1 to 10, how determined are you to give another option (other than suicide) a try first?
- Let us suppose you went for the last resort option and actually died. You are at your own funeral as a spirit looking down from about 10 feet up at the mourners below. What might you be thinking about another option you could have tried first? At this funeral, who would be the most upset among the mourners? What advice would they have wanted to give you regarding other options?
- When was the last time, before this current time in your life, that you thought of ending it all?
- What did you do that made a difference and enabled you to pull yourself back?
- Suicide is the last resort as we know; what other ways have you tried so far to crack this problem?

Similar questions can be used in the assessment of eating disorders (Jacob, 2001), hearing voices (White, 1995; Bullimore, 2002), and murderous intent (Milner, 2003, 2004a). Even in cases of acute psychosis, openness and confidence in the person's ability to manage their own risks makes it possible to assess intent, as this brief extract from an interview with Alan demonstrates (Macdonald, 2006, pp. 152–4).

Alan has been disturbed for several days before being detained under legal powers at his home. He resisted transfer by ambulance and was brought to the secure unit in handcuffs by police. This extract is from an interview the following day after questions have established that a diagnosis of paranoid illness can be made and his needs and wishes have been elicited (sorting out his money and getting some sleep):

Interviewer: So thinking about a scale of 1 to 10 where 10 is you get out of hospital and things are going well, and 0 is as bad as things were before, where are you right now on that scale?

Alan: Nought.

Interviewer: So how have you kept going when you were at nought?

Alan: Getting some sleep helped.

Interviewer: So sleep is really important for you. When you move up half a point on the scale what will be different for you?

Alan: I won't feel like hitting people.

Interviewer: Who do you feel like hitting?

Alan: The neighbours and that policeman. He had no right to put handcuffs on me.

Interviewer: How come the police were there?

Alan: I told the ambulance man I would cut him if he tried to come into my flat.

Interviewer: Have you cut anyone before? Or hit anyone?

Alan: No, but I could have done it.

Interviewer: How come you did not do that?

Alan: They came in before I could get a knife from the kitchen.

Interviewer: Do you still think about getting a knife or cutting someone?

Alan: I sometimes think about it.

Interviewer: How do you manage to think about it but not do it?

Alan: I think to myself that they will put me in hospital again if I cut someone. The neighbours might get me for it while I was sleeping.

Interviewer: Are their specific people that you think of cutting, neighbours or anyone else?

Alan: I felt like hitting that policeman.

Interviewer: Have you thought about cutting or hitting anyone in this hospital?

Alan: No.

Interviewer: How can we tell if you are thinking about cutting or hitting someone?

Alan: I don't know.

Interviewer: Will you tell us if you are thinking like that?

Alan: [no reply]

Interviewer:	When you are thinking like that, what can we do to help?	
Alan:	Let me stay in my room; the other people here are strange.	
Interviewer:	Will you tell us when you need to stay in your room?	
Alan:	Yes.	
Interviewer:	OK; we will ask you if we're not sure. I guess that hitting or cutting someone will not help you get out of hospital sooner.	
Alan:	[nods]	
Interviewer:	Anything else to mention today?	
Alan:	No. I'm tired just now.	

As can be seen from these examples, checklists and predictive tools are not always necessary for assessing risks and needs when the assessing worker shows no fear of the worst scenario and talks sincerely and genuinely with service users about their pain as well as their dangerousness, joining with them to generate other possibilities at the same time as ensuring that they are responsible for any decisions they make (Henden, 2005), in other words, using social work skills in direct practice rather than relying on tools as a means of case management.

Further reading for those working with people with mental illness

Bailey, D. (ed.) (2000) *At the Core of Mental Health Practice*. Brighton: Pavilion.
Foster, A. and Roberts, V. Z. (eds) (1998) *Managing Mental Health in the Community: Chaos and Containment*. London: Routledge.
Hawkes, D., Marsh, T. and Wilgosh, R. (1998) *Solution Focused Therapy: A Handbook for Health Care Professionals*. Oxford: Butterworth Heinemann.
Macdonald, A. (2006) *Solution-Focused Therapy: Theory, Research and Practice*. London: Sage.

People with dual diagnosis

> Substance abuse by users of mental health services (dual diagnosis) can seriously affect the ability of services to assess, treat and care for patients safely and effectively. (DoH, 2006)

The term dual diagnosis is used to describe people who misuse substances *and* have mental health problems (Wake, 2004); originally they were referred to as having 'complex needs' (Rassool, 2002). Not only can substance misuse make symptoms worse; it can lead to suicide or violence and increased risk-taking behaviours, thus treatment of substance misuse often ameliorates psychiatric problems (Crome, 1999). The initial guidance (DoH, 2002) aimed to provide an integrated service within mental health and substance misuse services so that people were not shunted between different sets of services or put at risk of dropping out of care completely (DoH, 2002). Despite guidance on how to undertake a comprehensive risk and needs assessment of the person and their family, between 22 per cent and 44 percent of inpatients are said to misuse substances and between 60 percent and 80 per cent have a history of substance misuse prior to admission, but fewer than 20 per cent receive treatment for their misuse. Later guidance from the government (DoH, 2006) advises that substance misuse specialists should be responsible for assessment and treatment of the misuse. Black and ethnic minority groups were identified as being particularly poorly served in this area.

There is a suggestion that assessment of substance misuse should form part of the care programme approach assessment and the assessment should include a risk assessment and a plan for managing the risk. Workers are advised not to assume that only one drug is being misused and therefore report headings should include:

- The number of drugs being misused.
- What these drugs are.
- The quantity used.
- The frequency.
- By what route.
- How long the misuse has been going on for.

Service users should also be asked whether they see the misuse as a problem. Assessors are to:

- Ascertain whether the person understands the potential for serious damage to themselves.
- Explore past usage and its relationship to the course of the mental illness.
- Explore why the person misuses, be it to help with coping with the illness, or just part of a life-style, or whether it is done out of boredom.
- Consult relatives and other carers, although their views are not to be shared with the patient.
- Consider whether samples should be taken for testing.

It is also suggested that some who do not misuse drugs should still be assessed for risk of future misuse because, for example, of association with misusers. Personalised education programmes and preventative interventions should also figure in plans.

People with physical impairment

For several decades 'disabled' people have been saying that what they want is access to the world, socially, educationally and economically, rather than be recipients of social welfare. We use quotation marks to signify our view that those with physical impairments are people who are disabled by social attitudes as much as by their physical problems. A social construction of people with physical impairments as dependent, and therefore deficient in some way, may enter the minds of disabled people themselves. Thus, although social work has embraced a social model of disability (Swain *et al.*, 2003) and has worked at getting people the help they need (for example wheelchairs), as well as seeking to change attitudes and change public facilities such as transport, so that those with impairments can go about living as full a life as anyone else, service users may feel that they have lost their entire identity as a person. They may resent support, and hence work may be needed to shift their constructs and stereotypes so that they could believe in the possibility of being an autonomous person still, rather than becoming their own oppressor. When those whose identity is bound up with being able-bodied become impaired, guiding them towards an alternative understanding of impairment and disability can be a most important step.

When social workers are involved in assessing need they, therefore, need to make sure that they have a social model of disability fixed in their minds, and that they are able to ensure that they do not come across to service users as 'representing an organization that is embedded in an individual model approach to disability issues' (Sapey, 2002, p. 187). We need to ensure that we bring an attitude that regards disabled people as complete human beings in every way, but who may be disadvantaged by the perceptions of many people in society and in the failure to remove the obstacles that block their way in life. Sapey reminds us that disability can be a universal experience, as any one of us can become disabled at some stage – in this respect disability is different from other oppressions such as gender. Disabled people are not, however, one homogenous group; the disability can be chronic or temporary, longstanding or recent, and static or deteriorating. Long periods of physical impairment and/or ill health threaten psychological and sexual wellbeing as much as physical needs, so effective assessments are flexible, and look for the impact of these differences in disability on service users. For example, when assessing service users with disabilities from childhood, chronic lack of independence and privacy may have denied many opportunities. Blackburn (2002) interviewed a hundred young adults with spina bifida or hydrocephalus and found that she was the first person for most of them who had ever talked with them about their sexual activity – or lack of opportunity for such activity. These young people had not received sex education appropriate to their needs; the materials used had shown only able-bodied, white subjects and there had been no information provided on the particular difficulties these people would experience should they find a sexual partner. Equally worrying was Blackburn's finding that this group was particularly vulnerable to sexual abuse, there being both historic and current experiences of such abuse in this group.

Disability also disadvantages women disproportionately to men in the following ways:

- Disabled men are more likely than women to establish satisfying relationships.
- Disabled women are more likely to be divorced than disabled men.
- Men's negative reactions are more extreme towards disability.

- Disabled women are more likely to lack 'desirable' female qualities, such as physical grace and ease, so their body image is harder hit than that of disabled men.
- Disabled married women with a non-disabled partner are the subjects of curiosity, scrutiny and public misunderstanding (Asch and Fine, 1988).
- The quest for physical perfection makes it especially hard for disabled women, resulting in negative self-image or poor self-esteem (Thomas, 1999). Thus it is as important for assessments to focus on body image as on mobility.

Where a disability situation is a deteriorating one, assessments need to be both speedy and frequently updated. Advances in palliative care mean that there are more very ill people living in the community, and there is little point in providing a wheelchair for someone after they have become too ill to use it. A study of palliative care (Clausen *et al.*, 2005) found that carers' needs were neglected and that they too require regular and speedy reassessments to assist them to adjust to a rapidly changing situation.

Many assessments of people with physical impairment are undertaken by occupational therapists, but they and social workers need to collaborate to provide the best service, because, despite the politics of disability and arguments that social work contributes to disablement by seeing people as needy, social provision is needed to support those who cannot provide equipment and house modifications for themselves because of lack of income – support without which they could not make progress in their lives. It can be said that people need help not just because of an impairment, but because of social factors such as poverty.

In assessing people who are physically impaired, social workers can empower them by bringing a political view of impairments as well as a view that dependency is not inevitable, a view that stresses their rights to have society adjust to them. In this way, they can be better informed about what is happening to them 'out there'. Then they may be interested in joining groups that stand up for their rights and thereby deal with feelings of disempowerment. Linking people with positive role models can be helpful, but simply administering care can in itself be disabling. However, grouping disabled people together socially also runs the danger of compounding disability. As a disabled writer commented, '[O]ne disabled person is a disabled person, two disabled people are a field trip, and three disabled people are a rehabilitation centre' (Knight, 1981, pp. 9–10).

Again, as with other service user groups, spending time getting to know people's strengths, showing interest in those strengths, appreciating how they are doing some things that are good for them, how they show impressive qualities in some way – all this shows respect for a fellow human being who is not regarded as 'other'. Developing a personal basis for their professional relationship symbolically separates the social worker from the potentially oppressive organization (Sapey, 2002, p. 188). We can work at countering oppression and discrimination in our direct work with disabled peopled also, for example by encouraging self-assessment of needs. Some useful questions that help avoid a focus simply on deficits could usefully include:

- In what ways has your disability made you a stronger person?
- What is good about your body?
- What needs to happen for you to live a fuller life?

Further reading for those working with people with physical impairment/disabilities

Oliver, M. and Sapey, B. (1999) *Social Work with Disabled People*, 2nd edn. Basingstoke: Palgrave Macmillan.

Barnes, C. and Mercer, G. (2003) *Disability*. Cambridge: Polity.

People with learning difficulties

We use the term *learning difficulty* rather than learning disability here on the grounds that, as Stainton (2002) says, this group of people have been more vulnerable than most to negative, stigmatizing and exclusionary constructions. They themselves have adopted People First as the name of their movement for equality, to show that while they are people who have a difficulty they are also full citizens, with full human rights. Linguistics and constructs have tremendous power for good or ill, so social workers need to be able to deconstruct negative identities that are imposed on people. This might include some colleagues from our own or another services who have not been trained in anti-discriminatory practice. Our organization may carry subtle oppressive constructs that can affect our responses and assessments without our being aware of it. Stainton (2002) suggests that we ask ourselves who is the person behind this construction. And then ask how we can help the person overcome the negative features attributed to him/her and begin to construct a fully human identity, which has strengths and positive qualities.

Difficulties may be categorized by a single impairment, such as, Down's syndrome, but these definitions lean towards seeing disability as a pathology, with no reference to the social implications or to the many possible degrees of difficulty that can be involved. As we will see below in the case of Andrew, another classification is based on intelligence tests which are derived from normative assumptions and can ignore the person behind the number. Yet another definition is based on the social model which sees disability less as a personal tragedy, than as a matter of how the problem is constructed by society and its arrangements (Swain *et al.*, 2003). People are stigmatized and discriminated against in areas of work, education and isolation generally, and it is this that disables them from being fully accepted into society.

In this field, there are three main approaches, namely the medical/psychological approach, the normalization approach and the self-determining citizen with rights approach.

The *medical approach* responds with psychological and behavioural interventions, preventative measures and hospital treatments. Prenatal detection fits in this model, as do interventions for challenging behaviour.

The *normalization approach* focuses on social roles, on countering negative roles and replacing them with a positive image. This includes an emphasis on dressing normally, mixing with the public and having normal daily routines and, especially, engaging in meaningful activities and valued roles in the community. This means spending less or no time in day centres or on courses that only emphasize the problem. So we can ask whether a certain activity supports a negative or a positive image of the person.

The *self-determining citizen with rights approach* is becoming the dominant approach in many services. It focuses on ensuring that the people know and use their full rights as citizens. There used to be a liberal belief that people with learning difficulties, and those with severe mental illness, can never become free of parental-type care or be capable of relationships or parenthood. (We will return to parents with learning difficulties later.) This meant they were deprived of *opportunities* to choose to live as they wanted or to make self-determined plans, irrespective of *outcomes*. Structural barriers were put in their way by agencies and communities.

It is important to be aware of all three approaches and how they can influence assessments. We would encourage a greater use of the third approach with its emphasis on the traditional social work value of self-determination and assessing what support people need to be able to determine their own futures and daily lives.

This involves, yet again, gaining an understanding of people as individuals, focusing on how to achieve what they want rather than deciding what is best for them, assessing how the needs they perceive can best be met and assessing how they can be empowered towards being autonomous citizens with full human rights. As we saw earlier, lacking speech or the ability to read is no reason for not including the person fully in an assessment (see Brewster, 2004, for details of 'talking mats', and so on). The research shows that carers of people with severe learning difficulty overestimate their verbal comprehension ability (Banat *et al.*, 2002), but these aspects of learning difficulty can be accommodated with time and care:

- Inattention (poor ability to tune in and recognize what is important) can be combatted by providing limited amounts of information, looking at the person directly and using practical examples.
- Lack of perception (poor ability to make sense of and understand information) can be combatted by limiting the amount of information presented, using short chunks of information and giving visual prompts to jog the memory.
- Limited comprehension (poor ability to understand what is being said) can be combatted by reducing the speed of what is said, modifying language used, clarifying complex ideas and continually repeating and rephrasing key learning points.

- Difficulties in expressing themselves (poor ability to communicate messages to other people) can be combated by using symbols, pictures and drawings to help explain complex concepts such as emotions and thoughts.

- Poor ability to cope with change can be combated by keeping changes to the minimum. Keene (2001) makes the point that people with complex needs often do not want to make major changes, or at least at the same time as professionals, and therefore the assessment needs to look at maintenance rather than change interventions in many instances.

- Poor ability to practise self-control techniques cognitively can be combated by frequent repetition of simple information until it is assimilated and the principles applied to a variety of contexts (Tudway and Darmoody, 2005).

Many adults with learning disability arrive in adult services from children's services, with an SAP assessment and specialist assessments. There may be assessments of mental capacity, not only by the health service but by specialists in housing, for example, who assess capacity to live in certain conditions, or the capacity for dealing with other aspects of independent living. Adult services will usually do an up-to-date comprehensive assessment. Some service users will be involved in a CPA programme coordinated by mental health professionals – for example, the broker may be a social worker or another professional, or a parent. Much of the work is NHS/social-work-integrated.

In assessment work with this group, as well as with other vulnerable adults, the focus needs to be not only on enabling them to live as full a life as possible but also very much on *safeguarding* them from abuse of any sort. It is estimated that 2 to 4 per cent of vulnerable older people, and their carers, are at risk of mistreatment, largely neglect (Mowlan *et al.*, 2007; O'Keefe *et al.*, 2007), and social workers need the skills and sensitivity to check it out not only for those in institutions but also for those in the community, including those living with partners or other relatives. We need vigilance to pick up tell-tale signs and ask people about how safe they feel. The 'risk of abuse' box may be ticked by some worker as 'safe' but situations can change rapidly and all agencies need to be proactive and not leave frequent review to everyone else or to someone commissioned to provide service.

The Learning Disability Coalition claim (*The Guardian*, 19 March 2008) that people with learning disability who have parents, are being put in lower eligibility categories, or sometimes given no category of need, on the basis that if they have others they don't need services, even though the parents may be in their seventies, eighties or even nineties. Any assessment needs to consider the whole situation and avoid pushing family carers to breaking-point and involving greater costs in the long term.

CASE STUDY: THEORY INTO PRACTICE

Andrew is a looked-after child who has lived as a single resident with 24-hour supervision in a specialist children's home following his sexual and physical abuse of his siblings at the age of 13. Previously he had been sexually abused by his father from the ages of 3 to 7. Although he has a complex learning difficulty, he has been educated in mainstream schooling where he has a full-time mentor to assist with both his learning and his aggressive behaviour towards other pupils. School has entered him for nine GCSEs, but his expected grades are below the minimum pass mark. He has been subject to numerous assessments, the latest stating that he is at high risk of sexually reoffending as he takes any opportunity to leave school and visit his family, and has little understanding of the impact of his offending behaviour. He is now approaching his sixteenth birthday, at which point the children and families team will have to hand over his care to another team, so a multidisciplinary team meeting is being held to decide on which branch of social services will be responsible for his care in the future, and what type of further education will be most suitable for him.

His Connexions' worker informs the meeting that Andrew hopes to become a policeman or enter the armed forces so he has obtained Andrew a place on an access course preparing young people for a carer in the armed forces at the local college.

His carers comment that Andrew is unable to use public transport as he does not understand the direction signs on buses and that, as the college is on three sites, he will either get lost or walk to his family home where his mother is unable to refuse him entrance as she is fearful of him.

The representative from the leaving care team says that Andrew is not suitable for the provision they use for preparing young people for independent living.

The representative from the learning disabilities team says that they cannot accept Andrew as his IQ is one point above their cutoff point of 70. Although it is pointed out that his IQ score of 71 is inflated by his superficial verbal ability and that his conceptual ability is very much lower, the team remain adamant that he does not qualify for their service.

The representative from the vulnerable adults team says that their services are geared towards elderly people and that they would be unable to provide him with the services he may require.

The meeting concludes with the recommendation that a further assessment be undertaken.

■ What level of risk do you consider Andrew to pose?

■ What are his needs?

■ Bearing in mind the resource limitations listed above, how could you use the single assessment process or the common assessment framework to establish both the needs and risks?

Further reading for those working with people with learning difficulties

Stainton, T. (2000) 'Learning disabilities', in Adams, R., Dominelli, L. and Payne, M. *Critical Practice in Social Work*. Basingstoke: Palgrave Macmillan.

Grant, G., Coward, P. and Richardson, M. (2005) *Learning Disability: A Life Cycle Approach to Valuing People*. Maidenhead: Open University Press.

Parents with learning difficulties

This is a group for whom both children's services and adults' services cooperate. The starting principle (DoH, 2007b) is that these parents have a right to be supported in their role, just as their children have a right to live in a safe and supportive environment. And such parents can be good parents, so the outcome for them would be bringing up their children successfully, with appropriate support and the outcomes for the children are the same five outcomes outlined by the government in *Every Child Matters* (DoH, 2005a) – see Chapter 10 of this volume. However, the research shows that this group of parents is most likely to be subject to pre-birth assessments and to lose their children to adoption (Booth and Booth, 1994, 2004). The guidance suggests that where assessments focus primarily on the learning difficulty, it is difficult to bring about changes, but if the focus is on things that can be changed or improved – housing for example – there are more possibilities for effective parenting: 'When problems are seen as rooted in deficit ... they may seem intractable' (Booth and Booth, 1997, p. 38).

Good practice requires:

- Accessible information for the family and good communication.
- Clear, coordinated referrals and assessment procedures and processes, eligibility criteria and care pathways.
- Support designed to meet needs, based on an assessment of strengths as well as needs.
- Independent advocacy.

The organization CHANGE, along with a group of parents with learning difficulties, devised the following guidelines:

- Social workers doing assessments should be respectful, turn up on time, speak directly to the parents, not use jargon, think before they speak, listen and 'hear' what people say, explain what is happening, do what they say they will do, be patient and take enough time to communicate clearly.
- Identification of need should start as soon as pregnancy is confirmed.
- Before starting an assessment, permission should be obtained from the parents/parents-to-be, unless it is ordered by a court, and the purpose of the assessment should be fully explained in clear language.
- Eligibility criteria should be clearly understood and referred to in considering needs.
- Learning difficulty does not mean that new skills cannot be learned for meeting a child's needs.
- Workers need to allow for parents being highly anxious about the possibility of their child being removed from them.
- Person-centred planning should be made available, not only after the assessment but during it, as it enables the identification of strengths, needs and barriers that might otherwise be missed.

The government guidance suggests the use of an initial screening tool (see for example McGaw *et al.*, 1998, 2007) to see if an expert assessment is needed as well as the CAF assessment. The roles of significant others should also be explored and the advice of a specialist sought if necessary.

Further reading for those working with parents with learning difficulties:

Booth, T. and Booth, W. (1997) *Exceptional Childhoods, Unexceptional Children*. London: Policy Studies Centre.

Department of Health (2007b) *Good Practice Guidance on Working with Parents with a Learning Disability*. London: Department of Health.

McGaw, S. (2006) Decision-Making: Parents with Learning Difficulties, in Murphy, G. and Clare, I. (eds) *Decision-Making: People with Learning Difficulties*. London: Sage.

People with challenging behaviour

Challenging behaviour was defined by Emerson *et al.* (1987) as behaviour of such intensity, frequency or duration that the physical safety of the person, and others, is likely to be placed in serious jeopardy, or behaviour that is seriously likely to limit or delay access to ordinary community facilities. Challenging behaviour has become the subject of government guidance (DoH, 2007a) which advises that all public services, including housing departments, have a responsibility towards disabled people who have challenging behaviour, although services designed to help this group are usually provided by the independent sector. It is stressed that the rights of people with this problem are the same as anyone else, including the right to personal relationships.

Challenging behaviour, like all the 'problems' in this section, is to a large extent socially constructed, owing partly to attitudes to disabilities generally as well as especially puzzling problems like autism, and partly to environmental factors in the services around these people and the attitudes of staff in those services. The service often amounts to little more than unskilled caring, with frequent changes of service and changes of carers. Medication is often used, but in many cases it serves only to mask the problem, not cure it.

An appropriate goal of this work is the achievement of as good a quality of life as possible *in spite of* the problem. Plans need to be highly individualized and made on the basis of getting to know the person and gathering accurate information about the individual in assessment, rather than on the basis of norms. Behavioural change usually needs other changes – improved communication skills, for example. One way of eliciting the hopes and wishes of this group of people is to use *social stories* as a means of talking about preferred futures (Grey, 2001). The prevention of worsening behaviour is a priority; for example, sexual reoffending in young people with a learning difficulty is higher, and within a shorter time, than their non-disabled peers and they require more external controls and a longer time scale for work to be effective (Craig and Hutchinson, 2005). They are also especially vulnerable to sexual violence themselves (for an overview see Myers and Milner, 2007), and the effects are long-lasting and severe (O'Callaghan *et al.*, 2003). Government guidance also advises local links and access to other public services need to be maintained.

THINKING POINT

- Look again at the case example of Andrew.
- How would you conduct your assessment to ensure that his rights as a young person, to attend college and live a full life, are balanced against the need to safeguard other young people?

Further reading for those working with people with challenging behaviour:

Emerson, E. *et al.* (1987) *Developing Services for People with Severe Learning Difficulties and Challenging Behaviour.* Canterbury: Institute of Social and Applied Psychology.

Department of Health (2007c) *Services for People with Learning Disability and Challenging Behaviour or Mental Health Needs.* London.

Critical comment

Views on assessment tools

In a large literature review at Sterling, Barry (2007) looked more closely at social workers' views of approaches to risk assessment. While social work literature continues to stress that the relationship between worker and service user is crucial to develop trust, cooperation and motivation to make changes, Barry found that social workers feel that the politics of risk are eroding such a relationship. Workers felt that agency accountability systems are reactive, adversarial and stifle professional autonomy, and that they do not allow for a culture of learning from mistakes that would enable confidential reporting of 'near misses'. Barry found that there was no confidence in the prediction ability of the assessment tools, and that these tools tend unfortunately to replace rather than inform professional judgement. Workers felt that the relationship that is so essential for effective working was being eroded by long proforma, and they felt that a more participatory, holistic and proactive approach which allows dialogue between workers, service users and managers is needed. On the other hand, there is some agreement that *prompts* are useful, in that they ensure the agenda is covered and there is less rushing back to people apologizing for forgetting something that is basic.

General issues

One reaction of social workers to lengthy assessment protocols, which we have noticed, is that there is never enough time to complete them properly. This is a major waste of resources. Perhaps the paperwork is so lengthy because the designers want to ensure that nothing is ever missed. We are not confident that the goal is achievable in a limited number of visits, let alone one visit.

Since the National Health Service and Community Care Act 1990, social work has been required to gate-keep services for those most in need and this imperative, along with limited resources, creates a tension between the professional values of social work and management's focus on eligibility (Ray and Phillips, 2002, p. 201). It takes a strong, even brave, worker to refrain from becoming reductionist, a short-term solution that can be more costly in the long term. The social work profession, therefore, would do well to set up a regular forum where managers, social workers and service users could discuss and negotiate ways of improving collaborative assessment.

We believe, however, that managerialism and procedural assessment are here to stay – that is the way all public service is moving, owing partly to the need for accountability for the massive costs to the taxpayer of quality services. So, rather than fighting against the trend, we want our criticism to be seen as helpful and we feel that concerned professionals and academics need to focus on ways of improving the quality of what we have in ways that make assessment more economical and more effective in terms of good outcomes for service users. We suggest that some methods drawn from brief therapies could be built in – any method is worth looking at that can mobilize the considerable resources of service users in finding constructive ways of reducing dependence on services, getting better involvement by service users and their carers in change efforts and better value for money at the same time.

This 'involvement' has come to be described as 'engagement' which used to mean relationship. 'We got no engagement' is a confusing way of saying the service user would not do what we asked. Worse still is the statement, especially in health services, 'We got no concordance', when what is meant is no compliance. This strange use of language seems to us to be a subtle way of saying the service user is at fault, without being accused of oppressive practice. This can appear too in work with those who are mentally ill and in child protection work (Platt, 2004). Ferguson (2007) says it gives a new meaning to an old word while sounding like a value.

The standardized approaches of procedural assessments can give rise to several difficulties:

- The theme of independence is fine and is in line with government guidance, but in the SAP documents the emphasis is on the risks to it, rather than what improvements can be made. So SAP tends to feed into the assumption that independence is inevitably in decline, and that residential care is inevitable when needs become more complex.

- Restrictions on resources can lead managers to expect assessors to make funding considerations their starting-point rather than the ideas of service users about their needs and solutions.

- Service imperatives to prove eligibility can skew the assessment away from service users' potential, ability to take risks and individual aspirations. 'Proving eligibility can carry with it a disincentive to highlight the older person's strengths, abilities and lifelong continuities which may be harnessed to cope with current challenges' (Ray and Phillips, 2002, p. 201)

- Standardized approaches make it difficult for workers to use theoretical frameworks (as discussed in the 'maps' chapters), or at least they distract the work from this.

- Routines assessment practices can divert attention from the rights of the individual to a real say in dealing with their concerns over their quality of life.

- These approaches drive work towards short-term assessment relationships, but problems of memory loss, communication and concerns about intrusive strangers make it nigh-on impossible for this to work effectively (see Ray and Phillips, 2002, p. 203).

- Whereas biography and life course work are a means of maintaining continuities for older people, and of giving workers better understanding of people's individual ways of managing change (Bornat, 1999), snapshot assessments allow neither the time nor the space for such work – work which would assist in resolving some of the dilemmas of ageing.

- Routine assessment means that workers need to make a special effort to avoid disempowering older people by misunderstandings, rushed work, selective listening and not having time to clearly explain the realities of what services they can and cannot provide.

In this chapter we have attempted to illustrate the individuality of adults requiring services, whatever their impairment, and for each assessment to represent this uniqueness. Despite its complexity, the Single Assessment Process goes some way to aiding this but the structure of Social Care department teams, and the effect of this on resource provision, makes it especially difficult. For example, dementia patients get specialized medical care until they are 65 and then they are referred to teams providing services for elderly people, where they fall between services for those with physical and mental illnesses. This has the effect of making it even more difficult to individualize carers and enable them to be full participants in assessments. For example, dementia carers prefer home-based respite care to residential-based respite care (www.fordementia.org.uk) but are restricted in their choices by available resources.

And neither are carers a homogenous group. Although the majority are women, who have been 'negotiated' into caring simply because they were unable to say 'no' (Ungerson, 1987), many are children. This is partly because of the added disadvantages of disability for women; young carers are highly likely to live in a single-parent household headed by a mother. Where there is a father, he may be not only an invisible non-carer but he may also be an abuser of the young carer. Thus, young carers occupy several positions in families – carer, teenager, victim, all of which have different needs (for an overview see Milner, 2001). Carers can also be abusers, of older partners (Glendenning, 1997; Hearn, 1999), or of HIV sufferers (Hanson and Maroney, 1999), for example. When undertaking an assessment, it is important to be sensitive to the possible vulnerablities and needs of carers, as well as the people they care for – who may not only be cared for but also be abusive (Mowlan *et al.*, 2007). And the emphasis on women as carers should not lead to men's caring capacities being underestimated.

> **CASE EXAMPLE**
>
> Kenneth was severely depressed following the deaths of his widowed mother and, later, his male partner, both of whom he had provided with intimate care over long periods. His social worker had referred him for counselling which he found unhelpful as his counsellor storied him as a feminized elderly man (on account of his both his sexuality and his history of caring) who had lost his purpose in life (a feminized version of the empty nest syndrome). He explained that he was not grieving for the loss of his mother and partner in terms of not having anyone to care for, but it in terms of loss of interdependency: 'I propped them up physically and they propped me up emotionally.'

Adult care is not simply about some people caring and other people being cared for; about some people being competent and others dependent; it is about family relationships in which members are interconnected and interdependent. To be effective, assessments need to recognize this complexity:

> It is important to emphasise that, whereas specialist expert knowledge is better informed than that of most clients, the clients themselves may have greater understanding of their own ability to cope and their maintenance needs. (Keene, 2001, p. 138)

It is also worth remembering that, although direct payments are intended to empower and improve autonomy, this is also subject to resource restrictions. Ellis (2007) found that the process resembled 'street-level bureaucracy', especially since the Bill *Safeguarding Vulnerable Groups* (DoH, 2006) has promised the flexible use of monies, as the degree of adequate support for recipients is difficult to assess. Equity is impossible to maintain if every applicant wants everything they could be entitled to while resources are limited. Managers see self-assessment of need as a threat to resource management. The time it takes to do an assessment has meant that some initial assessments have been made by telephone. Ellis found that in general there was considerable disquiet among staff over assessments for direct payments, which has affected take-up.

SUMMARY

- This chapter has dealt with several categories of adult service users.
- It has set out the relevant legislation and government policies.
- It has mentioned the main government guidance for work with various service user groups.
- It has explained the types of assessments involved.

- It has addressed in some detail the operation of the single assessment process, fair access to care services, and the self-assessment process.

- Some social policy issues are raised as critical comment on this rapidly changing area of social work practice.

FURTHER LEARNING ACTIVITIES

Debate the statement 'If it's not good enough for your own grandmother, it's not good enough for your service user.'

Read again the case of Mrs Young (page 224)

Three weeks after the planning meeting, during a SW visit, Mrs Young 'begged for help'. She had become incontinent of urine. She was taken to a residential home.

When reviewed in the residential home, the SW, CPN and psychiatrist all noted a marked deterioration in her general level of awareness and memory. The psychiatrist hadn't seen Mrs Young this bad before – she wasn't aware of where 'home' was. She was not asking to go home and seemed to have settled in the care home. She was asking for food and sleeping better. She had a urinary tract infection which probably caused the incontinence and the confusion. This was being treated.

- What do you think will happen if, as the infection clears up, her confusion also clears up?

Decide which service and/or professional would be best placed to take lead responsibility for assessing Mrs Young's care.

FURTHER READING

McDonald, A. (2006) *Understanding Community Care*, 2nd edn. Basingstoke: Palgrave Macmillan.

Sharkey, P. (2007) *The Essentials of Community Care*. Basingstoke: Palgrave Macmillan.

NATIONAL OCCUPATIONAL STANDARDS

For students working with the British National Occupation Standards for Social Work (see Appendix)

- This chapter relates to *practice* elements 1.1–3; 2.1–4; 3.1–2; 4.2–4; 5.1–2; 6.1–5; 7.1; 9.1–3; 11.1–4; 12.1–3; 13.1–3; 17.1–4; 19.1–5.

- With which of the *knowledge* requirements does this chapter help you?

Conclusion – Essentials to Think About

Keeping an open mind can never be taken for granted. How can we make sound judgements without being judgemental?

First, let the lead social workers, having consulted all those involved, accept responsibility for their own judgements, so that the decision is theirs, not the group's. This is not to say that decisions can be taken in isolation, or that it is not a team effort – consulting with a team is not the same as having a team decision.

Second, be aware of the importance of your first assessment because this will underpin all your subsequent decisions and may hinder the process of evaluation. The only way you can reasonably engage in evaluation of your assessments, we suggest, is by ensuring that you have multiple frames at the outset. Consider the maps outlined earlier even where they do not fit comfortably with your theories about people.

Third, check your case files for language usage that pathologizes rather than individualizes the subject.

Fourth, set out your report in a logical order using some adapted version of the headings in Chapter 3. These are based loosely on the work of Meyer (1993) and, as the reader will have realized by now, they reflect the layout of this book and mirror the six stages of the process of making assessments. In particular, in stage 2 (presenting the data) beware how the various 'domains', 'dimensions' and subheadings on assessment guidelines/proformas can conspire towards a biased picture. In each heading, ensure a balanced account by reporting strengths and potential as well as difficulties and shortcomings, and signs of safety as well as signs of danger.

In conclusion, the main hallmark of effective *professional* practice is when theoretical knowledge acts as a basis of professional expertise (Sibeon, 1991) – for, as theory informs practice, so practice develops theory. We hope, therefore, that practitioners will become less ambivalent about theory, that they will seek to own it rather than abandon it to academics. We hope that by focusing on making assessments useful we have been able to cut away some of the mystique and bring theory down to earth, making it more useable in the real world.

Messy uncertainty remains part of reality, and the best we can do is 'continue to struggle through our confusion, to insist on being human', as R. D. Laing used to say. In social work, we are dealing with unique difficulties each day, and we therefore need to carry on what Sibeon (1992, p. 163) calls a 'reflective conversation with the situation'. This approach embraces uncertainty, encouraging its creative use.

We must remain aware of how the structure of psychocultural assumptions and biases constrains our view of others and take action to counteract them when they lead to inequality. In other words, we need to avoid assuming that our theories, social roles and expectations are not problematic for others. Such practice is about seeking to make the best use of the theory that is available, learning how to make it more useful or helpful and learning from our mistakes. To do this, we need to work in partnership with service users, for they are well, if not best, placed to reflect on the usefulness of the partnership. They will tell us which ways of working best meet their needs.

Appendix

Knowledge requirements of the National Occupational Standards for Social Work

I. The legal, social, economic and ecological context of social work practice

a. Country, UK, and EU legislation, statutory codes, standards, frameworks and guidance relevant to social work practice and related fields, including multi-disciplinary and multi-organizational practice, data protection and confidentiality of information.

b. Social policy, including policy on social care, criminal justice, education, health, housing, income support.

c. Demographic and social trends.

d. Theories of poverty, unemployment, health, impairment and other sources of discrimination and disadvantage and their impact on social exclusion.

e. Policies on diversity, discrimination and promoting independence/autonomy of adults, children, families, groups and communities, and research on their effectiveness.

2. The context of social work practice for this area of work

a. Historical perspectives of social work and social welfare.

b. International law and social policy, in broad terms, for the purpose of comparison.

c. Contemporary issues and trends in social work.

d. Understanding of why people use social work and social care services.

e. Psychological and sociological explanations of:

– human growth and development and the factors that impact on it

– mental health and well being

– social interactions and relationships

– discrimination and oppression

– human behaviour.

f. Knowledge of the range of local resources and services.

g. Theories about how systems work.

h. Organizational structures, policies and procedures for referral.

i. Policies, procedures and legal requirements for the security and confidentiality of information.

j. How to access and use information and communications technology (ICT) and other electronic systems that may help in the collection of information.

3. Values and ethics

a. Awareness of your own values, prejudices, ethical dilemmas and conflicts of interest and their implications on your practice.

b. Respect for, and the promotion of:
   – each person as an individual
   – independence and quality of life for individuals, whilst protecting them from harm
   – dignity and privacy of individuals, families, carers, groups and communities.

c. Recognize and facilitate each person's use of language and form of communication of their choice.

d. Value, recognize and respect the diversity, expertise and experience of individuals, families, carers, groups and communities.

e. Maintain the trust and confidence of individuals, families, carers, groups and communities by communicating in an open, accurate and understandable way.

f. Understand and make use of strategies to challenge discrimination, disadvantage and other forms of inequality and injustice.

4. Social work theories, models and methods for working with individuals, families, carers, groups and communities

a. Principles, theories and methods of social work practice.

b. Theories about the impact of authority and power in the social work role.

c. Theories about the impact of discrimination, and methods of working with diversity.

d. Theories and methods about working with the main groups of people using services. These include child care, mental health, learning difficulties, older people, minority and ethnic groups, drug and alcohol use, disability and impairment.

e. Principles about balancing the rights of individuals, families, carers, groups and communities with the interests of society and the requirements of practice.

f. Lessons learned from both serious failure of service and practice, and from successful interventions.

g. Approaches to evidence and knowledge based practice.

h. Theories of organizations, group behavior and organizational change. Theories and methods of promoting personal, social and emotional well being.

Practice requirements of the National Occupational Standards for Social Work

These consist of four key roles, each with a set of units.

Each unit has a set of performance requirements, or *elements.*

The elements will be available on your course, or they can be downloaded as follows:

– Access the Topss site www.topssengland.net and go to the left side menu and 'National Occupational Standards'. A submenu will appear; click on 'Social Work'.

– Scroll down to the end of that page and you will be able to click on 'Enter The National Occupational Standards for Social Work' pages.

– You will notice that there is some overlap between the knowledge requirements and the practice requirements; they are not entirely separate.

Note: Scotland has *The Framework for Social Work Education in Scotland* which has an integrated Standards in Social Work Education in Scotland (SiSWE).

References

Adams, R., Dominelli, L. and Payne, M. (2002) *Critical Practice in Social Work*. Basingstoke: Palgrave Macmillan.

Aggleton, P. and Chambers, H. (1986) *Nursing Models and Nursing Process*. London: Macmillan.

Ahmad, B. (1990) *Black Perspectives in Social Work*. London: Venture.

Ainsworth, M. D., Blehar, M. C., Waters, E. and Wall, S. (1978) *Patterns of Attachment: Assessed in a Strange Situation and at Home*. Hillsdale, NJ: Erlbaum.

Aldridge, A. (2006) 'Religion', in Payne, G. (ed.) *Social Divisions*. Basingstoke: Palgrave Macmillan.

Arber, S. and Ginn, J. (1991) *Gender and Later Life*. London: Sage.

Asch, A. and Fine, M. (1988) 'Introduction: beyond pedestals', in Fine, M. and Asch, A. (eds) *Women with Disabilities: Essays in Psychology*. Philadelphia, PA: Temple.

Audit Commission (1992) *The Community Revolution: Personal Social Services and Community Care*. London: HMSO.

Augusta-Scott, T. (2007) 'Letters from prison: re-authoring identity with men who have perpetrated sexual violence', in Brown, C. and Augusta-Scott, T. (eds) *Narrative Therapy: Making Meaning, Making Lives*. London: Sage.

Babcock, J. C., Jacobson, N. S., Gottman, J. M. and Yerington, T. P. (2000) 'Attachment, emotional regulation, and the function of marital violence's differences between secure, pre-occupied, and dismissing violent and non-violent husbands', *Journal of Family Violence*, 15:391–410.

Bailey, D. (ed.) (2000) *At the Core of Mental Health Practice*. Brighton: Pavilion.

Baker, L., Lynch, K. and Cantillon, J. (2004) *Equity: From Theory to Action*. Basingstoke: Palgrave Macmillan.

Baldwin, S. (1993) *The Myth of Community Care: An Alternative Neighbourhood Model of Care*. London: Chapman & Hall.

Banat, D., Summers, S. and Pring, T. (2002) 'An investigation into carers' perceptions of the verbal comprehension ability of adults with severe learning disability', *British Journal of Learning Disability*, 30:78–81.

Bandura, A. (1969) *Principles of Behavior Modification*. New York: Holt, Rinehart & Winston.

Bandura, A. (1977) *Social Learning Theory*. Englewood Cliffs, NJ: Prentice Hall.

Barber, J. G. (1991) *Beyond Casework*. London: Macmillan/British Association of Social Workers.

Barnes, C. and Mercer, G. (2002) *Disability*. Cambridge: Polity.

Barrett, D. (1997) *Child Prostitution in Britain*. London: Children's Society.

Barry, M. (2007) *Effective Approaches to Risk Management in Social Work: An International Literature Review*. Stirling: Scottish Government Publications.

Bartholomew, K. and Horowitz, L. M. (1991) 'Attachment styles among young adults: a test of a four-category model', *Journal of Personal and Social Psychology*, 61:226–44.

Bass, E. and Davis, L. (1988) *The Courage to Heal: A Guide for Women Survivors of Child Sexual Abuse*. New York: HarperCollins.

Bateson, G. (1977) *Steps to an Ecology of Mind*. New York: Ballantine.

Bebington, A. and Miles, J. (1989) 'The background of children who enter local authority care', *British Journal of Social Work*, 19:349–69.

Beck, A. T. (1967) *Depression: Clinical, Experimental and Theoretical Aspects*. London: Hoeber.

Beck, A. T. (1993) *Therapy and Emotional Disorders*. New York: Guilford.

Beck, A. T. and Beck, J. S. (2005) *Cognitive Therapy for Challenging Problems*. New York: Guilford.

Beck, A. T. and Tomkin, A. (1989) *Cognitive Therapy and Emotional Disorders*. London: Penguin.

Belsky, J. and Nezworski, T. (eds) (1988) *Clinical Implications of Attachment*. Hillsdale, NJ: Erlbaum.

Bentall, R. (2003) *Madness Explained: Psychosis and Human Nature*. London: Allen Lane.

Bentovim, A. and Bingley Miller, L. (2001) *Assessment of Family Competence, Strengths and Difficulties*. London: Routledge–Taylor and Francis.

Berg, I. K. and Miller, S. D. (1992) *Working with the Problem Drinker*. New York: Norton.

Berg, I. K. and Reuss, N. M. (1998) *Solutions Step by Step: A Substance Abuse Treatment Manual*. New York: Norton.

Berne, E. (1964) *Games People Play*. New York: Grove Books.

Berne, E. (1978) *A Layman's Guide to Psychiatry and Psychoanalysis*. London: Penguin.

Bessant, D. (2004) 'Risk technologies and youth work practice', *Youth and Policy*, 83:60–77.

Bibring, G. L. (1961) 'A study of psychological processes in pregnancy'. In *The Psychological Study of the Child 10.16*. New York: International University Press.

Biehal, N. (2007) 'Reuniting children with their families: reconsidering the evidence on timing, contact, and outcomes', *British Journal of Social Work*, 37:807–23. (2000).

Bird, J. (2000) *The Heart's Narrative: Therapy and Navigating Life's Contradictions*. Auckland: Edge.

Blackburn, M. (2002) *Sexuality and Disability*. Oxford: Butterworth Heinemann.

Blair, M. (1996) 'Interviews with black families', in Cohen, R., Hughes, M., Ashworth, L. and Blair, M. *School's Out: The Family Perspective on School Exclusions*. London: Family Service Units and Barnardo's.

Blaug, R. (1995) 'Distortion of the face to face: communicative reason and social work practice', *British Journal of Social Work*, 25:3–39.

Blumenthol, S. and Lavender, T. (2000) *Violence and Mental Disorder: A Critical Aid to the Assessment and Management of Risk*. London: Jessica Kingsley.

Blyth, E. and Milner, J. (1996) 'Black boys excluded from school: race and masculinity issues', in Blyth, E. and Milner, J. (eds) *School Exclusions: Interprofessional Issues for Policy and Practice*. London: Routledge.

Boddy, J., Potts, P. and Statham, J. (2006) *Models of Good Practice in Joined Up Assessment: Working for Children with 'Significant and Complex Needs'*. London: Thomas Coram Research Unit/University of London.

Booth, T. and Booth, W. (1997) *Exceptional Childhoods, Unexceptional Children*. London: Policy Studies Centre.

Booth, W. and Booth, T. (2004) 'A family at risk: multiple perspectives on parenting in child protection', *British Journal of Learning Disability*, 32:9–15.

Bornat, J. (ed.) (1999) *Biographical Interviews: The Link between Research and Practice*. London: Centre for Policy on Aging.

Bowey, L. and McGlaughin, A. (2007) 'Older carers of adults with a learning disability confront the future: issues and preferences in planning', *British Journal of Social Work*, 37:39–54.

Bowlby, J. (1963) 'Pathological mourning and childhood mourning', *Journal of the American Psychoanalytic Association*, 118:500–41.

Bowlby, J. (1979) *The Making and Breaking of Affectional Bonds*. London: Tavistock.

Bowlby, J. (1982) *Attachment and Loss*. London: Hogarth.

Bowlby, J. (1988) *A Secure Base: Clinical Implications of Attachment Theory*. London: Routledge.

Boykim, W. and Toms, F. D. (1985) 'Black child socialisation: a conceptual framework', in McAdoo, H. P. and McAdoo, J. L. (eds) *Black Children: Social, Educational and Parental Environments*. London: Sage.

Brandon, M. *et al.* (2007) *Evaluating the Common Assessment Framework and Lead Professionals' Guidance and Implementation in 2005–6*. London: DfES, RR740.

Braye, S. and Preston-Shoot, M. (1995) *Empowering Practice in Social Care*. Buckingham: Open University Press.

Bretherton, I. (1992) 'The origins of attachment theory: John Bowlby and Mary Ainsworth', *Developmental Psychology*, 28:759–75.

Bretherton, I. and Waters, E. (eds) (1985) 'Growing points of attachment theory and research', *Growing Points in Attachment: Theory and Research*. Monographs of the Society for Research in Child Development 50.

Brewster, S. J. (2004) 'Putting words into their mouths? Interviewing people with learning disabilities and little/no speech', *British Journal of Learning Disability*, 32:166–9.

British Association for Adoption and Fostering (1996) *Working with Children*. London.

Brown, C. and Augusta-Scott, T. (eds) (2007) *Narrative Therap:. Making Meaning, Making Lives*. London: Sage.

Browne, K. and Hamilton, C. E. (1998) 'Physical violence between young adults and their parents: associations with a history of child maltreatment', *Journal of Family Violence*, 13:59–80.

Bruner, E. (1986) 'Ethnography as narrative', in Turner, V. and Bruner, E. (eds) *The Anthropology of Experience*. Urbana, IL: University of Illinois Press.

Bryman, A. (2004) *Social Research Methods*, 2nd edn. Oxford: Oxford University Press.

Buchanan, A. (1999) *What Works for Troubled Children? Family Support for Children with Emotional Behavioural Problems*. London: Barnardo's and Wiltshire County Council.

Bullimore, P. (2002) 'Altering the balance of power: working with voices', *Journal of Narrative Therapy and Community Work*, 3:22–8.

Burke, B. and Harrison, P. (2002) 'Anti-oppressive practice', in Adams, R., Dominelli, L. and Payne, M. (eds) *Critical Practice in Social Work*. Basingstoke: Palgrave Macmillan.

Burnard, P. A. (1991) 'Method of analysing interview transcripts in qualitative research', *Nurse Education Today*, 11:461–6.

Burns, D. D. (1999) *Feeling Good: The New Mood Therapy*. London: HarperCollins.

Burr, V. (2003) *An Introduction to Social Constructionism*, 2nd edn. London: Routledge.

Bushman, B. J., Baumeister, R. F. and Stack, A. D. (1999) 'Catharsis, aggression and persuasive influence: self-fulfilling or self-defeating prophecies?', *Journal of Personality and Social Psychology*, 76:367–76.

Butler, J. (1990) *Gender Trouble: Feminism and the Subversion of Identity*. London: Routledge.

Butt, T. (2003) *Understanding People*. Basingstoke: Palgrave Macmillan.

Byng-Hall, J. (1985) 'The family script: a useful bridge between theory and practice', *Journal of Family Therapy*, 7:301–5.

Caldwell, B. M. and Bradley, R. H. (1984) *Home Observation for Measurement of the Environment: Administration Manual*. Arkansas, AR: University of Arkansas.

Cann, J., Falshaw, L. and Friendship, C. (2003) *Understanding What Works: Accredited Cognitive Behavioural Skills Programmes for Adult Men and Young Offenders*. Home Office Research Findings 226. London: Home Office.

Caplan, G. (1961) *An Approach to Community Mental Health*. London: Tavistock.

Cavanagh, K. and Gee, V. (eds) (1996) *Working with Men: Feminism and Social Work*. London: Routledge.

Cavanagh, K. and Lewis, R. (1996) 'Interviewing violent men: challenge or compromise?', in Cavanagh, K. and Cree, V. (eds) *Working with Men: Feminism and Social Work*. London: Routledge.

Challis, D. *et al.* (1990) *Case Management in Social and Health Care*. University of Kent at Canterbury: Personal Social Services Research Unit.

Channer, Y. (1995) *I am a Promise. The School Achievement of Black African Caribbeans*. London: Trentham Books.

Chapman, T. and Hough, M. (2001) *Evidence Based Practice: A Guide to Effective Practice*. London: HM Inspectorate of Probation.

Christodoulides, T. E. *et al.* (2005) 'Risk assessment with adolescent sex offenders', *Journal of Sexual Aggression*, 11:37–48.

Cicirelli, V. G. (1991) 'Attachment theory in old age: protection of the attachment figure', in Pillemer, K. and McCartney, K. (eds) *Parent–Child Relations Across the Life Course*. Hillsdale, NJ: Erlbaum.

Cigno, C. (1998) 'Cognitive behaviour Practice', in Adams, R., Dominelli, L. and Payne, M. (eds). *Social Work: Themes, Issues and Critical Debates*. Basingstoke: Macmillan.

Cigno, K. and Bourn, D. (1998) *Cognitive-Behaviour Social Work in Practice*. Aldershot: Ashgate.

Clark, H., Dyer, S. and Hansaran, L. (1996) *Going Home: Older People Leaving Hospital*. London: Polity in conjunction with the Joseph Rowntree Foundation and *Community Care* Magazine.

Clarkson, P. *et al.* (2007) *Assessment, Performance Measurement and User Satisfaction in Older People's Services*. PSSRU@manchester.ac.uk.

Clausen, H. *et al.* (2005) 'Would palliative care patients benefit from social workers retaining the traditional "casework" role rather than working as care managers? A prospective social qualitative interview study', *British Journal of Social Work*, 35:277–85.

Cleaver, H. (2002) 'Assessing children's needs and parents' responses', in Ward, H. and Rose, W. (eds) *Approaches to Needs Assessment in Children's Services*. London: Jessica Kingsley.

Cleaver, H. and Freeman, P. (1995) *Parental Perspectives in Cases of Suspected Child Abuse*. London: HMSO.

Cleaver, H. and Walker, P. with Meadows, P. (2004) *Assessing Children's Needs and Circumstances: The Impact of the Assessment Framework*. London: Jessica Kingsley.

Cleaver H., Unell, I. and Algate, J. (1999) *Parenting Capacity: The Impact of Parental Mental Illness, Problem Alcohol and Drug Use, and Domestic Violence on Children's Development*. London: Stationery Office.

Clifford, D. (1994) 'Towards an anti-oppressive social work assessment method', *Practice*, 6(3):226–38.

Clifford, D. (1998) *Social Assessment Theory and Practice: A Multidisciplinary Framework*. Aldershot: Ashgate.

Cockburn, C. (1991) *In the Way of Women: Men's Resistance to Sex Equality in Organisations*. Basingstoke: Macmillan.

Commission for Social Care Inspection (2006a) *Social Services Performance Indicators: Children*. www.csci.org.uk.

Commission for Social Care Inspection (2006b) *Social Services Performance Indicators: Adults*. www.csci.org.uk.

Compton, B. R. and Galloway, B. (1999) *Social Work Processes*. London: Brooks/Cole.

Connell, R. W. (1987) *Gender and Power*. Cambridge: Polity.

Cooper, S. (2005) 'Understanding, treating, and managing sex offenders who deny their offence', *Journal of Sexual Aggression*, 11:85–94.

Corby, B. (2000) *Child Abuse: Towards a Knowledge Base*, 2nd edn. Buckingham: Open University Press.

Cordery, J. and Whitehead, A. (1992) 'Boys don't cry: empathy, collusion and crime', in Senior, P. and Woodhill, B. (eds) *Gender, Crime and Probation Practice*. Sheffield City Polytechnic: PAVIC Publications.

Coulshed, V. and Mullender, A. with Jones, D. and Thompson, N. (2006) *Management in Social Work*, 3rd edn. Basingstoke: Palgrave Macmillan.

Coulshed, V. and Orme, J. (1998) *Social Work Practice: An Introduction*. 3rd. edn. Basingstoke: Macmillan.

Coulshed, V. and Orme, J. (2006) *Social Work Practice: An Introduction*. 4th edn. Basingstoke: Palgrave Macmillan.

Couzens, A. (1999) 'Sharing the load: group conversations with young Indigenous men', *Extending Narrative Therapy: A Collection of Practice-Based Papers*. Adelaide: Dulwich Centre.

Cox, A. and Bentovim, A. (2000) *The Family Pack of Questionnaires and Scales*. London: HMSO.

Craig, L. and Hutchinson, R. B. (2005) 'Sexual offenders with learning disabilities: risk, recidivism and treatment', *Journal of Sexual Aggression*, 11:289–304.

Craig, L. A., Browne, K. D., Stringer, I. and Beech, A. (2005) 'Sexual recidivism: a review of static, dynamic and actuarial predictors', *Journal of Sexual Aggression*, 11:65–84.

Crawford, K. and Walker, J. (2003) *Social Work and Human Development*, 2nd edn. Exeter: Learning Matters.

Cree, V. (2002) *Sociology for Social Workers and Probation Officers*. London: Routledge

Cree V. and Myers, S. (2008) *Social Work: Making a Difference*. Bristol: Polity.

Crisp, B. R., Anderson, M. R., Orme, J. and Green Lister, P. (2005) *Learning and Teaching in Social Work Education: Textbooks and Frameworks on Assessment*. London: Social Care Institute of Excellence.

Crittenden, P. M. (1999) 'Child neglect: causes and contributors', in Dubowitz, H. (ed.) *Neglected Children: Research, Practice and Policy*. Thousand Oaks, CA: Sage.

Crome, D. H. (1999) 'Substance misuse and psychiatric comorbidity: towards improved service provision', *Drugs, Education, Prevention and Policy*, 68:151–74.

Cross, R. (2007) *Psychology: The Science of Mind and Behaviour*, 5th edn. Abingdon: Hodder Arnold.

D'Cruz, H., Gillingham, P. and Melendes, S. (2007) 'Reflexivity, it's meaning and relevance for social work: a critical review of the literature, *British Journal of Social Work*, 37:73–90.

Da Valda, M. (2003) 'From paranoid schizophrenia to hearing voices – and other class distinctions', *International Journal of Narrative Therapy and Community Work*, 3:13–17.

Dale, P., Morrison, T. and Waters, J. (1986) *Dangerous Families: Assessment and Treatment of Child Abuse*. London: Tavistock.

Dalrymple, J. and Burke, B. (1995) *Anti-oppressive Practice. Social Care and the Law*. Buckingham: Open University Press.

Darmody, M., Madden, B. and Sharry, J. (2002) *Becoming a Solution Detective*. London: Brief Therapy Press.

Davidson, G. and Campbell, J. (2007) 'An examination of the use of coercion by assertive outreach by community mental health teams in Northern Ireland', *British Journal of Social Work*, 37:537–55.

Davies, D. (1999) 'Homophobia and heterosexism', in Davies, D. and Neal, C. (eds) *Pink Therapy: A Guide for Counsellors and Therapists Working with Lesbian, Gay, and Bisexual Clients*. Buckingham: Open University Press.

Davies, M. (1981) *The Essential Social Worker: A Guide to Positive Practice*. London: Heinemann.

Davies, M. (ed.) (1997) *The Blackwell Companion to Social Work*. Oxford: Blackwell.

Davis, A. and Ellis, K. (1995) 'Enforced altruism or community care', in Hugman, R. and Smith, D. (eds) *Ethical Issues in Social Work*. London: Routledge.

De Boer, C. and Coady, N. (2007) 'Good helping relationships in child welfare: learning from stories of success', *Child and Family Social Work*, 12:32–42.

De Jong, P. and Berg, I. K. (2002) *Interviewing for Solutions*, 2nd edn. Pacific Grove, CA.: Brooks/Cole.

de Shazer, S. (1985) *Keys to Solution in Brief Therapy.* New York: Norton.

de Shazer, S. (1988) *Clues: Investigating Solutions in Brief Therapy.* New York: Norton.

de Shazer, S. (1991) *Putting Difference to Work.* New York: Norton.

de Shazer, S. (1993) Verbal Communication, Glasgow Conference, Solutions in Brief Therapy.

de Shazer, S. (1994) *Words Were Originally Magic.* New York: Norton.

Denborough, D. *et al.* (2006) 'Linking stories and invitations: a narrative approach to working with the skills and knowledge of community', *International Journal of Narrative Therapy and Community Work*, 2:19–51.

Denman, G. and Thorpe, D. (1993) 'Participation and patterns of intervention in child protection in Gwent'. *A Research Report for the Area Child Protection Committee, Gwent.* University of Lancaster.

Denney, D. (1992) *Racism and Anti-Racism in Probation.* London: Routledge.

Department for Education and Science (2005) *Children's Trusts: Leadership, Co-operation, Planning and Safeguarding.* Nottingham: DES.

Department of Health (1988) *Protecting Children. A Guide for Social Workers undertaking a Comprehensive Assessment.* London: HMSO.

Department of Health (1990a) *Community Care in the Next Decade and Beyond.* London: HMSO.

Department of Health (1990b) *Child Abuse: A Study of Abuse Reports 1980–1989.* London: HMSO.

Department of Health (1991) *The Patient's Charter.* London: HMSO.

Department of Health (1995a) *Child Protection: Messages from Research.* London: HMSO.

Department of Health (1995b) *Looking After Children.* London: HMSO.

Department of Health (1998) *Modernising Mental Health Services: Safe, Sound and Supportive.* http://www.doh.gov.uk/nsf/mentalh.htm.

Department of Health (1999) *Me, Survive, Out There? New Arrangements for Young People Living in and Leaving Care.* London: HMSO.

Department of Health (2000a) *Framework for the Assessment of Children in Need and Their Families.* London: HMSO.

Department of Health (2000b) *No Secrets: Guidance on Developing and Implementing Multi-Agency Policies and Procedures to Protect Vulnerable Adults from Abuse.* London: HMSO.

Department of Health (2000c) *Safeguarding Children Involved in Prostitution. Supplementary Guidance to Working Together to Safeguard Children.* London: HMSO.

Department of Health (2001a) *Health and Social Care Act.* London: HMSO.

Department of Health (2001b) *Treatment Choice in Psychological Therapies and Counselling: Evidence-based Clinical Practice Guidelines.* London: HMSO.

Department of Health (2001c) *The National Framework for Older People.* London: DoH.

Department of Health (2002) *Mental Health Policy Implementation Guide: Dual Diagnosis Good Practice Guide.* www.doh.gov.uk/mentalhealth.

Department of Health (2003) *Fair Access to Care Services:, Guidance on Eligibility Criteria for Adult Social Care.* London: HMSO.

Department of Health (2004) *Mental Health Policy Implementation Guide.* London: HMSO.

Department of Health (2005a) *Every Child Matters.* London: HMSO.

Department of Health (2005b) *The Mental Capacity Act.* London: HMSO.

Department of Health (2006a) *Dual Diagnosis in Mental Health Inpatient and Day Hospital Settings.* London: HMSO.

Department of Health (2006b) *Safeguarding Vulnerable Groups.* London: HMSO.

Department of Health (2006c) *Our Health, Our Care, Our Say.* London: HMSO.

Department of Health (2007a) *Direct Payments. Policy Paper.* London: HMSO.

Department of Health (2007b) *Good Practice Guidance on Working with Parents with a Learning Disability.* London: HMSO.

Department of Health (2007c) *Mental Health Act*. London: HMSO.

Department of Health (2007d) *Services for People with Learning Disability and Challenging Behaviour or Mental Health Needs*. London: HMSO.

Department of Health, Cox, A. and Bentovim, A. (2000d) *The Family Assessment Pack of Questionnaires and Scales*. London: HMSO.

Dermer, S. B., Hemesath, C. W. and Russell, C. S. (1998) 'A feminist critique of solution-focused therapy', *American Journal of Family Therapy*, 26:239–50.

Derrida, J. (1973) *Writing and Difference*. Chicago, IL: University of Chicago Press.

Devore, W. and Schlesinger, E. G. (1991) *Ethnic-sensitive Social Work*. New York: Macmillan.

Dobash, R. E., Dobash, R. P., Cavanagh, K. and Lewis, R. (2000) *Changing Violent Men*. London: Sage.

Doel, M. and Marsh, P. (1992) *Task Centred Social Work*. London: Ashgate.

Dogra, N., Parkin, A., Gale, F. and Frake, C. (2002) *A Multidisciplinary Handbook of Child and Adolescent Mental Health for Front Line Professionals*. London: Jessica Kingsley.

Dolan, Y. (1991) *Resolving Sexual Abuse*. New York: Norton.

Dolan, Y. (1998) *Beyond Survival: Living Well Is the Best Revenge*. Workshop held at Brief Therapy Practice, Institute of Child Health, London, 2–3 July.

Dominelli, L. (2002) 'Values in social work: contested entities with enduring qualities', in Adams, R., Dominelli, L. and Payne, M. (eds) *Critical Practice in Social Work*. Basingstoke: Palgrave Macmillan.

Dryden, W. and Mytton, J. (1999) *Four Approaches to Counselling and Psychotherapy,*. London: Routledge.

Dryden, W. and Yankura J. (1993) *Counselling Individuals: A Rational Emotive Behavioural Handbook*, 2nd edn. London: Whurr.

Dumbrill, G. (2006) 'Parental experience of child protection intervention: a qualitative study', *Child Abuse and Neglect*, 30:27–37.

Durrant, M. (1993) *Creative Strategies for School Problems*. Epping, NSW: Eastwood Centre.

Dutton, D. and Corvo, K. (2007) 'The Duluth model: a data impervious paradigm and a failed strategy', *Aggression and Violent Behavior*, 12:658–67.

Dutton, D. G., Saunders, K., Starzowski, A. and Bartholomew, K. (1994) 'Intimacy–anger and insecure attachment as precursors of abuse in intimate relationships', *Journal of Applied Social Psychology*, 24:1367–86.

Ellis, A. and Dryden, W. (2007) *The Practice of Rational Emotive Therapy*. New York: Springer.

Ellis, A. (1962) *Reason and Emotion in Psychotherapy*. New York: Lyle Stuart.

Ellis, A. (2006) *How to Stubbornly Refuse to Make Yourself Miserable about Anything: Yes, Anything*. New York: Citadel/Kensington.

Ellis, K. (2007) 'Direct payments and social work practice: the significance of "street-level bureaucracy" in determining eligibility', *British journal of Social Work*, 37:405–22.

Emerson, E. *et al.* (1987) *Developing Services for People with Severe Learning Difficulties and Challenging Behaviour*. Canterbury: Institute of Social and Applied Psychology.

Engle, G. (1980) 'The clinical application of the biopsychosocial model', *American Journal of Psychiatry*, 137, 535–44.

Epstein, L. (1988) *Helping People: The Task Centred Approach*. Columbus, OH: Merrill.

Epston, D. (1998) *Catching Up with David Epston: A Collection of Narrative-Based Papers, 1991–1996*. Adelaide: Dulwich Centre.

Epston, D., Lakusta, C. and Tomm, K. (2006) 'Haunting from the future: a congenial approach to parent-child conflicts', *International Journal of Narrative Therapy and Community Work*, 2:61–70.

Erickson, M. H. (1959) *Hypnotherapy: An Exploratory Casebook*. New York: Irvington.

Erikson, E. H. (1948) *Children and Society*. Harmondsworth: Penguin.

Erikson, E. H. (1977) *Childhood and Society*. London: Granada.

Essex, S., Gumbelto, J. and Luger, C. (1996) 'Resolutions: working with families where responsibility is denied', *Child Abuse Review*. 5:191–201.

Evans, J. (1995) *Feminist Theory Today*. London: Sage.

Fahlberg, V. (1981a) *Attachment and Separation*. London: British Association for Adoption and Fostering.

Fahlberg, V. (1981b) *Helping Children When They Must Move*. London: British Association for Adoption and Fostering.

Fahlberg, V. (1982) *Child Development*. London: British Association for Adoption and Fostering.

Fahlberg, V. (1984) 'The child who is "stuck"', in Adcock, M. and White, R. (eds) *In Touch with Parents*. London: British Association for Adoption and Fostering.

Fahlberg, V. (1988a) *Putting the Pieces Together*. London: British Association for Adoption and Fostering.

Fahlberg, V. (1988b) *The Child in Placement*. London: British Association for Adoption and Fostering.

Falkov, A. (2002) 'Addressing family needs where a parent is mentally ill', in Ward, H. and Rose, W. (eds) *Approaches to Needs Assessment in Children's Services*. London: Jessica Kingsley.

Falshaw, L., Friendship, C., Travers, R. and Nugent, F. (2004) *Searching for 'What Works': An Evaluation of Cognitive Skills Programmes*. Home Office Research Findings 206. London: HMSO.

Farrall, S. (2004) 'Supervision, motivation and social context: what matters most when probationers desist?', in Mair, G. (ed.) *What Matters in Probation*. Cullompton: Willan.

Fawcett, B., Featherstone, B., Hearn, J. and Toft, C. (eds) (1996) *Violence and Gender Relations Theories and Interventions*. London: Sage.

Featherstone, B. and Trinder, L. (1997) 'Familiar subjects? Domestic violence and child welfare', *Child and Family Social Work*, 2:147–59.

Ferguson, H. (2003) 'Welfare, social exclusion and reflexivity: the case of child and woman protection', *Journal of Social Policy*, 32(2):199–216.

Ferguson, H. (2004) *Protecting Children in Time: Child Abuse, Child Protection and the Consequences of Modernity*. Basingstoke: Palgrave Macmillan.

Ferguson, I. (2007) 'Increasing user choice or privatising risk? The antinomies of personalization', *British Journal of Social Work*, 37:387–403.

Field, P. A. and Morse, J. M. (1985) *Nursing Research: The Application of Qualitative Approaches*. London: Croom Helm.

Finkelhor, D. (1983) 'Common features of family abuse', in Finkelhor, D., Gelles, R., Hotaling, G. and Straus, M. (eds) *The Dark Side of Families: Current Family Violence Research*. Beverly Hills, CA: Sage.

Fisher, J. and Goceros, H. (1975) *Planned Behavior Change*. New York: Free Press.

Fisher, D. J., Himle, J. A. and Hanna, G. L. (1998) 'Group behavioural therapy for adolescents with obsessive-compulsive disorder', *Research on Social Work Practice*, 8(6):629–36.

Falkov, A. (2002) 'Addressing family needs where a parent is mentally ill', in Ward, H. and Rose, W. (eds) *Approaches to Needs Assessment in Children's Services*. London: Jessica Kingsley.

Fonagy, P. (2001) *Attachment Theory and Psychoanalysis*. New York: Other Press.

Ford, P. and Postle, K. (2000) 'Task-centred practice and care management', in Stepney, P. and Ford, D. (eds) *Social Work Models, Methods and Theories: A Framework for Practice*. Lyme Regis: Russell House.

Forster, N. (1994) 'An analysis of company documentation', in Cassell, C. and Symon, G. (eds) *Qualitative Methods in Organizational Research: a Practice Guide*. London: Sage.

Foster, A. and Roberts, V. Z. (eds) (1998) *Managing Mental Health in the Community: Chaos and Containment*. London: Routledge.

Foucault, M. (1972) *The Archaeology of Knowledge and the Discourse of Language*. New York: Pantheon.

Foucault, M. (1973) *The Birth of the Clinic*. London: Tavistock.

Foucault, M. (1980) *Power/Knowledge*. New York: Pantheon.

Foucault, M. (1988) 'Technologies of self', in Martin, L., Gutman, H. and Hutton, P. (eds) *Technologies of the Self*. Amherst, MA: University of Massachusetts.

Fraiberg, S. (1980) *Clinical Studies in Infant Mental Health*. London: Tavistock.

Frankl, V. F. (1997) *Man's Search for Meaning*. New York: Simon & Schuster.

Freeman, J., Epston, D. and Lobovits, D. (1997) *Playful Approaches to Serious Problems*. New York: Norton.

Freire, P. (1972) *Pedagogy of the Oppressed*. Harmondsworth: Penguin.

Freud, A. (1936) *Ego and the Mechanisms of Defence*. New York: International Universities Press.

Freud, A. (1968) *Ego and the Mechanisms of Defence*, 2nd edn. London: Hogarth.

Freud, S. (1937) 'Constructions of analysis, vol. 23', in Strachey, J. (ed.) *The Standard Edition of the Complete Psychological Works of Sigmund Freud*. London: Hogarth.

Friendship, C., Blud, L., Erikson, M. and Travers, R. (2002) *An Evaluation of Cognitive Behavioural Treatment for Prisoners*. Home Office Research Findings 161. London.

Furman, B. and Ahola, T. (1992) *Solution Talk*. New York: Norton.

Gallwey, P. (1997) 'Bad parenting and pseudo-parenting', in Wall, N. (ed.) *Rooted Sorrows: Psychoanalytic Perspectives on Child Protection, Assessment and Treatment*. Bristol: Family Law.

Glaser, B. and Strauss, A. L. (1969) *The Discovery of Grounded Theory: Strategies for Qualitative Research*. Chicago, IL: Aldine.

Glass, N. (2001) 'What works for children – the political issues', *Children and Society*, 15(1):14–20.

Glendenning, F. (1997) 'What is elder abuse and neglect?', in Decalmer, P. and Glendenning F. (eds) *The Mistreatment of Elderly People*, 2nd edn. London: Sage.

Goldberg, E. M., Gibbons, J. and Sinclair, I. (1985) *Problems, Tasks and Outcomes: The Evaluation of Task-Centred Casework in Three Settings*. London: Allen & Unwin.

Goldman, A. I. (1970) *A Theory of Human Action*. Englewood Cliffs, NJ: Prentice Hall.

Goldstein, J., Freud, A. and Solnit, A. (1973) *Beyond the Best Interests of the Child*. London: Collier-Macmillan.

Goldstein, J., Freud, A. and Solnit, A. (1979) *Before the Best Interests of the Child*. New York: Free Press.

Goldstein, J., Freud, A. and Solnit, A. (1985) *In the Best Interests of the Child*. New York: Free Press.

Gondolf, E. (2007) 'Theoretical and research support for the Duluth model: a reply to Dutton and Corvo', *Aggression and Violent Behavior*, 12:644–57.

Gorer, G. (1966) 'Psychoanalysis in the world', in Rycroft, C., Gorer, G., Storr, A., Wren-Lewis, J. and Lomas, P. (eds) *Psychoanalysis Observed*. Harmondsworth: Penguin.

Gorey, K. M., Thyer, B. A. and Pawluck, D. E. (1998) 'Differential effectiveness of prevalent social work practice models: a meta-analysis', *Social Work*, 43(3):269–78.

Grady, A. (2002) 'Female-on-male domestic violence: uncommon or ignored?', in Young, R. and Foyle, C. (eds) *New Visions of Crime Victims*. Oxford: Hart.

Grant, G., Coward, P., Richardson, M. and Ramcharan, P. (2005) *Learning Disability: A Life Cycle Approach to Valuing People*. Maidenhead: Open University Press.

Grey, C. (2001) *The New Social Story Book*. Arlington, TX: Future Horizons.

Griggs, L. (2000) 'Assessment in community care', in Davies, M. (ed.) *The Blackwell Encyclopaedia of Social Work*. Oxford: Blackwell.

Grossman, K., Grossman, K. E. and Spangler, G. (1985) 'Maternal sensitivity and newborns' orientation responses as related to quality of attachment in Northern Germany', in Bretherton, I. and Waters, E. (eds) *Growing Points of Attachment Theory and Research*. Monographs of the Society for Research in Child Development 50. Chicago, IL: University of Chicago Press.

Grubin, D. (1998) *Sex Offending Against Children: Understanding the Risk*. Home Office Police Research Paper 99. London: HMSO.

5555555555555555

Hackett, S. (2004) *What Works for Children and Young People with Sexually Harmful Behaviours?* Barkingside: Barnardo's.

Hall, C. S. (1954) *A Primer of Freudian Psychology.* London: New English Library.

Halliday, M. A. K. (1978) 'Antileagues', in Halliday, M. A. K. (ed.) *Language as Social Semiotic: The Social Interpretation of Language and Meaning.* London: Arnold.

Hamner, J. and Statham, D. (1988) *Women and Social Work.* London: Macmillan.

Hanson, B. and Maroney, T. (1999) 'HIV and same-sex domestic violence',. in Leventhal, B. and Lundy, S. E. (eds) *Same-Sex Domestic Violence: Strategies for Change.* London: Sage.

Hanson, R. K. and Bussiere, M. T. (1998) 'Predicting relapse: a meta-analysis of sexual offending recidivism studies', *Journal of Consultancy and Clinical Psychology,* 66:348–63.

Hanson, R. K. (2004) 'Sex offender risk assessment', in Hollin, C. R. (ed.) *The Essential Handbook of Offender Assessment and Treatment.* Chichester: Wiley.

Haralambos, M. and Holborn, M. (1990) *Sociology: Themes and Perspectives.* London: Unwin Hyman.

Harris, T. A. (1970) *I'm OK - You're OK.* London: Pan.

Harrison, H. (1995) 'Child assessment and family support.' Paper given at conference Assessing the Needs of Individual Children, 31 October. London: National Children's Bureau.

Hawkes, D., Marsh, T. I. and Wilgosh, R. (1998) *Solution Focused Therapy: A Handbook for Health Care Professionals.* Oxford: Butterworth Heinemann.

Hayes, N. (2000) *Foundations in Psychology,* 3rd edn. London: Thompson Learning.

Hazan, C. and Shaver, P. (1987) 'Romantic love conceptualized as an attachment process', *Journal of Personal and Social Psychology,* 52:511–24.

Healy, K. (2005) *Social Work Theories in Context: Creating Frameworks for Practice.* Basingstoke: Palgrave Macmillan.

Hearn, J. (1999) 'Agism, violence and abuse – theoretical and practical perspectives on the links between "child abuse" and "elder abuse"', in Violence Against Children Study Group, *Children, Child Abuse and Child Protection: Placing Children Centrally.* Chichester: Wiley.

Henden, J. (2008) *Preventing Suicide: The Solution Focused Approach.* Chichester: Wiley.

Henning, K., Jones, A. R. and Holdford, R. (2005) ' "I didn't do it, but if I did I had good reason": minimisation, denial and attribution of blame among male and female domestic violence offenders', *Journal of Family Violence,* 20:131–9.

Hepworth, D. H., Rooney, R. H. and Larsen, J. A. (2002) *Direct Social Work Practice: Theory and Skills.* London: Brooks/Cole.

Hesse, E. (1999) 'The adult attachment interview: historical and current perspectives', in Cassidy, J. and Shaver, P. R. (eds) *Handbook of Attachment: Theory, Research and Clinical Implications.* New York: Guilford.

Hicks, S. (2005) 'Genealogy's desire: practices of kinship amongst lesbian and gay foster carers and adopters', *British Journal of Social Work,* 36:761–76.

Hicks, S. (2007) 'Thinking through sexuality', *Journal of Social Work,* 8:85–102.

Hilsenroth, M. F. *et al.* (2001) 'Evaluating the phase model of change during short-term psycho-dynamic psychotherapy', *Psychotherapy Research,* 11(1):29–41.

Hobart, C. and Frankel, J. (2004) *A Practical Guide to Child Observation and Development,* 3rd edn. Cheltenham: Nelson Thornes.

Hobbs, T. (2002) 'Parental Alienation Syndrome and UK Family Courts', *Family Law,* 32:82–9 and 32:381–7.

Holland, S. (2000) 'The assessment relationship: interaction between social workers and parents in child protection assessments', *British Journal of Social Work,* 30:149–63.

Hollis, F. (1964) *Social Casework: A Psychosocial Therapy.* New York: Random House.

Home Office, Department of Health and the Welsh Office (1995) *National Standards for the Supervision of Offenders in the Community.* London: Home Office Probation Services Division.

hooks, bell (1991) *Yearning.* London: Turnaround.

hooks, bell (1993) *Sisters of the Yam: Black Women and Self-Recovery.* London: Turnaround.

Hothersall, S. J. (2006) *Social Work with Children, Young People and Their Families in Scotland.* Exeter: Learning Matters.

Howe, D. (1995) *Attachment Theory for Social Work Practice.* Basingstoke: Macmillan.

Howe, D. (2000) 'Attachment', in, Horwath, J. (ed.) *The Child's World: Assessing Children In Need.* London: National Society for the Prevention of Cruelty to Children.

Huberman, A. M. and Miles, M. B. (1994) 'Data management and analysis methods', in Denzin, N. K. and Lincoln, Y. S. (eds) *Handbook of Qualitative Research.* London: Sage.

Hudson, B. L. and Macdonald, G. M. (1986) *Behavioural Social Work: An Introduction.* London: Macmillan.

Hughes, B. (1995) *Older People and Community Care: Critical Theory and Practice.* Buckingham: Open University Press.

Hughes, B. and Mtezuka, M. (1992) 'Social work and older women: where have older women gone?', in Langan, M. and Day, L. (eds) *Women, Oppression and Social Work: Issues in Anti-Discriminatory Practice.* London: Tavistock/Routledge.

Hugman, R. (1991) *Power in Caring Professions.* Basingstoke: Macmillan.

Hussain, N. (1996) 'An investigation of the placement arrangements made for children and young people "looked after" in relation to cultural and religious origins.' Dissertation. Department of Behavioural Sciences, University of Huddersfield.

Ingleby, D. (1985) 'Professionals as socialisers: the "psy complex"', in Spitzer, S. and Scull, A. T. (eds) *Research in Law, Deviance, and Social Control.* New York: Jai.

Ingleby, D. (2006) *Applied Psychology for Social Work.* Exeter: Polity.

Iveson, C. (1990) *Whose Life? Community care of Older People and their Families.* London: Brief Therapy Press.

Iveson, C. (2002) 'Solution-focused brief therapy', *Advances in Psychiatric Treatment,* 8(2):149–56.

Jack, G. and Gill, O. (2003) *The Missing Side of the Triangle: Assessing the Importance of Family and Environmental Factors in the Lives of Children.* London: Barnardo's.

Jackson, P. Z. and McKergow, M. (2002) *The Solutions Focus: the Simple Way to Make Positive Change.* London: Brearly.

Jacob, F. (2001) *Solution-Focused Recovery from Eating Distress.* London: Brief Therapy Press.

Jacobs, M. (1999) *Psychodynamic Counselling in Action.* London: Sage.

Janis, I. L. and Mann, L. (1977) *Decision Making.* New York: Free Press.

Jasper, K. (2007) 'The blinding power of genetics: manufacturing and privatising stories of eating disorders', in Brown, C. and Augusta-Scott, T. (eds) *Narrative Therapy: Making Meaning, Making Lives.* London: Sage.

Jenkins, A. (1990) *Invitations to Responsibility.* Adelaide: Dulwich Centre.

Jenkins, A. (1996) 'Moving towards respect: a quest for balance', in McClean, C., Carey, M. and White, C. (eds) *Men's Ways of Being.* Boulder, CO: Westview.

Jones, D. P. H. (1998) 'The effectiveness of intervention', in Adcock, M. and White, R. (eds) *Significant Harm: Its Management and Outcome.* Croydon: Significant Publications.

Jones, D. P. H. (2000) 'The assessment of parenting capacity', in Howarth, J. (ed.) *The Child's World: Assessing Children in Need.* London: National Society for the Prevention of Cruelty to Children.

Jones, D. P. H. and Ramchandani, P. (1999) *Child Sexual Abuse: Informing Practice from Research.* Oxford: Radcliffe Medical Press.

Jones, P. (2003) *Introducing Social Theory.* Cambridge: Polity.

Jones, W. (1994) 'Research expertise on the World Bank', in Walford, G. (ed.) *Researching the Powerful in Education.* University College London Press.

Jordan, B. (1990) *Social Work in an Unjust Society.* Hemel Hempstead: Harvester Wheatsheaf.

Jordan, J. (1989) *Moving Towards Home. Political Essays.* London: Virago.

Jordan, J. V. (1997) 'A relational perspective for understanding women's development', in Jordan, J. V. *et al.*(eds) *Women's Growth and Diversity: More Writings from the Stone Centre.* New York: Guilford.

Kahneman, D. and Tversky, A. (1982) 'The psychology of preferences', *Scientific American*, 246:160–73.

Kahneman, D. and Tversky, A. (1979) 'Prospect theory: an analysis of decisions under risk', *Econometrician*, 47, 263–91.

Katz, I. (1996) *The Construction of Racial Identity in Children of Mixed Parentage: Mixed Metaphors.* London: Jessica Kingsley.

Kazdin, A. E. (1997) *Conduct Disorder in Childhood and Adolescence.* Newbury Park, CA: Sage.

Kearney, R. (2002) *On Stories.* London: Routledge.

Keene, J. (2001) *Clients with Complex Needs. Interprofessional Practice.* Oxford: Blackwell.

Kelly, L. (1994) 'The interconnectedness of domestic violence and child abuse: challenges for research, policy and practice', in Mullender, A. and Morley, K. (eds) *Children Living with Domestic Violence: Putting Men's Abuse of Children on the Child Care Agenda.* London: Whiting & Birch.

Kelly, N. (2000) 'Decision making in child protection practice', PhD thesis, University of Huddersfield.

Kelly, N. and Milner, J. (1996a) 'Decision-making in child protection practice: the effectiveness of the case conference in the UK.' Paper presented at ISPCAN Eleventh International Congress on Child Abuse and Neglect. University College, Dublin 18–21 August.

Kelly, N. and Milner, J. (1996b) 'Child protection decision-making', *Child Abuse Review*, 5:91–102.

Kemshall, H. (1998) *Risk in Probation Practice.* Aldershot: Ashgate.

Kemshall, H. (2002) *Risk, Social Policy and Welfare.* Buckingham: Open University Press.

Kennedy, R. (1997) 'Assessment of parenting', in, Wall, N. (ed.) *Rooted Sorrows: Psychoanalytic Perspectives on Child Protection, Assessment and Treatment.* Bristol: Family Law.

Kesner, D. E. and McKenry, P. C. (1998) 'The role of childhood attachment factors in predicting male violence toward female intimates', *Journal of Family Violence*, 13:417–32.

Kitwood, T. (1998) 'Professional and moral development for care work: some observations on the process', *Journal of Moral Education*, 27:401–11.

Klein, M. (1988) *Love, Guilt and Reparation and Other Works: 1921–1945.* London: Virago.

Knight, S. E. (1981) 'Introduction', in Bullard, D. G. and Knight, S. E. (eds) *Sexuality and Physical Disability. Personal Perspectives.* London: Mosby.

Kohlberg, L. (1968) 'The child as a moral philosopher', *Psychology Today*, 2, 25–30.

Kral, R. (1989) *Strategies that Work: Techniques for Solution in the Schools.* Milwaukee, WI: Brief Family Therapy Centre.

Laing, R. D. (1961) *The Self and Others.* London: Tavistock.

Lawrence, M. (1992) 'Women's psychology and feminist social work', in Langan, M. and Day, L. (eds) *Women, Oppression and Social Work. Issues for Anti-Discriminatory Practice.* London: Tavistock/Routledge.

Lee, M. Y., Sebold, J. and Uken, A. (2003) *Solution Focused Treatment of Domestic Violence Offenders: accountability and change.* Oxford University Press.

Leiss, W. and Chociolko, C. (1994) *Risk and Responsibility.* Montreal: McGill–Queen's University Press.

Lester, H. and Glasby, J. (2006) *Mental Health Policy and Practice.* Basingstoke: Palgrave Macmillan.

Letham, J. (1994) *Moved to Tears, Moved to Action. Solution Focused Brief Therapy with Women*. London: Brief Therapy Press.

Leventhal, B. and Lundy, S. E. (eds) (1999) *Same-Sex Domestic Violence: Strategies for Change*. London: Sage.

Lewis, A., Shemmings, D. and Thoburn, J. (1991) *Participation in Practice – Involving Families in Child Protection: A Training Pack*. Norwich: Social Work Development Unit, University of East Anglia.

Lewis, J. and Utting, W. (2001) 'Made to measure? Evaluating community initiatives for children. Introduction', *Children and Society*, 15(1):1–4.

Lindow, V. (2000) 'User perspectives on social work', in Davies, M. (ed.) *The Blackwell Encyclopaedia of Social Work*. Oxford: Blackwell.

Lipchik, E. and Kubicki, A. D. (1996) 'Solution focused domestic violence: bridges towards a new reality in couples therapy', in Miller, S. D. and Duncan, B. L. (eds) *Handbook of Solution Focused Therapy*. San Francisco, CA: Jossey Bass.

Lockwood, R. and Ascione, F. R. (eds) (1998) *Cruelty to Animals and Interpersonal Violence: Readings in Research and Application*. West Lafayette, IN: Purdue University Press.

Logan, S. L. *et al.* (1990) *Social Work Practice with Black Families*. New York: Longman.

Lymbery, M. (2001) 'Social work at the crossroads', *British Journal of Social Work*, 31:369–84.

Mac an Ghaill, M. (ed.) (1996) *Understanding Masculinities*. Buckingham: Open University press.

Macdonald, A. J. (1997) 'Brief therapy in adult psychiatry - further outcomes', *Journal of Family Therapy*. 19:213–22.

Macdonald, A. J. (2007) *Solution Focused Therapy: Theory, Research and Practice*. London: Sage.

Macdonald, G. (1998) 'Promoting evidence-based practice in child protection', *Clinical Child Psychology and Psychiatry*. 3(1):71–85.

Macdonald, G. (2000) 'Evidence based practice', in Davies, M. (ed.) *The Blackwell Encyclopaedia of Social Work*. Oxford: Blackwell.

Mackinnon, C. (1987) *Feminism Unmodified: Discourses on Life and Law*. Cambridge, MA: Harvard University Press.

Macleod, M. and Saroga, E. (1988) 'Challenging the orthodoxy: towards a feminist theory and practice', *Feminist Review*, 28:16–56.

Main, M. and Weston, D. (1981) 'Quality of attachment to mother and to father: related to conflict behaviour and the readiness for establishing new relationships', *Child Development*, 52:932–40.

Main, M., Kaplan, N. and Cassidy, J. (1985) 'Security in infancy, childhood and adulthood: a move to the level of representation', in Bretherton, I. and Waters, E. (eds) *Growing Points in Attachment: Theory and Research*. Monographs of the Society for Research in Child Development 50. Chicago, IL: University of Chicago Press.

Mair, G. (2004) 'The origins of what works in England and Wales: a house built on sand?', in Mair, G. (ed.) *What Matters in Probation*. Cullompton: Willan.

Mantle, G. *et al.* (2007) 'Whose wishes and feelings? Children's autonomy and parental influence', *British Journal of Social Work*, 37:785–805.

Marsh, P. and Doel, M. (2005) *The Task Centred Book (Social Work Skills)*. Abingdon: Routledge.

Marshall, J. (1981) 'Pansies, perverts and macho men: changing conceptions of male homosexuality', in Plummer, K. (ed.) *The Making of the Modern Homosexual*. London: Hutchinson.

Marshall, W. (1996) 'Professionals, children and power', in Blyth, E. and Milner, J. (eds) *School Exclusions: Interagency Issues for Policy and Practice*. London: Routledge.

Marvin, R. S. and Stewart, R. B. (1990) 'A family system framework for the study of attachment', in Greenberg, M., Cichetti, D. and Cummings M. (eds) *Attachment Beyond the Pre-School Years*. Chicago, IL: University of Chicago Press.

Maslow, A. H. (1954) *Motivation and Personality*. New York: Harper.

Masson, H. and O'Byrne, P. (1984) *Applying Family Therapy*. London: Pergamon.

Maturana, H. and Varela, F. (1987) *The Tree of Knowledge: Biological Roots of Human Understanding*. Boston, MA: New Science Library.

Mayer, J. E. and Timms, N. (1970) *The Client Speaks: Working Class Impressions of Casework*. London: Routledge & Kegan Paul.

Maynard, M. and Purvis, J. (1995) *Researching Women's Lives from a Feminist Perspective*. London: Taylor & Francis.

McAuley, C., Pecora, P. and Rose, W. (2006) *Enhancing the Well-being of Children and Families through Effective Interventions. International Evidence for Practice*. London: Jessica Kingsley.

McDonald, A. (2006) *Understanding Community Care*, 2nd edn Basingstoke: Palgrave Macmillan.

McGaw, S. (2006) 'Decision-making: parents with learning difficulties', in Murphy, G. and Clare, I. *Decision-Making: People with Learning Difficulties*. London: Sage.

McGuire, J.+e)d (1995) *What Works: Reducing Re-offending. Guidelines from Research and Practice*. Chichester: Wiley.

McKeowan, K. *et al.* (2001) *Distressed Relationships: Does Counselling Help?* Dublin: Marital and Relationship Counselling Service.

McLeod, J. (2003) *An Introduction to Counselling*, 2nd edn. Buckingham: Open University Press.

McNay, M. (1992) 'Social work and power relations', in Langan, M. and Day, L. (eds) *Women, Oppression and Social Work Issues in Anti-Discriminatory Practice*. London: Tavistock/Routledge.

McNeil, F. and Whyte, B. (2007) *Reducing Offending: Social Work with Offenders in Scotland*. Edinburgh: Willan.

Mead, G. H. (1934) *Mind, Self and Society*. Chicago, IL: Chicago University Press.

Meredith, B. (1993) *The Community Care Handbook: The New System Explained*. London: Age Concern.

Messerschmidt, J. W. (2000) *Nine Lives: Adolescent Masculinities, the Body, and Violence*. Boulder, CO: Westview.

Meyer, C. (1993) *Assessment in Social Work Practice*. New York: Columbia University Press.

Middleton, L. (1997) *The Art of Assessment*. Birmingham: Venture.

Millar, M. and Corby, B. (2007) 'The framework for the assessment of children in need and their families: a basis for "therapeutic" encounters?', *British Journal of Social Work*, 36:887–99.

Miller, D. T. and Ross, M. (1975) 'Self-serving biases in attribution of causality: fact or fiction?', *Psychological Bulletin*, 82, 213–18.

Miller, J. Baker (ed.) (1973) *Psychoanalysis and Women*. Harmondsworth: Penguin.

Milner, J. (1993) 'A disappearing act: the differing career paths of fathers and mothers in child protection investigations', *Critical Social Policy*, 38:48–68.

Milner, J. (2001) *Women and Social Work. Narrative Approaches*. Basingstoke: Palgrave Macmillan.

Milner, J. (2003) 'Narrative group work with young women – and their mobile phones', *International Journal of Narrative Therapy and Community Work*, 3:54–60.

Milner, J. (2004a) 'From "disappearing" to "demonized": the effects on men and women of professional interventions based on challenging men who are violent', *Critical Social Policy*, 24:79–101.

Milner, J. (2004b) 'Groupwork with young women', *Context*, 74:14–17.

Milner, J. (2008a) 'Working with people who are violent to their partners: a safety building approach', *Liverpool Law Review*, 29:67–80.

Milner, J. (2008b) 'Domestic violence: solution focused practice with men and women who are violent', *Journal of Family Therapy*, 30:29–53.

Milner, J. (2009) 'Solution focused approaches to caring for children whose behaviour is sexually harmful', *Adoption and Fostering*, 32(4):42–50.

Milner, J. and O'Byrne, P. (2002) *Assessment in Social Work*, 2nd edn. Basingstoke: Palgrave Macmillan.

Milner, J. and O'Byrne, P. (2002) *Brief Counselling: Narratives and Solutions*. Basingstoke: Palgrave Macmillan.

Milner, J. and Jessop, D. (2003) 'Domestic violence: narratives and solutions', *Probation Journal*, 50:127–51.

Milner, J. and Myers, S. (2007) *Working with Violence*. Basingstoke: Palgrave Macmillan.

Morgan, D. L. (1998) *The Focus Guidebook*. London: Sage.

Moscovici, S. and Zavalloni, M. (1969) 'The group as polariser of attitudes', *Journal of Personality and Social Psychology*, 12, 125–35.

Mowlan, A., Tennant, R., Dixon, J. and McCreadie, C. (2007) *UK Study of Abuse and Neglect of Older People: Qualitative Findings*. London: National Centre for Social Research, Kings College.

Mullender, A. (1996) *Rethinking Domestic Violence: The Social Work and Probation Response*. London: Routledge.

Muptic, L. R. *et al.* (2007) 'An exploratory study of women arrested for intimate partner violence: violent women or violent resistance?', *Journal of Interpersonal Violence*, 22:753–74.

Murray Parkes, C. (1986) *Bereavement*. London: Tavistock.

Myake, K., Chen, S., Campos, J. and Waters, E. (1985) 'Infants' temperament, mothers' mode of interaction and attachment in Japan: an interim report', in Bretherton, I. and Waters, E. (eds) *Growing Points of Attachment Theory and Research*. Monographs of the Society for Research in Child Development 50. Chicago, IL: University of Chicago Press.

Myers, J. (2007) *Theory into Practice: Solution Focused Approaches*. Lyme Regis: Russell House.

Myers, S. (2005) 'Signs of safety approach to assessing children with sexually concerning or harmful behaviour', *Child Abuse Review*, 14:97–112.

Myers, S. (2007a) '(De)Constructing the risk categories in the AIM Assessment Model for children with sexually harmful behaviour', *Children in Society*, 21:365–77.

Myers, S. (2007b) *Solution Focused Approaches*. Lyme Regis: Russell House.

Myers, S. and Milner, J. (2007) *Sexual Issues in Social Work*. Bristol: Polity.

Myers, S., MacLaughlin, M. and Warwick, K. (2003) 'The day the Touching Monster came: narrative and solution focused approaches to working with children and young people with sexually inappropriate behaviour', *Journal of Educational Psychology*, 20:76–89.

Netton, A., Francis, J., Jones, K. and Bebbington, A. (2004) *Performance and Quality: User Experiences of Home Care Services. Final Report*: Personal Social Services Research Unit Discussion Paper, 2104/3 www.PSSRU.ac.uk.

Newburn, T. (2001) 'What do we mean by evaluation?', *Children and Society*, 15(1):5–13.

Newman, T., Moseley, A., Tierney, S. and Ellis, A. (2005) *Evidence-Based Social Work. A Guide for the Perplexed*. Lyme Regis: Russell House.

Nice, V. (1988) 'Them and us: women as carers: clients and social workers', *Practice*, 2(1):58–73.

Nicholson, P., Brayne, R. and Owen, J. (2006) *Applied Psychology for Social Workers*. Basingstoke: Palgrave Macmillan.

O'Callaghan, A. C., Murphy, G. and Clare, I. C. H. (2003) 'The impact of abuse on men and women with severe learning disabilities and their families', *British Journal of Learning Disability*, 3:175–80.

O'Callaghan, D. and Print, B. (1994) 'Adolescent sexual abusers: research, assessment and treatment', in Morrison, T., Erooga, M. and Beckett, R. (eds) *Sexual Offending Against Children: Assessment and Treatment of Male Abusers*. London: Routledge.

O'Connell, B. (1998) *Solution Focused Therapy*. London: Sage.

O'Connell, B. (2001) *Solution Focused Stress Counselling*. London: Continuum.

O'Hagan, K. and Dillenburger, K. (1995) *The Abuse of Women Within Child Care Work*. Buckingham: Open University Press.

O'Hanlon, B. (1995) *Breaking the Bad Trance*. London: Brief Therapy conference.

O'Hanlon, B. and Beadle, S. (1994) *A Field Guide to Possibility Land*. Omaha, NB: Possibility Press.

O'Keefe, M. *et al.* (2007) *UK Study of Abuse and Neglect of Older People: Prevalence Report*. London: National Centre for Social Research, Kings College.

O'Leary, E. (1996) *Counselling Older Adults:. Perspectives, Approaches and Research*. London: Chapman & Hall.

O'Sullivan, T. (1999) *Decision Making in Social Work*. Basingstoke: Macmillan.

Oliver, M. and Sapey, B. (1999) *Social Work with Disabled people*, 2nd edn. Basingstoke: Palgrave Macmillan.

Parad, H. J. (1965) *Crisis Intervention: Selected Readings*. New York: Family Service Association of America

Parsloe, P. (1999) *Risk Assessment in Social Work and Social Care (research highlights)*. London: Jessica Kingsley.

Parton, N. (1998) 'Risk, advanced liberalism and child welfare: the need to rediscover uncertainty and ambiguity', *British Journal of Social Work*, 28:5–27.

Parton, N. and Marshall, W. (1998) 'Postmodernism and discourse approaches to social work', in Adams, R., Dominelli, L. and Payne M. (eds) *Social work: Themes, Issues and Critical Debates*. Basingstoke: Macmillan.

Parton, N. and O'Byrne, P. (2000) *Constructive Social Work*. Basingstoke: Palgrave Macmillan.

Parton, N., Thorpe, D. and Wattam, C. (1997) *Child Protection: Risk and the Moral Order*. Basingstoke: Macmillan.

Pavlov, I. P. (1960) *Conditional Reflexes: An Investigation of the Psychological Activity of the Cerebral Cortex* (translation). New York: Hover Publications.

Payne, G. (ed.) (2006) *Social Divisions*. Basingstoke: Palgrave Macmillan.

Payne, Mm. (2005) *Modern Social Work Theory*. Basingstoke: Palgrave Macmillan.

Payne, Mn. (2006) *Narrative Therapy*, 2nd edn. London: Sage.

Payne, Mn. (2000) *Narrative Therapy: An Introduction for Counsellors*. London: Sage.

Peck, E., Gulliver, P. and Towell, D. (2002) 'Information, consultation and control: user involvement in mental health services in England at the turn of the century', *Journal of Mental Health*, 11(4):441–51.

Penfield, W. (1952) 'Memory mechanisms', *AMA Archives of Neurology and Psychiatry*, 67:178–98.

Phair, L. and Good, V. (1998) *Dementia:. A Positive Approach*. London: Whurr.

Piaget, J. (1977) *The Origin of Intelligence in the Child*. Harmondsworth: Penguin.

Pincus, A. and Minahan, A. (1973) *Social Work Practice: Model and Method*. Itasca, IL: Peacock.

Pinsof, W. M. (1994) 'An overview of integrated problem solving therapy', *Journal of Family Therapy*, 16:103–20.

Platt, D. (2007) 'Congruence and cooperation in social workers' assessments of children in need', *Child and Family Social Work*, 12:326–35.

Pocock, D. (1995) 'Searching for a better story', *Journal of Family Therapy*, 17:149–74.

Pozatek, E. (1994) 'The problem of certainty', *Social Work*, 39, 396–404.

Prince, K. (1996) *Boring Records? Communication, Speech and Writing in Social Work Records*. London: Jessica Kingsley.

Quinn, C. (1996) *The Care Must Be There*. www.fordementia.org.uk.

Randall, P. (1997) *Adult Bullying: Perpetrators and Victims*. London: Routledge.

Rassool, G. H. (2002) *Dual Diagnosis: Substance Misuse and Psychiatric Disorder*. Oxford: Blackwell.

Ray, M. and Phillips, J. (2002) 'Older people', in Adams, R., Dominelli, L. and Payne, M. (eds) *Critical Practice in Social Work*. Basingstoke: Palgrave Macmillan.

Read, J. (2000) *Disability, the Family and Society: Listening to Mothers*. Buckingham: Open University Press.

Reder, P., Duncan, S. and Gray, M. (1993) *Beyond Blame: Child Abuse Tragedies Revisited*. London: Routledge.

Reid, W. J. (1963) 'An experimental study of the methods used in casework treatment.' Doctrinal dissertation. New York: Columbia University Press.

Reid, W. J. (1978) *The Task-Centred System*. New York: Columbia University Press.

Reid, W. J. (1992) *Task Strategies*. New York: Columbia University Press.

Reid, W. J. and Epstein, L. (1972) *Task-Centred Casework*. New York: Columbia University Press.

Reid, W. J. and Shyne, A. (1969) *Brief and Extended Casework*. New York: Columbia University Press.

Renzetti, C. M. (1992) *Violent Betrayal. Partner Abuse in Lesbian Relationships.* London: Sage.

Renzetti, C. M. and Lee, R. (1993) *Researching Sensitive Topics*. London: Sage.

Richards, J. (1980) *The Sceptical Feminist*. London: Routledge.

Richards, S. (2000) 'Bridging the divide: elders and the assessment process', *British Journal of Social Work*, 30:37–49.

Robson, C. (2002) *Real World Research*, 2nd edn. Oxford: Blackwell.

Romme, M. and Escher, S. (2000) *Making Sense of Voices: A Guide for Mental Health Professionals working with Voice-Hearers.* London: Mind Publications.

Rose, W. and Gray, J. with McAuley, C. (2006) 'Child welfare in the UK: legislation, policy and practice', in McAuley, C., Pecora, P. and Rose, W. (eds) *Enhancing the Well-being of Children and Families through Effective Interventions. International Evidence for Practice.* Lyme Regis: Jessica Kingsley.

Rutter, M. (1981) *Maternal Deprivation Reassessed*. London: Penguin.

Rycroft, C. (1966) 'Introduction: causes and meaning', in Rycroft, C. *et al.* (eds) *Psychoanalysis Observed* Harmondsworth: Penguin.

Sagi, A., Lamb, M. E. and Lewkowicz, K. S. (1985) 'Security of infant–mother – father and – metaplet among Kibbutz reared Israeli children', in Bretherton, I. and Waters, E. (eds) *Growing Points of Attachment Theory and Research.* Monographs of the Society for Research in Child Development 50. Chicago, IL: University of Chicago Press.

Sainsbury, E. (1970) *Social Diagnosis in Casework*. London: Routledge & Kegan Paul.

Sampson, A. *et al.* (1991) 'Gender issues in inter-agency relations: police, probation and social services', in Abbott, P. and Wallace, C. (eds) *Sex, Gender and Care Work: Research Highlights in Social Work.* London: Jessica Kingsley.

Sanders, C. J. (2007) 'A poetics of resistance: compassionate practice in substance misuse therapy', in Brown, C. and Augusta-Scott, T. (eds) *Narrative Therapy: Making Meaning, Making Lives.* London: Sage.

Sapey, B. (2002) 'Physical disability', in Adams, R., Dominelli, L. and Payne, M. (eds) *Critical Practice in Social Work.* Basingstoke: Palgrave Macmillan.

Sawicki, J. (1991) *Disciplining Foucault: Feminism, Power and the Body.* London: Sage.

Schaffer, H. R. (1998) *Making Decisions about Children*, 2nd edn. Oxford: Blackwell.

Schwartz, A. and Goldiamond, I. (1975) *Social Casework: A Behavioural Approach.* New York: Columbia University Press.

Scott, D. (1998) 'A qualitative study of social work assessment in cases of alleged child abuse', *British Journal of Social Work*, 28:73–88.

Scottish Executive (2004) *Getting it Right for Every Child*. Edinburgh.

Scottish Executive (2006) *Changing Lives: Report of the 21st Century Social Work Review.* Edinburgh.

Scourfield, J. (2003) *Gender and Child Protection*. Basingstoke: Palgrave Macmillan.

Sebold, J. and Uken, A. (2000) *Treating Domestic Violence Offenders*. (Audio Tape.) Milwaukee, WI: Brief Family Therapy Centre.

Selekman, M. D. (2002) *Living on the Razor's Edge*. London: Norton.

Seligman, M. E. P. (1992) *Helplessness: On Depression, Development and Death.* New York: Freeman.

Shaffer, H. R. (1998) *Making Decisions about Children* (2nd *ed*) Oxford: Blackwell.

Sharkey, P. (2007) *The Essentials of Community Care*. Basingstoke: Palgrave Macmillan.

Sheldon, B. (1982) *Behaviour Modification: Theory, Practice and Philosophy.* London: Tavistock.

Sheldon, B. (1995) *Cognitive-Behavioural Therapy, Research, Practice and Philosophy.* London: Routledge.

Sheppard, M. (1995) *Care Management and the New Social Work: A Critical Analysis.* London: Whiting & Birch/Social Care Association + education).

Sibeon, R. (1992) *Towards a New Sociology of Social Work.* Aldershot: Avebury.

Silvester, J., Bentovim, A., Stratton, P. and Hanks, H. (1995) 'Using spoken attributions to classify abusive families', *Child Abuse and Neglect*, 19:1221–32.

Sinclair, I. *et al.* (1990) *The Kaleidoscope of Care: A Review of Research in Welfare Provision for Elderly People.* London: HMSO for National Institute of Social Work.

Sinclair, R., Garrett, L. and Berridge, D. (1995) *Social Work and Assessment with Adolescents.* London: National Children's Bureau.

Skinner, B. F. (1953) *Science and Human Behaviour.* New York: Macmillan.

Skinner, B. F. (1958) 'Reinforcement theory', *American Psychologist*, 13:94–9.

Skuse, D. *et al.* (1998) 'Risk factors for development of sexually abusive behaviour in sexually victimised boys: cross sectional study', *British Medical Journal*, 317:175–9.

Smale, G. and Tuson, G. with Brehal, N. and Marsh, P. (1993) *Empowerment, Assessment, Care Management and the Skilled Worker.* London: National Institute for Social Work.

Smale, G. *et al.* (1994) *Negotiating Care in the Community.* London: HMSO for National Institute for Social Work.

Smart, C., Neale, B. and Wade, A. (2001) *The Changing Experience of Childhood: Families and Divorce.* Cambridge: Polity.

Smith, D. (ed.) (2004) *Social Work and Evidence-Based Practice.* London: Jessica Kingsley.

Smith, P. B. (2005) 'Good answers to bad invitations', *International Journal of Narrative Therapy and Community Work*, 1:23–30.

Social Services Inspectorate. (1991) *Getting the Message Across:. A Guide to Developing and Communicating Policies, Principles and Procedures on Assessment.* London: HMSO.

Soothill K. *et al.* (2000) 'Sex offenders: specialists, generalists, or both?', *British Journal of Criminology*, 40:56–67.

Speedy, J. (2004) 'Using therapeutic documents in narrative practice', in Bolton, G., Howlett, S., Lago, C. and Wright, J. (eds) *The Writing Cure: An Introductory Handbook of Writing in Counselling and Therapy.* London: Routledge.

Spence, M. F. (1995) 'Finding a healthy path through racism and sexism', *Social Work Education*, 14(4):106–13.

Spender, D. (1985) *Man Made Language*, 2nd edn. London: Routledge & Kegan Paul.

Stainton, T. (2002) Learning Disabilities, in Adams, R., Dominelli, L. and Payne, M. (eds) *Critical Practice in Social Work.* Basingstoke: Palgrave Macmillan.

Stanley, L. and Wise, S. (1991) 'Method, methodology and epistemology in feminist research process', in Stanley, L. (ed.) *Feminist Praxis: Research, Theory and Epistemology.* London: Routledge.

Stanley, T. (2005) 'Making decisions: social work processes and the construction of risk in child protection work.' PhD thesis, University of Canterbury, Christchurch, New Zealand.

Stanley, T. (2006) 'Assisting risk assessment work: social workers talking about the Risk Estimation System (RES)', *Social Work Now (Practice Journal of Child Youth and Family Services)*, 35:8–12.

Stanley, T. (2007) 'Risky work: child protection practice', *The Social Policy Journal of New Zealand Te Puna Whakaaro*, 30:163–77.

Steward, I. and Joines, V. (1999) *TA Today: A New Introduction to TA.* Nottingham: Lifespace.

Stiver, I. P. (1991) 'The meanings of "dependency" in female-male relationships', in Jordan, J. V. *et al. Women's Growth in Connection: Writings from the Stone Centre.* New York: Guilford.

Storr, A. (1966) 'The concept of cure', in Rycroft, C. *et al.* (eds) *Psychoanalysis Observed*. Harmondsworth: Penguin.

Strand, P. S. (1997) 'Toward a developmentally informed narrative therapy', *Family Process*, 36:325–39.

Strand, P. S. (1997) 'Casework with ego-fragmented parents', *Social Casework*, 36: 325–39.

Strean, H. F. (1968) 'Casework with ego-fragmented parents', *Social Casework*, April, 1968.

Strom-Gottfried, K. (1999) *Social Work Practice. Cases, Activities, and Exercises*. Thousand Oaks, CA: Pine Forge.

Stuart, R. B. (1974) 'Behaviour modification: a technology for social change', in Turner, F. J. (ed.) *Social Work Treatment*. New York: Free Press.

Sutton, C. (2000) *Child and Adolescent Behaviour Problems*. Leicester: British Psychological Society.

Swain, J., French, S. and Cameron, C. (2003) *Controversial Issues in a Disability Society*. Buckingham: Open University Press.

Szasz, T. (1960) 'The myth of mental illness', *American Psychologist*, 15:564–80.

Tamasese, K. and Waldergrave, C. (1996) 'Culture and gender accountability in the "just therapy" approach', in McLean, C., Carey, M. and White, C. (eds) *Men's Ways of Being*. Boulder, CO: Westview.

Taylor, C. (2004) 'Underpinning knowledge of child care practice: reconsidering child development theory', *Child and Family Social Work*, 9:225–35.

Taylor, C. and White, S. (2000) *Practicing Reflexivity in Health and Welfare: Making Knowledge*. Buckingham: Open University Press.

Thoburn, J., Lewis, A. and Shemmings, D. (1995) *Paternalism or Partnership? Family Involvement in the Child Protection Process*. London: HMSO.

Thoburn, J., Norford, L. and Rashid, S. (2000) *Permanent Family Placement for Children of Ethnic Minority Origin*. London: Jessica Kingsley.

Thomas, C. (1999) *Female Forms:. Experiencing and Understanding Disability*. Buckingham: Open University Press.

Thompson, N. (1995) *Theory and Practice in Health and Social Care*. Buckingham: Open University Press.

Thompson, N. (2003a) *Promoting Equality: Challenging Discrimination and Oppression*. Basingstoke: Palgrave Macmillan.

Thompson, N. (2003b) *Communication and Language: A Handbook of Theory and Practice*. Basingstoke: Palgrave Macmillan.

Thompson, N. (2006a) *Anti-Discriminatory Practice*, 4th edn. Basingstoke: Palgrave Macmillan.

Thompson, N. (2006b) *People Problems*. Basingstoke: Palgrave Macmillan.

Thyer, B. A. (1998) *Handbook of Social Work Practice*. Chichester: Wiley.

Thyer, B. A. (2002) *Handbook of Social Work Research*. London: Sage.

Trepper, T. S. and Barrett, M. J. (eds) (1986) *Treating Incest*, Binghamton, NY: Haworth.

Trevithick, P. (2007) *Social Work Skills: A Practice Handbook*. Maidenhead: Open University Press.

Tudway, J. A. and Darmoody, M. (2005) 'Clinical assessment of adult sex offenders with learning difficulties', *Journal of Sexual Aggression*, 11:177–288.

Tunstill, J. and Aldgate, J. (2000) *Children in Need: From Policy to Practice*. London: HMSO.

Tunstill, J. (1993) 'Local authority policies on children in need', in Gidden, J. (ed.) *The Children Act 1989 and Family Support*. London: HMSO.

Turnell, A. and Edwards, S. (1999) *Signs of Safety: A Solution and Safety Orientated Approach to Child Protection Casework*. New York: Norton.

Turnell, A. and Essex, S. (2006) *Working with 'Denied' Child Abuse: The Resolutions Approach*. Maidenhead: Open University Press.

Turner, B. (1986) *Equality*. London: Tavistock.

Ungerson, C. (1987) *Policy is Personal: Sex, Gender and Informal Care.* London: Tavistock.

Vennard, J., Sugg, D. and Hedderman, C. (1997) *The Use of Cognitive Behavioural Approaches with Offenders: Message from the Research Unit.* London: Home Office.

Wake, D. (2004) 'The influence of dual diagnosis', in Kirby, S. D., Hart, D. A., Cross, D. and Mitchell G. (eds) *Mental Health Nursing: Competence for Practice.* Basingstoke: Palgrave Macmillan.

Walford, G. (1994) 'A new focus on the powerful', in Walford, G. (ed.) *Researching the Powerful in Education.* London: University College London Press.

Ward. H. (1995) *Looking After Children: Research into Practice.* London: HMSO.

Ward, H. and Rose, W. (eds) (2002) *Approaches to Needs Assessment in Children's Services.* London: Jessica Kingsley.

Ward, T. (2002) 'Good lives and the rehabilitation of offenders: promises and problems', *Aggression and Violent Behavior,* 7:513–28.

Ward, T. and Mann, R. E. (2004) 'Good lives and the rehabilitation of offenders: a positive approach to treatment', in Lindley, P. A. and Joseph, S. (eds) *Positive Psychology in Practice.* New York: Wiley.

Ward, T. and Stewart, C. A. (2003) 'The treatment of sex offenders: risk management and good lives', *Professional Psychology: Research and Practice,* 34(4):353–60.

Ward, T., Mann, R. E. and Gannon, T. A. (2007) 'The good lives model of offender rehabilitation: clinical implications', *Aggression and Violent Behavior,* 12:87–107.

Wasserman, S. L. (1974) 'Ego psychology', in Turner, F. J. (ed.) *Social Work Treatment.* New York: Free Press.

Webb, S. (2001) 'Some considerations on the validity of evidence-based practice in social work', *British Journal of Social Work,* 31:57–79.

Webb, S. (2006) *Social Work in a Risk Society: Social and Political Perspectives.* Basingstoke: Palgrave Macmillan.

Webb, Y. *et al.* (2000) 'Comparing patients' experience in mental health services in England: a five-trust survey', *International Journal of Health Care Quality Assurance,* 13:273–81.

Weiss, J. S. (1991) 'The attachment bond in childhood and adulthood', in Murray-Parkes, C., Stevenson-Hinde, J. and Marris, P. (eds), *Attachment Across the Life Cycle.* London: Routledge.

Weiss, R. S. (1982) 'Attachment in adult life', in Murray-Parkes, C. and Stevenson-Hinde, J. (eds) *The Place of Attachment in Human Behaviour.* New York: Wiley.

Werner, H. D. (ed.) (1970) *New Understandings of Human Behaviour.* New York: Association Press.

Westwood, S. (1996) 'Feckless parents: masculinities and the British state', in Mac an Ghaill, M. (ed.) *Understanding Masculinities.* Buckingham: Open University Press.

White, M. (1988) 'The externalizing of the problems and the re-authoring of lives and relationships', *Dulwich Centre Newsletter* (Adelaide), Summer: 3–21.

White, M. (1993) 'Deconstruction and therapy', in Gilligan, S. and Price, R. (eds) *Therapeutic Conversations.* New York: Norton.

White, M. (1995) *Re-Authoring Lives: Interviews and Essays,* Adelaide: Dulwich Centre.

White, M. (1996) Verbal communication. Conference on Narrative Work. Doncaster.

White, M. and Epston, D. (1990) *Narrative Means to Therapeutic Ends.* New York: Norton.

White, V. (1995) 'Commonality and diversity in feminist social work', *British Journal of Social Work,* 25:143–56.

Whitfield, C., Anda, R. F., Dube, S. R. and Felitti, V. J. (2003) 'Violent childhood experience and the risk of intimate partner violence in adults: assessment in a large health maintenance organization', *Journal of Interpersonal Violence,* 18:166–85.

Whyte, G. (1989) 'Groupthink reconsidered', *Academy of Management Review,* 14(1):40–56.

Whyte, G. (1993) 'Decision failures, why they occur and how to prevent them', *Academy of Management Executive,* 5(3):23–31.

Wigfall, V., Monck, E. and Reynolds, J. (2006) 'Putting programmes into practice: the introduction of concurrent planning into mainstream adoption and fostering services', *British Journal of Social Work*, 36:41–55.

Wilgosh, R., Hawkes, D. and Marsh. I. (1993) 'Session two and beyond', *Context*, 17, 31–3.

Williams, F. (1993) 'Women and community', in Borat, J., Pereira, C., Pilgrim, D. and Williams, F. (eds) *Community Care: A Reader*. Basingstoke: Macmillan.

Wilson, K. and James, A. (2007) *The Child Protection Handbook*. Edinburgh: Baillière Tindall.

Winnicott, C. (1986) 'Face to face with children', in *Working with Children*. London: British Association for Adoption and Fostering.

Winnicott, D. W. (1964) *The Child, the Family and the Outside World*. Harmondsworth: Penguin.

Winnicott, D. W. (1971) *Playing and Reality*. London: Tavistock.

Wise, S. (1995) 'Feminist ethics in practice', in Hugman, R. and Smith, D. (eds) *Ethical Issues in Social Work*. London: Routledge.

Wittgenstein, L. (1980) *Remarks on the Philosophy of Psychology*. Oxford: Blackwell.

Wright, J. (2003) 'Considering issues of domestic violence and abuse in palliative care and bereavement situations', *Journal of Narrative Therapy and Community Work*, 3:72–4.

Wright, K., Haycox, A. and Leadman, I. (1994) *Evaluating Community Care Service for People with Learning Difficulties*. Buckingham: Open University Press.

Yan, E. and So-Kum Tang, C. (2003) 'Proclivity to elder abuse', *Journal of Interpersonal Violence*, 18:999–1017.

Yapko, M. (1988) *When Living Hurts: Directives for Treating Depression*. New York: Brunner/Mazel.

Young, V. (1999) 'Working with older lesbians', in Davies, D. and Neale, C. (eds) *Pink Therapy: A Guide for Counsellors and Therapists Working with Lesbian, Gay, and Bisexual Clients*. Buckingham: Open University Press.

Yuen, A. and White, C. (eds) (2007) *Conversations about Gender, Culture, Violence and Narrative Practice*. Adelaide: Dulwich Centre.

Zeig, J. K. (1985) *Ericksonian Psychotherapy. Volume 1: Structures*. New York: Brunner/Mazel.

Author Index

Subject Index